About the Author

Anthony Shaw is an avid Pythonista and fellow of the Python Software Foundation.

Anthony has been programming since the age of twelve and found a love for Python while trapped inside a hotel in Seattle, Washington, fifteen years later. After ditching the other languages he'd learned, Anthony has been researching, writing about, and creating courses for Python ever since.

Anthony also contributes to small and large open source projects, including CPython, and is a member of the Apache Software Foundation.

Anthony's passion lies in understanding complex systems, then simplifying them and teaching them to people.

About the Review Team

Jim Anderson has been programming for a long time in a variety of languages. He has worked on embedded systems, built distributed build systems, done offshore vendor management, and sat in many, many meetings.

Joanna Jablonski is the executive editor of *Real Python*. She likes natural languages just as much as she likes programming languages. Her love for puzzles, patterns, and pesky little details led her to follow a career in translation. It was only a matter of time before she would fall in love with a new language: Python! She joined *Real Python* in 2018 and has been helping Pythonistas level up ever since.

Jacob Schmitt is a longtime editor of academic and technology-related educational materials both in print and on the Web. He joined *Real Python* in 2020 and edits tutorials, articles, and books written by a diverse array of talented writers and developers.

Contents

CPython Internals: Your Guide to the Python 3 Interpreter

Anthony Shaw

CPython Internals: Your Guide to the Python 3 Interpreter

Anthony Shaw

For online information and ordering of this and other books by Real Python, please visit realpython.com. For more information, please contact us at info@realpython.com.

ISBN: 9781775093343 (paperback)

ISBN: 9781775093350 (electronic)

Cover design by Aldren Santos

Additional editing and proofreading by Jacob Schmitt

What Readers Say About *CPython Internals: Your Guide to the Python 3 Interpreter*

"It's the book that I wish existed years ago when I started my Python journey. After reading this book your skills will grow and you will be able solve even more complex problems that can improve our world."

— **Carol Willing**, CPython core developer and member of the CPython steering council

"The 'Parallelism and Concurrency' chapter is one of my favorites. I had been looking to get an in depth understanding around this topic and I found your book extremely helpful.

Of course, after going over that chapter I couldn't resist the rest. I am eagerly looking forward to have my own printed copy once it's out!

I had gone through your 'Guide to the CPython Source Code' article previously, which got me interested in finding out more about the internals.

There are a ton of books on Python which teach the language, but I haven't really come across anything that would go about explaining the internals to those curious minded.

And while I teach Python to my daughter currently, I have this book added in her must-read list. She's currently studying information systems at Georgia State University."

— **Milan Patel**, vice president at (a major investment bank)

"What impresses me the most about Anthony's book is how it puts all the steps for making changes to the CPython code base in an easy-to-follow sequence. It really feels like a 'missing manual' of sorts.

Diving into the C underpinnings of Python was a lot of fun and it cleared up some longstanding questions marks for me. I found the chapter about CPython's memory allocator especially enlightening.

CPython Internals is a great (and unique) resource for anybody looking to take their knowledge of Python to a deeper level."

— **Dan Bader**, author of *Python Tricks* and editor in chief at *Real Python*

"This book helped me to better understand how lexing and parsing works in Python. It's my recommended source if you want to understand it."

— **Florian Dahlitz**, Pythonista

"A comprehensive walkthrough of the Python internals, a topic which surprisingly has almost no good resource, in an easy-to-understand manner for both beginners as well as advanced Python users."

— **Abhishek Sharma**, data scientist

Contents

Contents

Foreword

A programming language created by a community fosters happiness in its users around the world.

— Guido van Rossum, "King's Day Speech"[1]

I love building tools that help us learn, empower us to create, and move us to share knowledge and ideas with others. I feel humbled, thankful, and proud when I hear how these tools and Python are helping you to solve real-world problems, like climate change or Alzheimer's.

Through my four-decade love of programming and problem solving, I have spent time learning, writing a lot of code, and sharing my ideas with others. I've seen profound changes in technology as the world has progressed from mainframes to cell phone service to the wide-ranging wonders of the Web and cloud computing. All these technologies, including Python, have one thing in common.

At one moment, these successful innovations were nothing more than an idea. The creators, like Guido, had to take risks and leaps of faith to move forward. Dedication, learning through trial and error, and working together through many failures built a solid foundation for success and growth.

CPython Internals will take you on a journey to explore the wildly successful programming language **Python**. The book serves as a guide

---

[1]http://neopythonic.blogspot.com/2016/04/

to how CPython works under the hood. It will give you a glimpse of how the core developers crafted the language.

Python's strengths include its readability and the welcoming community dedicated to education. Anthony embraces these strengths when explaining CPython, encouraging you to read the source and sharing the building blocks of the language with you.

Why do I want to share Anthony's *CPython Internals* with you? It's the book that I wish existed years ago when I started my Python journey. More importantly, I believe we, as members of the Python community, have a unique opportunity to put our expertise to work to help solve the complex real-world problems facing us.

I'm confident that after reading this book, your skills will grow, and you will be able solve even more complex problems and improve our world.

It's my hope that Anthony motivates you to learn more about Python, inspires you to build innovative things, and gives you confidence to share your creations with the world.

> Now is better than never.
>
> — Tim Peters, *The Zen of Python*

Let's follow Tim's wisdom and get started now.

Warmly,

— **Carol Willing**, CPython core developer and member of the CPython steering council

Introduction

Are there certain parts of Python that just seem like magic, like how finding an item is so much faster with dictionaries than looping over a list? How does a generator remember the state of variables each time it yields a value? Why don't you ever have to allocate memory like you do with other languages?

The answer is that CPython, the most popular Python runtime, is written in human-readable C and Python code.

CPython abstracts the complexities of the underlying C platform and your operating system. It makes threading straightforward and cross-platform. It takes the pain of memory management in C and makes it simple.

CPython gives the developer writing Python code the platform to write scalable and performant applications. At some stage in your progression as a Python developer, you'll need to understand how CPython works. These abstractions aren't perfect, and they're leaky.

Once you understand how CPython works, you can fully leverage its power and optimize your applications. This book will explain the concepts, ideas, and technicalities of CPython.

In this book, you'll cover the major concepts behind the internals of CPython and learn how to:

- Read and navigate the source code
- Compile CPython from source code

- Make changes to the Python syntax and compile them into your version of CPython
- Navigate and comprehend the inner workings of features like lists, dictionaries, and generators
- Master CPython's memory management capabilities
- Scale your Python code with parallelism and concurrency
- Modify the core types with new functionality
- Run the test suite
- Profile and benchmark the performance of your Python code and runtime
- Debug C and Python code like a professional
- Modify or upgrade components of the CPython library to contribute them to future versions

Take your time with each chapter and try out the demos and interactive elements. You'll feel a sense of achievement as you grasp the core concepts that will make you a better Python programmer.

How to Use This Book

This book is all about learning by doing, so be sure to set up your IDE early on by reading the instructions, downloading the code, and writing the examples.

For the best results, we recommend that you avoid copying and pasting the code examples. The examples in this book took many iterations to get right, and they may also contain bugs.

Making mistakes and learning how to fix them is part of the learning process. You might discover better ways to implement the examples, try changing them, and see what effect it has.

With enough practice, you'll master this material—and have fun along the way!

How skilled in Python do I need to be to use this book?

This book is aimed at intermediate to advanced Python developers. Every effort has been taken to show code examples, but some intermediate Python techniques will be used throughout.

Do I need to know C to use this book?

You don't need to be proficient in C to use this book. If you're new to C, then check out the appendix, "Introduction to C for Python Programmers," for a quick introduction.

How long will it take to finish this book?

We don't recommend rushing through this book. Try reading one chapter at a time, trying the examples after each chapter and exploring the code simultaneously. Once you've finished the book, it will make a great reference guide for you to come back to in time.

Won't the content in this book be out of date really quickly?

Python has been around for more than thirty years. Some parts of the CPython code haven't been touched since they were originally written. Many of the principles in this book have been the same for ten or more years.

In fact, while writing this book, we discovered many lines of code that were written by Guido van Rossum (the author of Python) and left untouched since version 1.

Some of the concepts in this book are brand-new. Some are even experimental. While writing this book, we came across issues in the source code and bugs in CPython that were later fixed or improved.[2]

---

[2]https://realpython.com/cpython-fixes

That's part of the wonder of CPython as a flourishing open source project.

The skills you'll learn in this book will help you read and understand current and future versions of CPython. Change is constant, and expertise is something you can develop along the way.

Bonus Material and Learning Resources

This book comes with a number of free bonus resources that you can access at realpython.com/cpython-internals/resources/. On this web page you can also find an errata list with corrections maintained by the *Real Python* team.

Code Samples

The examples and sample configurations throughout this book will be marked with a header denoting them as part of the `cpython-book-samples` folder:

cpython-book-samples ▶ 01 ▶ example.py

```
import this
```

You can download the code samples at realpython.com/cpython-internals/resources/.

Code Licenses

The example Python scripts associated with this book are licensed under a Creative Commons Public Domain (CC0) License.[3] This means you're welcome to use any portion of the code for any purpose in your own programs.

---

[3]https://creativecommons.org/publicdomain/zero/1.0/

CPython is licensed under the Python Software Foundation 2.0 license.[4] Snippets and samples of CPython source code used in this book are done so under the terms of the PSF 2.0 license.

> **Note**
>
> The code in this book has been tested with Python 3.9 on Windows 10, macOS 10.15, and Linux.

Formatting Conventions

Code blocks are used to present example code:

```python
# This is Python code:
print("Hello, World!")
```

Operating system–agnostic commands follow the Unix-style format:

```
$ # This is a terminal command:
$ python hello-world.py
```

(The $ is not part of the command.)

Windows-specific commands have the Windows command-line format:

```
> python hello-world.py
```

(The > is not part of the command.)

Command-line syntax follows this format:

- `Unbracketed text` must be typed as it is shown.

- `<Text inside angle brackets>` indicates a variable for which you must supply a value. For example, you would replace `<filename>` with the name of a specific file.

---

[4]https://github.com/python/cpython/blob/master/LICENSE

- [Text inside square brackets] indicates an optional argument that you may supply.

Bold text denotes a new or important term.

Notes and alert boxes appear as follows:

> **Note**
>
> This is a note filled in with placeholder text. The quick brown fox jumps over the lazy dog. The quick brown Python slithers over the lazy hog.

> **Important**
>
> This is an alert also filled in with placeholder text. The quick brown fox jumps over the lazy dog. The quick brown Python slithers over the lazy hog.

Any references to a file within the CPython source code will be shown like this:

path ▸ to ▸ file.py

Shortcuts or menu commands will be given in sequence, like this:

File ≫ Other ≫ Option

Keyboard commands and shortcuts will be given for both macOS and Windows:

Ctrl + Space

Feedback and Errata

We welcome ideas, suggestions, feedback, and the occasional rant. Did you find a topic confusing? Did you find an error in the text or code? Did we leave out a topic you would love to know more about?

We're always looking to improve our teaching materials. Whatever the reason, please send in your feedback at the link below:

realpython.com/cpython-internals/feedback

About Real Python

At *Real Python*, you'll learn real-world programming skills from a community of professional Pythonistas from all around the world.

The realpython.com website launched in 2012 and currently helps more than three million Python developers each month with books, programming tutorials, and other in-depth learning resources.

Here's where you can find *Real Python* on the Web:

- realpython.com
- @realpython on Twitter
- The *Real Python Newsletter*[5]
- The *Real Python Podcast*[6]

---

[5]https://realpython.com/newsletter
[6]https://realpython.com/podcast

Getting the CPython Source Code

When you type `python` at the console or install a Python distribution from Python.org, you're running **CPython**. CPython is one of many Python implementations maintained and written by different teams of developers. Some alternatives you may have heard of are PyPy, Cython, and Jython.

The unique thing about CPython is that it contains both a runtime and the shared language specification that all other Python implementations use. CPython is the official, or reference, implementation of Python.

The **Python language specification** is the document that describes the Python language. For example, it says that `assert` is a reserved keyword and that `[]` is used for indexing, slicing, and creating empty lists.

Think about the features you expect from the Python distribution:

- When you type `python` without a file or module, it gives an interactive prompt (REPL).
- You can import built-in modules like `json`, `csv`, and `collections` from the standard library.
- You can install packages from the Internet using `pip`.
- You can test your applications using the built-in `unittest` library.

These are all part of the CPython distribution. It includes a lot more than just a compiler.

In this book, you'll explore the different parts of the CPython distribution:

- The language specification
- The compiler
- The standard library modules
- The core types
- The test suite

What's in the Source Code?

The CPython source distribution comes with a whole range of tools, libraries, and components that you'll explore in this book.

> **Note**
>
> This book targets version 3.9[a] of the CPython source code.
>
> ---
> [a]https://github.com/python/cpython/tree/3.9

To download a copy of the CPython source code, you can use `git` to pull the latest version:

```
$ git clone --branch 3.9 https://github.com/python/cpython
$ cd cpython
```

The examples in this book are based on Python version 3.9.

> **Important**
>
> Switching to the 3.9 branch is an important step. The master branch changes on an hourly basis. Many of the examples and exercises in this book are unlikely to work on master.

Note

If you don't have Git available on your computer, then you can install it from git-scm.com. Alternatively, you can download a ZIP file[a] of the CPython source directly from the GitHub website.

If you download the source as a ZIP file, then it won't contain any history, tags, or branches.

---
[a]https://github.com/python/cpython/archive/3.9.zip

Inside the newly downloaded `cpython` directory, you'll find the following subdirectories:

```
cpython/
├── Doc          Source for the documentation
├── Grammar      The computer-readable language definition
├── Include      The C header files
├── Lib          Standard library modules written in Python
├── Mac          macOS support files
├── Misc         Miscellaneous files
├── Modules      Standard library modules written in C
├── Objects      Core types and the object model
├── Parser       The Python parser source code
├── PC           Windows build support files for older versions of Windows
├── PCBuild      Windows build support files
├── Programs     Source code for the python executable and other binaries
├── Python       The CPython interpreter source code
├── Tools        Standalone tools useful for building or extending CPython
└── m4           Custom scripts to automate configuration of the makefile
```

Next, you'll set up your development environment.

Setting Up Your Development Environment

Throughout this book, you'll be working with both C and Python code. It's essential that you have your development environment configured to support both languages.

The CPython source code is about 65 percent Python (of which the tests are a significant part) and 24 percent C. The remainder is a mix of other languages.

IDE or Editor?

If you haven't yet decided which development environment to use, then there's one decision to make first: whether to use an integrated development environment (IDE) or a code editor.

- An **IDE** targets a specific language and toolchain. Most IDEs have integrated testing, syntax checking, version control, and compilation.

- A **code editor** enables you to edit code files, regardless of language. Most code editors are simple text editors with syntax highlighting.

Because of their full-featured nature, IDEs often consume more hardware resources. So if you have limited RAM (less than 8 GB), then a code editor is recommended.

IDEs also take longer to start up. If you want to edit a file quickly, then a code editor is a better choice.

There are hundreds of editors and IDEs available for free or at a cost. Here are some commonly used IDEs and editors suitable for CPython development:

Application	Style	Supports
Microsoft Visual Studio Code	Editor	Windows, macOS, and Linux
Atom	Editor	Windows, macOS, and Linux
Sublime Text	Editor	Windows, macOS, and Linux
Vim	Editor	Windows, macOS, and Linux
Emacs	Editor	Windows, macOS, and Linux
Microsoft Visual Studio	IDE (C, Python, and others)	Windows
PyCharm by JetBrains	IDE (Python and others)	Windows, macOS, and Linux
CLion by JetBrains	IDE (C and others)	Windows, macOS, and Linux

A version of Microsoft Visual Studio is also available for Mac, but it doesn't support Python Tools for Visual Studio or C compilation.

In the sections below, you'll explore the setup steps for the following editors and IDEs:

- Microsoft Visual Studio
- Microsoft Visual Studio Code
- JetBrains CLion
- Vim

Skip ahead to the section for your chosen application, or read all of them if you want to compare.

Setting Up Visual Studio

The newest version of Visual Studio, Visual Studio 2019, has built-in support for Python and the C source code on Windows. I recommend using it for the examples and exercises in this book. If you already have Visual Studio 2017 installed, then that would also work.

> **Note**
>
> None of the paid features of Visual Studio are required for compiling CPython or completing this book. You can use the free Community edition.
>
> However, the profile-guided optimization build profile requires the Professional edition or higher.

Visual Studio is available for free from Microsoft's Visual Studio website.[7]

Once you've downloaded the Visual Studio installer, you'll be asked to select which components you want to install. You'll need the following components for this book:

- The **Python development** workload
- The optional **Python native development tools**
- Python 3 64-bit (3.7.2)

You can deselect Python 3 64-bit (3.7.2) if you already have Python 3.7 installed. You can also deselect any other optional features if you want to conserve disk space.

The installer will then download and install all the required components. The installation can take up to an hour, so you may want to read on and come back to this section when it finishes.

Once the installation is complete, click Launch to start Visual Studio. You'll be prompted to sign in. If you have a Microsoft account, you

---

[7]https://visualstudio.microsoft.com/vs/

can either log in or skip that step.

Next, you'll be prompted to open a project. You can clone CPython's Git repository directly from Visual Studio by choosing the Clone or check out code option.

For the repository location, enter `https://github.com/python/cpython`, choose your local path, and select Clone .

Visual Studio will then download a copy of CPython from GitHub using the version of Git bundled with Visual Studio. This step also saves you the hassle of having to install Git on Windows. The download may take up to ten minutes.

Important

Visual Studio will automatically checkout the master branch. Before compiling, make sure you change to the 3.9 branch from within the Team Explorer window. Switching to the 3.9 branch is an important step. The master branch changes on an hourly basis. Many of the examples and exercises in this book are unlikely to work on master.

Once the project has downloaded, you need to point Visual Studio to the `PCBuild` ‣ `pcbuild.sln` solution file by clicking Solutions and Projects ⟩ ⟩ pcbuild.sln :

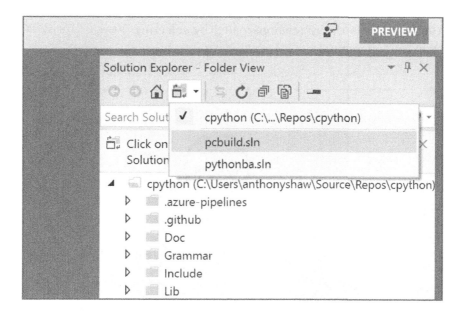

Now that you have Visual Studio configured and the source code downloaded, you can compile CPython on Windows by following the steps in the next chapter.

Setting Up Visual Studio Code

Microsoft Visual Studio Code is an extensible code editor with an online marketplace of plugins.

It makes an excellent choice for working with CPython as it supports both C and Python with an integrated Git interface.

Installing

Visual Studio Code, sometimes known as VS Code, is available with a simple installer at code.visualstudio.com.

Out of the box, VS Code has the necessary code editing capabilities, but it becomes more powerful once you install extensions.

You can access the Extensions panel by selecting View ⟩ Extensions from the top menu:

Inside the Extensions panel, you can search for extensions by name or by their unique identifier, such as `ms-vscode.cpptools`. In some cases there are many plugins with similar names, so use the unique identifier to be sure you're installing the right one.

Recommended Extensions for This Book

There are several useful extensions for working with CPython:

- **C/C++** (`ms-vscode.cpptools`) provides support for C/C++, including IntelliSense, debugging, and code highlighting.

- **Python** (`ms-python.python`) provides rich Python support for editing, debugging, and reading Python code.

- **reStructuredText** (`lextudio.restructuredtext`) provides rich support for reStructuredText, the format used in the CPython documentation.

- **Task Explorer** (`spmeesseman.vscode-taskexplorer`) adds a Task Explorer panel inside the Explorer tab, making it easier to launch make tasks.

After you install these extensions, you'll need to reload the editor.

Many of the tasks in this book require a command line. You can add an integrated terminal into VS Code by selecting Terminal ≫ New Terminal. A terminal will appear below the code editor:

Using Advanced Code Navigation and Expansion

With the plugins installed, you can perform some advanced code navigation.

For example, if you right-click a function call in a C file and select Go to References, then VS Code will find other references to that function in the codebase:

Go to References is very useful for discovering the proper calling form for a function.

If you click on or hover over a C macro, then the editor will expand that macro to the compiled code:

To jump to the definition of a function, hover over any call to it and press Cmd + Click on macOS or Ctrl + Click on Linux and Windows.

Configuring the Task and Launch Files

VS Code uses a `.vscode` folder in the workspace directory. If this folder doesn't exist, create it now. Inside this folder, you can create the following files:

- `tasks.json` for shortcuts to commands that execute your project
- `launch.json` to configure the debugger (see the chapter "Debugging")
- Other plugin-specific files

Create a `tasks.json` file inside the `.vscode` directory if one doesn't already exist. This `tasks.json` file will get you started:

cpython-book-samples ▸ 11 ▸ tasks.json

```
{
    "version": "2.0.0",
    "tasks": [
        {
            "label": "build",
            "type": "shell",
            "group": {
                "kind": "build",
                "isDefault": true
            },
            "windows": {
                "command": "PCBuild/build.bat",
                "args": ["-p", "x64", "-c", "Debug"]
            },
            "linux": {
                "command": "make -j2 -s"
            },
            "osx": {
                "command": "make -j2 -s"
            }
        }
    ]
}
```

Using the Task Explorer plugin, you'll see a list of your configured tasks inside the vscode group:

In the next chapter, you'll learn more about the build process for compiling CPython.

Setting Up JetBrains CLion

JetBrains makes an IDE for Python called PyCharm as well as an IDE for C/C++ development called CLion.

CPython has both C and Python code. You can't install C/C++ support into PyCharm, but CLion comes bundled with Python support.

> **Important**
>
> Makefile support is available only in CLion versions 2020.2 and above.

> **Important**
>
> This step requires that you have both generated a makefile by running `configure` and compiled CPython.
>
> Please read the chapter "Compiling CPython" for your operating system and then return to this chapter.

After compiling CPython for the first time, you'll have a makefile in the root of the source directory.

Open CLion and choose `Open or Import` from the welcome screen. Navigate to the source directory, select the makefile, and press `Open`:

CLion will ask whether you want to open the directory or import the makefile as a new project. Select Open as Project to import as a project.

CLion will ask which make target to run before importing. Leave the default option, clean, and continue:

Next, check that you can build the CPython executable from CLion. From the top menu, select Build ≫ Build Project.

In the status bar, you should see a progress indicator for the project build:

35

Once this task is complete, you can target the compiled binary as a run/debug configuration.

Select Run ⟩⟩ Edit Configurations to open the Run/Debug Configurations window. Inside this window, select + ⟩⟩ Makefile Application and complete the following steps:

1. Set the Name to cpython.

2. Leave the build target as all.

3. For the executable, select the dropdown and choose Select Other, then find the compiled CPython binary in the source directory. It will be called python or python.exe.

4. Enter any program arguments you wish to always have, such as -X dev to enable development mode. These flags are covered later in "Setting Runtime Configuration With the Command Line."

5. Set the working directory to the CLion macro $ProjectFileDir$:

Click OK to add this configuration. You can repeat this step as many times as you like for any of the CPython make targets. See the section

"CPython's Make Targets" in the chapter "Compiling CPython" for a full reference.

The cpython build configuration will now be available in the top right of the CLion window:

To test it out, click the arrow icon or select $\boxed{\text{Run}} \gg \boxed{\text{Run 'cpython'}}$ from the top menu. You should now see the REPL at the bottom of the CLion window:

Great! Now you can make changes and quickly try them out by clicking $\boxed{\text{Build}}$ and $\boxed{\text{Run}}$. If you put any breakpoints in the C code, then make sure you choose $\boxed{\text{Debug}}$ instead of $\boxed{\text{Run}}$.

Within the code editor, the shortcuts $\boxed{\text{Cmd}}+\boxed{\text{Click}}$ on macOS and $\boxed{\text{Ctrl}}$ $+\boxed{\text{Click}}$ on Windows and Linux will bring up in-editor navigation features:

```
708
709 ≒    static int do_raise(PyThreadState *tstate, PyObject *exc, PyObject *cause);
710 ≒    static int unpack_iterable(PyThreadState *, PyObject *, int, int, PyObject **);
711
712      #define _Py_TracingPossible(ceval) ((ceval)->tracing_possible)
713                                    Usages of _Py_TracingPossible in All Places (4 usages found)          ✗ ✗
714
715      PyObject *                  ceval.c  847    if (!tltrace && !_Py_TracingPossible(ceval) && !PyDTrace_LINE_ENABLED()) { \
716 ≒    PyEval_EvalCode(PyObj     ceval.c 1274    if (_Py_TracingPossible(ceval) &&
717      {                           tags    8231    _Py_TracingPossible ./Python/ceval.c /^#define _Py_TracingPossible(/;" d file:
718          return PyEval_Eva  Press ⌥⌘F7 again to search in Project Files
719          globals, locals,
720          (PyObject **)NULL, 0,
721          (PyObject **)NULL, 0,
722          (PyObject **)NULL, 0,
723          NULL, NULL);
724      }
725
726
727      /* Interpreter main loop */
728
```

Setting Up Vim

Vim is a powerful console-based text editor. For fast development, use Vim with your hands resting on the keyboard home keys. The shortcuts and commands are within reach.

> **Note**
>
> On most Linux distributions and within the macOS Terminal, `vi` is an alias for `vim`. We'll use the `vim` command in this book, but if you have the alias, then `vi` will also work.

Out of the box, Vim has only basic functionality, little more than a text editor like Notepad. With some configuration and extensions, however, Vim can become a powerful tool for both Python and C editing.

Vim's extensions are in various locations, including GitHub. To ease the configuration and installation of plugins from GitHub, you can install a plugin manager like Vundle.

To install Vundle, run this command at the terminal:

```
$ git clone https://github.com/VundleVim/Vundle.vim.git \
  ~/.vim/bundle/Vundle.vim
```

Once Vundle is downloaded, you need to configure Vim to load the Vundle engine.

You'll install two plugins:

1. **Fugitive:** A status bar for Git with shortcuts for many Git tasks

2. **Tagbar:** A pane for making it easier to jump to functions, methods, and classes

To install these plugins, first change the contents of your Vim configuration file (normally HOME ▶ .vimrc) to include the following lines:

cpython-book-samples ▶ 11 ▶ .vimrc

```
syntax on
set nocompatible           " be iMproved, required
filetype off               " required

" set the runtime path to include Vundle and initialize
set rtp+=~/.vim/bundle/Vundle.vim
call vundle#begin()

" let Vundle manage Vundle, required
Plugin 'VundleVim/Vundle.vim'

" The following are examples of different formats supported.
" Keep Plugin commands between vundle#begin/end.
" plugin on GitHub repo
Plugin 'tpope/vim-fugitive'
Plugin 'majutsushi/tagbar'
" All of your Plugins must be added before this line
call vundle#end()          " required
filetype plugin indent on  " required
" Open tagbar automatically in C files, optional
autocmd FileType c call tagbar#autoopen(0)
" Open tagbar automatically in Python files, optional
autocmd FileType python call tagbar#autoopen(0)
" Show status bar, optional
set laststatus=2
" Set status as git status (branch), optional
set statusline=%{FugitiveStatusline()}
```

To download and install these plugins, run the following command:

```
$ vim +PluginInstall +qall
```

You should see output for the download and installation of the plugins specified in the configuration file.

When editing or exploring the CPython source code, you will want to jump quickly between methods, functions, and macros. A basic text search won't distinguish a call to a function or its definition from the implementation. But you can use an application called ctags[8] to index source files across a multitude of languages into a plain text database.

To index CPython's headers for all the C files and Python files in the standard library, run the following code:

```
$ ./configure
$ make tags
```

Now open the Python▸ceval.c file in Vim:

```
$ vim Python/ceval.c
```

You'll see the Git status at the bottom and the functions, macros, and variables in the right-hand pane:

---

[8]http://ctags.sourceforge.net/

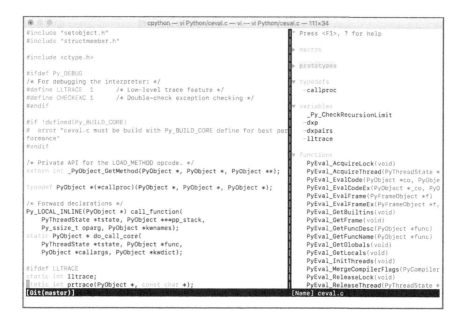

Next, open a Python file, such as Lib ▸ subprocess.py:

```
$ vim Lib/subprocess.py
```

Tagbar will show your imports, classes, methods, and functions:

Within Vim, you can switch between windows with Ctrl + W, move to the right-hand pane with L, and use the arrow keys to move up and down between the tagged functions.

Press Enter to skip to any function implementation. To move back to the editor pane, press Ctrl + W, then press H.

> **See Also**
>
> Check out VIM Adventures[a] for a fun way to learn and memorize the Vim commands.
>
> ---
> [a]https://vim-adventures.com/

Conclusion

If you're still undecided about which environment to use, then you don't need to make a decision right away. We used multiple environments while writing this book and working on changes to CPython.

Debugging is a critical feature for productivity, so having a reliable debugger that you can use to explore the runtime and understand bugs will save you a lot of time. If you're used to debugging in Python with `print()`, then it's important to note that this approach doesn't work in C. You'll cover debugging in full later in this book.

Compiling CPython

Now that you've downloaded a development environment and configured it, you can compile the CPython source code into an executable interpreter.

Unlike Python files, C source code must be recompiled each time it changes. You'll probably want to bookmark this chapter and memorize some of the steps, because you'll be repeating them a lot.

In the previous chapter, you saw how to set up your development environment with an option to run the build stage, which recompiles CPython. Before the build steps will work, you need a C compiler and some build tools.

The tools used depend on the operating system you're using, so skip ahead to the section for your operating system.

> **Note**
>
> If you're concerned that any of these steps will interfere with your existing CPython installations, don't worry. The CPython source directory behaves like a virtual environment.
>
> When compiling CPython or modifying the source or the standard library, this all stays within the sandbox of the source directory.
>
> If you want to install a custom version, this step is covered in this chapter.

Compiling CPython on macOS

Compiling CPython on macOS requires some additional applications and libraries. First, you'll need the essential C compiler tool kit. **Command Line Tools** is an app that you can update in macOS through the App Store. You need to perform the initial installation on the terminal.

> **Note**
>
> To open up a terminal in macOS, go to Applications ⟩ Other ⟩ Terminal. You'll want to save this app to your Dock, so Ctrl + Click the icon and select Keep in Dock.

Within the terminal, install the C compiler and tool kit by running the following:

```
$ xcode-select --install
```

After running this command, you'll be prompted to download and install a set of tools, including Git, Make, and the GNU C compiler.

You'll also need a working copy of OpenSSL to use for fetching packages from the PyPI website. If you plan on using this build to install additional packages, then SSL validation is required.

The most straightforward way to install OpenSSL on macOS is to use Homebrew.

> **Note**
>
> If you don't have Homebrew, then you can download and install it directly from GitHub with the following command:
>
> ```
> $ /usr/bin/ruby -e "$(curl -fsSL \
>     https://raw.githubusercontent.com/Homebrew/install/master/install)"
> ```

Once you have Homebrew installed, you can install the dependencies for CPython with the `brew install` command:

```
$ brew install openssl xz zlib gdbm sqlite
```

Now that you have the dependencies, you can run the `configure` script.

The Homebrew command `brew --prefix <package>` will give the directory where `<package>` is installed. You will enable support for SSL by compiling the location that Homebrew uses.

The flag `--with-pydebug` enables debug hooks. Add this flag if you intend on debugging for development or testing purposes. Debugging CPython is covered extensively in the "Debugging" chapter.

The configuration stage needs to be run only once, with the location of the zlib package specified:

```
$ CPPFLAGS="-I$(brew --prefix zlib)/include" \
  LDFLAGS="-L$(brew --prefix zlib)/lib" \
  ./configure --with-openssl=$(brew --prefix openssl) \
  --with-pydebug
```

Running `./configure` will generate a makefile in the root of the repository. You can use it to automate the build process.

You can now build the CPython binary by running the following command:

```
$ make -j2 -s
```

See Also

For more information on the options for `make`, see the section "A Quick Primer on Make."

During the build, you may receive some errors. In the build summary, `make` will notify you that not all packages were built. For example, the `ossaudiodev`, `spwd`, and `_tkinter` packages will fail to build with this set of instructions. That's okay if you aren't planning on developing against these packages. If you are, then check out the Python Developer's Guide[9] for more information.

The build will take a few minutes and generate a binary called python.exe. Every time you make changes to the source code, you'll need to rerun make with the same flags.

The python.exe binary is the debug binary of CPython. Execute python.exe to see a working REPL:

```
$ ./python.exe
Python 3.9 (tags/v3.9:9cf67522, Oct 5 2020, 10:00:00)
[Clang 10.0.1 (clang-1001.0.46.4)] on darwin
Type "help", "copyright", "credits" or "license" for more information.
>>>
```

> **Important**
>
> Yes, that's right, the macOS build has a .exe file extension. This extension is *not* because it's a Windows binary!
>
> Because macOS has a case-insensitive file system, the developers didn't want people to accidentally refer to the directory Python/ when working with the binary, so they appended .exe to avoid ambiguity.
>
> If you later run make install or make altinstall, then the file will be renamed python before it's installed onto your system.

[9]https://devguide.python.org/

Compiling CPython on Linux

To compile CPython on Linux, you first need to download and install `make`, `gcc`, `configure`, and `pkgconfig`.

Use this command for Fedora Core, RHEL, CentOS, or other YUM-based systems:

```
$ sudo yum install yum-utils
```

Use this command for Debian, Ubuntu, or other APT-based systems:

```
$ sudo apt install build-essential
```

Then install some additional required packages.

Use this command for Fedora Core, RHEL, CentOS or other YUM-based systems:

```
$ sudo yum-builddep python3
```

Use this command for Debian, Ubuntu, or other APT-based systems:

```
$ sudo apt install libssl-dev zlib1g-dev libncurses5-dev \
    libncursesw5-dev libreadline-dev libsqlite3-dev libgdbm-dev \
    libdb5.3-dev libbz2-dev libexpat1-dev liblzma-dev libffi-dev
```

Now that you have the dependencies, you can run the `configure` script, optionally enabling the debug hooks using `--with-pydebug`:

```
$ ./configure --with-pydebug
```

Next, you can build the CPython binary by running the generated makefile:

```
$ make -j2 -s
```

> **See Also**
>
> For more help on the options for make, see the section "A Quick
> Primer on Make."

Review the output to ensure that there were no issues compiling the
_ssl module. If there were, then check with your distribution for in-
structions on installing the headers for OpenSSL.

During the build, you may receive some errors. In the build summary,
make will notify you that not all packages were built. That's okay if you
aren't planning on developing against those packages. If you are, then
check out the package details for required libraries.

The build will take a few minutes and generate a binary called python.
This is the debug binary of CPython. Execute ./python to see a working
REPL:

```
$ ./python
Python 3.9 (tags/v3.9:9cf67522, Oct 5 2020, 10:00:00)
[Clang 10.0.1 (clang-1001.0.46.4)] on Linux
Type "help", "copyright", "credits" or "license" for more information.
>>>
```

Installing a Custom Version

If you're happy with your changes and want to use them inside your
system, then you can install the Python binary from your source repository as a custom version.

For macOS and Linux, use the altinstall command, which doesn't
create symbolic links for python3 and installs a standalone version:

```
$ make altinstall
```

For Windows, you have to change the build configuration from Debug to Release, then copy the packaged binaries to a directory on your
computer that is part of the system path.

A Quick Primer on Make

As a Python developer, you might not have come across make before. Or perhaps you have, but you haven't spent much time with it.

For C, C++, and other compiled languages, the list of commands you need to execute to load, link, and compile your code in the right order can be very long. When compiling applications from source, you need to link any external libraries in the system.

It would be unrealistic to expect the developer to know the locations of all of these libraries and to copy and paste them into the command line, so make and configure are commonly used in C/C++ projects to automate the creation of a build script.

When you executed ./configure, autoconf searched your system for the libraries that CPython requires and copied their paths into a makefile.

The generated makefile is similar to a shell script and is broken into sections called **targets**.

Take the docclean target as an example. This target deletes some generated documentation files using the rm command:

```
docclean:
    rm -rf Doc/build
    rm -rf Doc/tools/sphinx Doc/tools/pygments Doc/tools/docutils
```

To execute this target, run make docclean. docclean is a simple target as it runs only two commands.

This is the convention for executing a make target:

```
$ make [options] [target]
```

If you call make without specifying a target, then make will run the default target, which is the first target specified in the makefile. For CPython, this is the all target, which compiles all parts of CPython.

make has many options. Here are some you'll find useful throughout this book:

Option	Use
-d, --debug[=FLAGS]	Print various types of debugging information
-e, --environment-overrides	Environment variables override makefiles
-i, --ignore-errors	Ignore errors from commands
-j [N], --jobs[=N]	Allow N jobs at once or infinite jobs otherwise
-k, --keep-going	Keep going when some targets can't be made
-l [N], --load-average[=N], --max-load[=N]	Start multiple jobs only if load < N
-n, --dry-run	Print commands instead of running them
-s, --silent	Don't echo commands
-S, --stop	Stop when targets can't be made

In the next section and throughout the book, you'll run make with these options:

```
$ make -j2 -s [target]
```

The -j2 flag allows make to run two jobs simultaneously. If you have four or more cores, then you can change this to four or higher and the compilation will complete faster.

The -s flag stops the makefile from printing every command it runs to the console. If you want to see what's happening, then remove the -s flag.

CPython's Make Targets

For both Linux and macOS, you'll find yourself needing to clean up files, build, or refresh the configuration. The sections below contain tables outlining a number of useful make targets built into CPython's makefile.

Build Targets

The following targets are used for building the CPython binary:

Target	Purpose
all (default)	Build the compiler, libraries, and modules
clinic	Run Argument Clinic on all source files
profile-opt	Compile the Python binary with profile-guided optimization
regen-all	Regenerate all generated files
sharedmods	Build the shared modules

Test Targets

The following targets are used for testing your compiled binary:

Target	Purpose
coverage	Compile and run tests with gcov
coverage-lcov	Create coverage HTML reports
quicktest	Run a faster set of regression tests by excluding the tests that take a long time
test	Run a basic set of regression tests
testall	Run the full test suite twice, once without .pyc files and once with them
testuniversal	Run the test suite for both architectures in a universal build on OS X

Cleaning Targets

The primary cleaning targets are clean, clobber, and distclean. The clean target is for generally removing compiled and cached libraries and .pyc files.

If you find that clean doesn't do the job, then try clobber. The clobber target will remove your makefile, so you'll have to run ./configure again.

To completely clean out an environment before distribution, run the distclean target.

The following list includes the three primary targets listed above, as well as some additional cleaning targets:

Target	Purpose
check-clean-src	Check that the source is clean when building out of source
clean	Remove .pyc files, compiled libraries, and profiles
cleantest	Remove test_python_* directories of previous failed test jobs
clobber	Same as clean but also remove libraries, tags, configurations, and builds
distclean	Same as clobber but also remove anything generated from source, such as makefiles
docclean	Remove built documentation in Doc/
profile-removal	Remove any optimization profiles
pycremoval	Remove .pyc files

Installation Targets

There are two flavors of installation targets: the default version, such as install, and the alt version, such as altinstall. If you want to install the compiled version onto your computer but don't want it to become the default Python 3 installation, then use the alt version of the commands:

Target	Purpose
altbininstall	Install the python interpreter with the version affixed, such as python3.9
altinstall	Install shared libraries, binaries, and documentation with the version suffix
altmaninstall	Install the versioned manuals
bininstall	Install all the binaries, such as python, idle, and 2to3
commoninstall	Install shared libraries and modules
install	Install shared libraries, binaries, and documentation (will run commoninstall, bininstall, and maninstall)
libinstall	Install shared libraries
maninstall	Install the manuals
sharedinstall	Load modules dynamically

After you install with `make install`, the command `python3` will link to your compiled binary. If you use `make altinstall`, however, only `python$(VERSION)` will be installed, and the existing link for `python3` will remain intact.

Miscellaneous Targets

Below are some additional `make` targets that you may find useful:

Target	Purpose
`autoconf`	Regenerate `configure` and `pyconfig.h.in`
`python-config`	Generate the `python-config` script
`recheck`	Rerun `configure` with the same options as last time
`smelly`	Check that exported symbols start with `Py` or `_Py` (see PEP 7)
`tags`	Create a tags file for vi
`TAGS`	Create a tags file for Emacs

Compiling CPython on Windows

There are two ways to compile the CPython binaries and libraries from Windows:

1. Compile from the command prompt. This still requires the Microsoft Visual C++ compiler, which comes with Visual Studio.

2. Open `PCbuild ▸ pcbuild.sln` from Visual Studio and build directly.

In the sections below, you'll explore both of these options.

Installing the Dependencies

For both the command prompt compile script and the Visual Studio solution, you need to install several external tools, libraries, and C headers.

Inside the PCbuild folder is a .bat file that automates this process for you. Open a command prompt window inside PCbuild and execute PCbuild ▸ get_externals.bat:

```
> get_externals.bat
Using py -3.7 (found 3.7 with py.exe)
Fetching external libraries...
Fetching bzip2-1.0.6...
Fetching sqlite-3.28.0.0...
Fetching xz-5.2.2...
Fetching zlib-1.2.11...
Fetching external binaries...
Fetching openssl-bin-1.1.1d...
Fetching tcltk-8.6.9.0...
Finished.
```

Now you can compile from either the command prompt or Visual Studio.

Compiling From the Command Prompt

To compile from the command prompt, you need to select the CPU architecture you want to compile against. The default is win32, but chances are that you want a 64-bit (amd64) binary.

If you do any debugging, then the debug build comes with the ability to attach breakpoints in the source code. To enable the debug build, you add -c Debug to specify the debug configuration.

By default, build.bat will fetch external dependencies, but because we've already done that step, it will print a message skipping downloads:

```
> build.bat -p x64 -c Debug
```

This command will produce the Python binary PCbuild ▸ amd64 ▸ python_d.exe. Start that binary directly from the command prompt:

```
> amd64\python_d.exe
```

```
Python 3.9 (tags/v3.9:9cf67522, Oct 5 2020, 10:00:00)
 [MSC v.1922 64 bit (AMD64)] on win32
Type "help", "copyright", "credits" or "license" for more information.
>>>
```

You're now inside the REPL of your compiled CPython binary.

To compile a release binary, use this command:

```
> build.bat -p x64 -c Release
```

This command will produce the binary PCbuild ‣ amd64 ‣ python.exe.

> **Note**
>
> The suffix _d specifies that CPython was built in the debug configuration.
>
> The released binaries on Python.org are compiled in the profile-guided optimization (PGO) configuration. See the "Profile-Guided Optimization (PGO)" section at the end of this chapter for more details on PGO.

Arguments

The following arguments are available in build.bat:

Flag	Purpose	Expected value
-p	Build platform CPU architecture	x64, Win32 (default), ARM, ARM64
-c	Build configuration	Release (default), Debug, PGInstrument or PGUpdate
-t	Build target	Build (default), Rebuild, Clean, CleanAll

Flags

Here are some optional flags you can use for build.bat:

Flag	Purpose
-v	Verbose mode: show informational messages during build
-vv	Very verbose mode: show detailed messages during build
-q	Quiet mode: show only warnings and errors during build
-e	Download and install external dependencies (default)
-E	*Don't* download or install external dependencies
--pgo	Build with profile-guided optimization
--regen	Regenerate all grammar and tokens (used when you update the language)

For a full list, run build.bat -h.

Compiling From Visual Studio

Inside the PCbuild folder is a Visual Studio solution file, PCbuild ▸ pcbuild.sln, for building and exploring CPython source code.

When the solution file is loaded, it will prompt you to retarget the projects inside the solution to the version of the C/C++ compiler that you have installed. Visual Studio will also target the release of the Windows SDK that you have installed.

Be sure to change the Windows SDK version to the newest installed version and the platform toolset to the latest version. If you missed this window, then you can right-click the solution file in the Solutions and Projects window and select Retarget Solution.

Navigate to Build ⟩ Configuration Manager and ensure the Active Solution Configuration drop-down list is set to Debug and the Active Solution Platform list is set to either x64 for 64-bit CPU architecture or win32 for 32-bit.

Next, build CPython by pressing Ctrl + Shift + B or choosing Build ⟩ ⟩ Build Solution. If you receive any errors about the Windows SDK being missing, make sure you set the right targeting settings in the Re-target Solution window. You should also see a Windows Kits folder in your Start menu with Windows Software Development Kit inside it.

The build stage could take ten minutes or more the first time. Once the build completes, you may see a few warnings that you can ignore.

To start the debug version of CPython, press F5, and CPython will launch the REPL in debug mode:

You can run the release build by changing the build configuration from Debug to Release on the top menu bar and rerunning Build > Build Solution. You now have both debug and release versions of the CPython binary within PCbuild ▸ amd64.

You can set up Visual Studio to be able to open a REPL with either the release or debug build by choosing Tools > Python > Python Environments from the top menu. In the Python Environments panel, click Add Environment and then target the debug or release binary. The debug binary will end in _d.exe, such as python_d.exe or pythonw_d.exe.

You'll most likely want to use the debug binary as it comes with debugging support in Visual Studio and will be useful as you read through this book.

In the Add Environment window, target the `python_d.exe` file as the interpreter inside `PCbuild` ▸ `amd64` and the `pythonw_d.exe` as the windowed interpreter:

Start a REPL session by clicking Open Interactive Window in the Python Environments window and you'll see the REPL for the compiled version of Python:

Throughout this book, there will be REPL sessions with example commands. I encourage you to use the debug binary to run these REPL sessions in case you want to put in any breakpoints within the code.

To make it easier to navigate the code, in the Solution view, click the toggle button next to the Home icon to switch to Folder view:

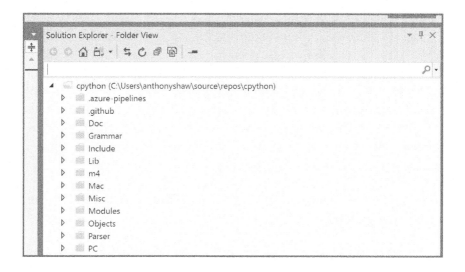

Profile-Guided Optimization

The macOS, Linux, and Windows build processes have flags for **profile-guided optimization (PGO)**. PGO isn't something created by the Python team, but a feature of many compilers, including those used by CPython.

PGO works by doing an initial compilation, then profiling the application by running a series of tests. The profile is then analyzed, and the compiler makes changes to the binary that improve performance.

For CPython, the profiling stage runs `python -m test --pgo`, which executes the regression tests specified in `Lib ▸ test ▸ libregrtest ▸ pgo.py`. These tests have been specifically selected because they use a commonly used C extension module or type.

> **Note**
>
> The PGO process is time-consuming, so to keep your compila-
> tion time short, I've excluded it from the lists of recommended
> steps offered throughout this book.
>
> If you want to distribute a custom-compiled version of CPython
> into a production environment, then you should run `./configure`
> with the `--with-pgo` flag in Linux and macOS and use the `--pgo`
> flag in `build.bat` on Windows.

Because the optimizations are specific to the platform and architecture that the profile was executed on, PGO profiles can't be shared
between operating systems or CPU architectures. The distributions
of CPython on Python.org have already been through PGO, so if you
run a benchmark on a vanilla-compiled binary, then it will be slower
than one downloaded from Python.org.

The Windows, macOS, and Linux profile-guided optimizations
include these checks and improvements:

- **Function inlining**: If a function is regularly called from another
  function, then it will be **inlined**, or copied into the calling function, to reduce the stack size.

- **Virtual call speculation and inlining**: If a virtual function call
  frequently targets a certain function, then PGO can insert a condi-
  tionally executed direct call to that function. The direct call can
  then be inlined.

- **Register allocation optimization**: Based on profile data results, the PGO will optimize register allocation.

- **Basic block optimization**: Basic block optimization allows
  commonly executed basic blocks that temporally execute within a
  given frame to be placed in the same **locality**, or set of pages. It
  minimizes the number of pages used, which minimizes memory
  overhead.

- **Hot spot optimization**: Functions that the program spends the most execution time on can be optimized for speed.

- **Function layout optimization**: After PGO analyzes the call graph, functions that tend to be along the same execution path are moved to the same section of the compiled application.

- **Conditional branch optimization**: PGO can look at a decision branch, like an if ... else if or switch statement, and spot the most commonly used path. For example, if there are ten cases in a switch statement, and one is used 95 percent of the time, then that case will be moved to the top so that it will be executed immediately in the code path.

- **Dead spot separation**: Code that isn't called during PGO is moved to a separate section of the application.

Conclusion

In this chapter, you've seen how to compile CPython source code into a working interpreter. You'll use this knowledge throughout the book as you explore and adapt the source code.

You might need to repeat the compilation steps dozens or even hundreds of times when working with CPython. If you can adapt your development environment to create shortcuts for recompilation, then it's better to do that now and save yourself a lot of time.

The Python Language and Grammar

The purpose of a compiler is to convert one language into another. Think of a compiler like a translator. You would hire a translator to listen to you speaking in English and then repeat your words in a different language, like Japanese.

To accomplish this, the translator must understand the grammatical structures of both the source and target languages.

Some compilers will compile into a low-level machine code that can be executed directly on a system. Other compilers will compile into an intermediary language to be executed by a virtual machine.

One consideration when choosing a compiler is the system portability requirements. Java and .NET CLR will compile into an intermediary language so that the compiled code is portable across multiple system architectures. C, Go, C++, and Pascal will compile into an executable binary. This binary is built for the platform on which it was compiled.

Python applications are typically distributed as source code. The role of the Python interpreter is to convert the Python source code and execute it in one step. The CPython runtime compiles your code when it runs for the first time. This step is invisible to the regular user.

Python code isn't compiled into machine code. It's compiled into a low-level intermediary language called **bytecode**. This bytecode is stored in .pyc files and cached for execution. If you run the same

Python application twice without changing the source code, then it will be faster on the second execution. This is because it loads the compiled bytecode instead of recompiling each time.

Why CPython Is Written in C and Not Python

The **C** in CPython is a reference to the C programming language, indicating that this Python distribution is written in the C language.

This statement is mostly true. The compiler in CPython is written in pure C. However, many of the standard library modules are written in pure Python or a combination of C and Python.

So Why Is the CPython Compiler Written in C and Not Python?

The answer is based on how compilers work. There are two types of compilers:

1. **Self-hosted compilers** are compilers written in the language they compile, such as the Go compiler. This is done by a process known as **bootstrapping**.

2. **Source-to-source compilers** are compilers written in another language that already has a compiler.

If you're writing a new programming language from scratch, then you need an executable application to compile your compiler! You need a compiler to execute anything, so when new languages are developed, they're often written first in an older, more established language.

There are also tools available that can take a language specification and create a parser, which you'll learn about later in this chapter. Popular compiler-compilers include GNU Bison, Yacc, and ANTLR.

> **See Also**
>
> If you want to learn more about parsers, then check out the Lark[a] project. Lark is a parser for context-free grammar written in Python.
>
> ---
> [a]https://github.com/lark-parser/lark

An excellent example of compiler bootstrapping is the Go programming language. The first Go compiler was written in C, then once Go could be compiled, the compiler was rewritten in Go.

CPython, on the other hand, kept its C heritage. Many of the standard library modules, like the `ssl` module or the `sockets` module, are written in C to access low-level operating system APIs.

The APIs in the Windows and Linux kernels for creating network sockets,[10] working with the file system,[11] or interacting with the display[12] were all written in C, so it made sense for Python's extensibility layer to be focused on the C language. Later in this book, you'll cover the Python standard library and the C modules.

There is a Python compiler written in Python called PyPy. PyPy's logo is an Ouroboros to represent the self-hosting nature of the compiler.

Another example of a cross-compiler for Python is Jython. Jython is written in Java and compiles from Python source code into Java bytecode. In the same way that CPython makes it easy to import C libraries and use them from Python, Jython makes it easy to import and reference Java modules and classes.

The first step to creating a compiler is to define the language. For example, this is not valid Python:

---

[10]https://realpython.com/python-sockets/
[11]https://realpython.com/working-with-files-in-python/
[12]https://realpython.com/python-gui-with-wxpython/

```
def my_example() <str> :
{
    void* result = ;
}
```

The compiler needs strict rules for the grammatical structure for the language before it tries to execute it.

> **Note**
>
> For the rest of this book, `./python` will refer to the compiled version of CPython. However, the actual command will depend on your operating system.
>
> For Windows:
>
> ```
> > python.exe
> ```
>
> For Linux:
>
> ```
> $ ./python
> ```
>
> For macOS:
>
> ```
> $ ./python.exe
> ```

The Python Language Specification

Contained within the CPython source code is the definition of the Python language. This document is the reference specification used by all the Python interpreters.

The specification is in both a human-readable and a machine-readable format. Inside the documentation is a detailed explanation of the Python language outlining what is allowed and how each statement should behave.

Language Documentation

The Doc ▸ reference directory contains reStructuredText explanations of the features in the Python language. These files form the official Python reference guide at docs.python.org/3/reference.

Inside the directory are the files you need to understand the whole language, structure, and keywords:

📁 *cpython/Doc/reference*

compound_stmts.rst	Compound statements like if, while, for, and function definitions
datamodel.rst	Objects, values, and types
executionmodel.rst	The structure of Python programs
expressions.rst	The elements of Python expressions
grammar.rst	Python's core grammar (referencing Grammar/Grammar)
import.rst	The import system
index.rst	Index for the language reference
introduction.rst	Introduction to the reference documentation
lexical_analysis.rst	Lexical structure like lines, indentation, tokens, and keywords
simple_stmts.rst	Simple statements like assert, import, return, and yield
toplevel_components.rst	Description of the ways to execute Python, like scripts and modules

An Example

Inside Doc ▸ reference ▸ compound_stmts.rst, you can see a simple example defining the with statement.

The with statement has many forms, the simplest being the instantiation of a context manager[13] and a nested block of code:

```
with x():
    ...
```

You can assign the result to a variable using the as keyword:

```
with x() as y:
    ...
```

---

[13]https://dbader.org/blog/python-context-managers-and-with-statement

You can also chain context managers together with a comma:

```
with x() as y, z() as jk:
    ...
```

The documentation contains the human-readable specification of the language. The machine-readable specification is housed in a single file, Grammar ▸ python.gram.

The Grammar File

Python's grammar file uses a parsing expression grammar (PEG) specification. In the grammar file you can use the following notation:

- * for repetition
- + for at-least-once repetition
- [] for optional parts
- | for alternatives
- () for grouping

As an example, think about how you would define a cup of coffee:

- It must have a cup.
- It must include at least one shot of espresso and can contain multiple shots.
- It can have milk, but this is optional.
- It can have water, but this is optional.
- If it contains milk, then the milk can be of various types, like full-fat, skimmed, or soy.

Defined in PEG, a coffee order could look like this:

```
coffee: 'cup' ('espresso')+ ['water'] [milk]
milk: 'full-fat' | 'skimmed' | 'soy'
```

> ### See Also
>
> In CPython 3.9, the CPython source code has two grammar files. One legacy grammar is written in a context-free notation called Backus-Naur Form (BNF). In CPython 3.10, the BNF grammar file (Grammar ▸ Grammar) has been removed.
>
> BNF isn't specific to Python and is often used as the notation for grammar in many other languages.

In this chapter, you'll visualize grammar with railroad diagrams. Here's a railroad diagram for the coffee statement:

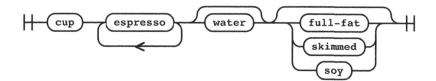

In a railroad diagram, each possible combination must go in a line from left to right. Optional statements can be bypassed, and some statements can be formed as loops.

Example: while Statement

There are a few forms of the while statement. The simplest contains an expression, then the : terminal, followed by a block of code:

```
while finished == True:
    do_things()
```

Alternatively, you can use an assignment expression, which is referred to in the grammar as a named_expression. This is a new feature as of Python 3.8:

```
while letters := read(document, 10):
    print(letters)
```

Optionally, while statements can be followed by an else statement and block:

```
while item := next(iterable):
    print(item)
else:
    print("Iterable is empty")
```

If you search for while_stmt in the grammar file, then you can see the definition:

```
while_stmt[stmt_ty]:
    | 'while' a=named_expression ':' b=block c=[else_block] ...
```

Anything in quotes is a string literal, known as a **terminal**. Terminals are how keywords are recognized.

There are references to two other definitions in these two lines:

1. **block** refers to a block of code with one or multiple statements.

2. **named_expression** refers to a simple expression or assignment expression.

Visualized in a railroad diagram, the while statement looks like this:

As a more complex example, the try statement is defined in the grammar like this:

```
try_stmt[stmt_ty]:
    | 'try' ':' b=block f=finally_block { _Py_Try(b, NULL, NULL, f, EXTRA) }
    | 'try' ':' b=block ex=except_block+ el=[else_block] f=[finally_block]..
except_block[excepthandler_ty]:
    | 'except' e=expression t=['as' z=target { z }] ':' b=block {
        _Py_ExceptHandler(e, (t) ? ((expr_ty) t)->v.Name.id : NULL, b,  ...
    | 'except' ':' b=block { _Py_ExceptHandler(NULL, NULL, b, EXTRA) }
finally_block[asdl_seq*]: 'finally' ':' a=block { a }
```

There are two uses of the `try` statement:

1. `try` with only a `finally` statement

2. `try` with one or many `except` clauses, followed by an optional `else`, then an optional `finally`

Here are those same options visualized in a railroad diagram:

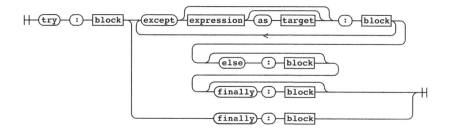

The `try` statement is a good example of a more complex structure.

If you want to understand the Python language in detail, then read through the grammar defined in Grammar ▸ python.gram.

The Parser Generator

The grammar file itself is never used by the Python compiler. Instead, a parser generator reads the file and generates a parser. If you make

73

changes to the grammar file, then you must regenerate the parser and recompile CPython.

The CPython parser was rewritten in Python 3.9 from a parser table automaton (the pgen module) into a contextual grammar parser.

In Python 3.9, the old parser is available at the command line by using the -X oldparser flag, and in Python 3.10 it's removed completely. This book refers to the new parser implemented in 3.9.

Regenerating Grammar

To see pegen, the new PEG generator introduced in CPython 3.9, in action, you can change part of the Python grammar. Search Grammar ▸ python.gram for small_stmt to see the definition of small statements:

```
small_stmt[stmt_ty] (memo):
    | assignment
    | e=star_expressions { _Py_Expr(e, EXTRA) }
    | &'return' return_stmt
    | &('import' | 'from') import_stmt
    | &'raise' raise_stmt
    | 'pass' { _Py_Pass(EXTRA) }
    | &'del' del_stmt
    | &'yield' yield_stmt
    | &'assert' assert_stmt
    | 'break' { _Py_Break(EXTRA) }
    | 'continue' { _Py_Continue(EXTRA) }
    | &'global' global_stmt
    | &'nonlocal' nonlocal_stmt
```

In particular, the line 'pass' { _Py_Pass(EXTRA) } is for the pass statement:

Change that line to accept the terminal (keyword) `'pass'` or `'proceed'` as keywords by adding a choice, `|`, and the `'proceed'` literal:

```
| ('pass'|'proceed') { _Py_Pass(EXTRA) }
```

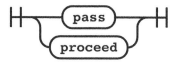

Next, rebuild the grammar files. CPython comes with scripts to automate grammar regeneration.

On macOS and Linux, run the `make regen-pegen` target:

```
$ make regen-pegen
```

For Windows, bring up a command prompt from the `PCBuild` directory and run `build.bat` with the `--regen` flag:

```
> build.bat --regen
```

You should see an output showing that the new `Parser` ▸ `pegen` ▸ `parse.c` file has been regenerated.

With the regenerated parser table, when you recompile CPython, it will use the new syntax. Use the same compilation steps you used for your operating system in the last chapter.

If the code compiled successfully, then you can execute your new CPython binary and start a REPL.

In the REPL, you can now try defining a function. Instead of using the `pass` statement, use the `proceed` keyword alternative that you compiled into the Python grammar:

```
$ ./python

Python 3.9 (tags/v3.9:9cf67522, Oct 5 2020, 10:00:00)
[Clang 10.0.1 (clang-1001.0.46.4)] on darwin
Type "help", "copyright", "credits" or "license" for more information.
>>> def example():
...     proceed
...
>>> example()
```

Congratulations, you've changed the CPython syntax and compiled your own version of CPython!

Next, you'll explore tokens and their relationship to grammar.

Tokens

Alongside the grammar file in the Grammar folder is the Grammar ▸ Tokens file, which contains each of the unique types found as leaf nodes in a parse tree. Each token also has a name and a generated unique ID. The names make it simpler to refer to tokens in the tokenizer.

> **Note**
>
> The Grammar ▸ Tokens file is a new feature in Python 3.8.

For example, the left parenthesis is called LPAR, and semicolons are called SEMI. You'll see these tokens later in the book:

```
LPAR              '('
RPAR              ')'
LSQB              '['
RSQB              ']'
COLON             ':'
COMMA             ','
SEMI              ';'
```

As with the Grammar file, if you change the Grammar ▸ Tokens file, you need to rerun pegen.

To see tokens in action, you can use the `tokenize` module in CPython.

> **Note**
>
> The tokenizer written in Python is a utility module. The actual Python parser uses a different process for identifying tokens.

Create a simple Python script called `test_tokens.py`:

cpython-book-samples ▶ 13 ▶ test_tokens.py

```python
# Demo application
def my_function():
    proceed
```

Input the `test_tokens.py` file to a module built into the standard library called `tokenize`. You'll see the list of tokens by line and character. Use the `-e` flag to output the exact token names:

```
$ ./python -m tokenize -e test_tokens.py
```

```
0,0-0,0:        ENCODING        'utf-8'
1,0-1,14:       COMMENT         '# Demo application'
1,14-1,15:      NL              '\n'
2,0-2,3:        NAME            'def'
2,4-2,15:       NAME            'my_function'
2,15-2,16:      LPAR            '('
2,16-2,17:      RPAR            ')'
2,17-2,18:      COLON           ':'
2,18-2,19:      NEWLINE         '\n'
3,0-3,3:        INDENT          '    '
3,3-3,7:        NAME            'proceed'
3,7-3,8:        NEWLINE         '\n'
4,0-4,0:        DEDENT          ''
4,0-4,0:        ENDMARKER       ''
```

In the output, the first column is the range of the line and column coordinates, the second column is the name of the token, and the final column is the value of the token.

In the output, the `tokenize` module has implied some tokens:

- The ENCODING token for `utf-8`
- A DEDENT to close the function declaration
- An ENDMARKER to end the file
- A blank line at the end

It's best practice to have a blank line at the end of your Python source files. If you omit it, then CPython adds one for you.

The `tokenize` module is written in pure Python and is located in `Lib ▸ tokenize.py`.

To see a verbose readout of the C parser, you can run a debug build of Python with the -d flag. Using the `test_tokens.py` script you created earlier, run it with the following:

```
$ ./python -d test_tokens.py

  > file[0-0]: statements? $
   > statements[0-0]: statement+
    > _loop1_11[0-0]: statement
     > statement[0-0]: compound_stmt
  ...
   + statements[0-10]: statement+ succeeded!
  + file[0-11]: statements? $ succeeded!
```

In the output, you can see that it highlighted `proceed` as a keyword. In the next chapter, you'll see how executing the Python binary gets to the tokenizer and what happens from there to execute your code.

To clean up your code, revert the change in `Grammar ▸ python.gram`, regenerate the grammar again, then clean the build and recompile.

Use the following for macOS or Linux:

```
$ git checkout -- Grammar/python.gram
$ make regen-pegen
$ make -j2 -s
```

Or use the following for Windows:

```
> git checkout -- Grammar/python.gram
> build.bat --regen
> build.bat -t CleanAll
> build.bat -t Build
```

Conclusion

In this chapter, you've been introduced to the Python grammar definitions and parser generator. In the next chapter, you'll expand on that knowledge to build a more complex syntax feature, an "almost-equal" operator.

In practice, changes to the Python grammar have to be carefully considered and discussed. There are two reasons for this level of scrutiny:

1. Having too many language features or a complex grammar would run counter to Python's ethos of being a simple and readable language.

2. Changes to grammar introduce backward incompatibilities, which create work for all developers.

If a Python core developer proposes a change to the grammar, then it must be proposed as a **Python Enhancement Proposal (PEP)**. All PEPs are numbered and indexed on the PEP index. PEP 5 documents the guidelines for evolving the language and specifies that changes must be proposed in PEPs.

You can see the drafted, rejected, and accepted PEPs for future versions of CPython in the PEP index.[14] Members can also suggest

---

[14]https://www.python.org/dev/peps/

changes to the language outside the core development group through the python-ideas mailing list.[15]

Once a PEP has consensus and the draft has been finalized, the steering council must accept or reject it. The mandate of the steering council, defined in PEP 13, states that council members shall work to "maintain the quality and stability of the Python language and CPython interpreter."

[15]https://www.python.org/community/lists/

Configuration and Input

Now that you've seen the Python grammar, it's time to explore how code gets into an executable state.

There are many ways Python code can be run in CPython. Here are some of the most commonly used approaches:

1. Running `python -c` and a Python string

2. Running `python -m` and the name of a module

3. Running `python <file>` with the path to a file that contains Python code

4. Piping Python code into the `python` executable over `stdin`, such as `cat <file> | python`

5. Starting a REPL and executing commands one at a time

6. Using the C API and using Python as an embedded environment

> **See Also**
>
> Python has so many ways to execute scripts that it can be a little overwhelming. For more on running Python scripts, check out *Real Python*'s "How to Run Your Python Scripts."[a]
>
> ---
> [a]https://realpython.com/run-python-scripts/

To execute any Python code, the interpreter needs three elements in place:

1. A module to execute

2. A state to hold information such as variables

3. A configuration, such as which options are enabled

With these three components, the interpreter can execute code and provide an output:

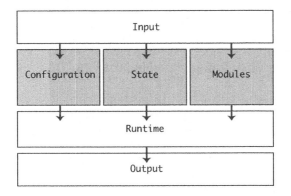

Similar to the PEP 8 style guide for Python code, there's a PEP 7 style guide for the CPython C code. It includes the following naming standards for C source code:

- The `Py` prefix is for public functions, not static functions.

- The `Py_` prefix is for global service routines, such as `Py_FatalError`. Specific groups of routines (like specific object type APIs) should use a longer prefix, such as `PyString_` for string functions.

- Public functions and variables should be written in Mixed-Case, with words separated by underscores, such as `PyObject_GetAttr()`, `Py_BuildValue()`, and `PyExc_TypeError()`.

- The `_Py` prefix should be reserved for internal functions that need to be visible to the loader, such as `_PyObject_Dump()`.

- Macros should have a MixedCase prefix and then use upper case, with all words separated by underscores, such as `PyString_AS_STRING` and `Py_PRINT_RAW`.

Unlike PEP 8, there are few tools for checking compliance with PEP 7. This task is instead done by the core developers as part of code reviews. As with any human-operated process, this type of review isn't error-proof, so you'll likely find code that doesn't adhere to PEP 7.

The only bundled tool for automating this process is a script called `smelly.py`, which you can execute using the `make smelly` target on Linux or macOS, or via the command line:

```
$ ./python Tools/scripts/smelly.py
```

This will raise an error for any symbols that are in `libpython` (the shared CPython library) that do not start with `Py` or `_Py`.

Configuration State

Before any Python code is executed, the CPython runtime first establishes the configuration of the runtime and any user-provided options.

The configuration of the runtime is in three locations, as defined in PEP 587:

1. `PyPreConfig`, used for preinitialization configuration

2. `PyConfig`, used for the runtime configuration

3. The compiled configuration of the CPython interpreter

Both data structures, `PyPreConfig` and `PyConfig`, are defined in Include▸ cpython▸initconfig.h.

Preinitialization Configuration

The preinitialization configuration is separate from the runtime configuration as its properties relate to the operating system or user environment.

`PyPreConfig` has three primary functions:

1. Setting the Python memory allocator

2. Configuring the LC_CTYPE locale to the system- or user-preferred locale

3. Setting the UTF-8 mode (PEP 540)

The `PyPreConfig` type contains the following fields, all of type `int`:

- **allocator:** Select a memory allocator, such as PYMEM_ALLOCATOR_MALLOC. Run `./configure --help` for more information on the memory allocator.

- **configure_locale:** Set the LC_CTYPE locale to the user preferred locale. If equal to 0, then set `coerce_c_locale` and `coerce_c_locale_warn` to 0.

- **coerce_c_locale:** If equal to 2, then coerce the C locale. If equal to 1, then read the LC_CTYPE locale to decide if it should be coerced.

- **coerce_c_locale_warn:** If nonzero, then emit a warning if the C locale is coerced.

- **dev_mode:** Turn on development mode.

- **isolated:** Enable isolated mode. sys.path contains neither the script's directory nor the user's site-packages directory.

- **legacy_windows_fs_encoding:** (Windows only) If nonzero, then disable UTF-8 mode and set the Python file system encoding to mbcs.

- **parse_argv:** If nonzero, then use command-line arguments.

- **use_environment:** If greater than zero, then use environment variables.

- **utf8_mode:** If nonzero, then enable UTF-8 mode.

Related Source Files

Below are the source files relating to PyPreConfig:

File	Purpose
Python ▸ initconfig.c	Loads the configuration from the system environment and merges it with any command-line flags
Include ▸ cpython ▸ initconfig.h	Defines the initialization configuration data structure

Runtime Configuration Data Structure

The second-stage configuration is the runtime configuration. The runtime configuration data structure in PyConfig includes several values, including the following:

- Runtime flags for modes like debug and optimized

- The mode of execution, such as a script file, stdin, or module

- Extended options, specified by -X <option>

85

- Environment variables for runtime settings

The configuration data is used by the CPython runtime to enable and disable features.

Setting Runtime Configuration With the Command Line

Python also comes with several command-line interface options.[16] For example, CPython has a mode called **verbose mode**. This is primarily aimed at developers for debugging CPython.

You can enable verbose mode with the -v flag, and Python will print messages to the screen when modules are loaded:

```
$ ./python -v -c "print('hello world')"

# installing zipimport hook
import zipimport # builtin
# installed zipimport hook
...
```

You'll see a hundred lines or more with all the imports of your user site packages and anything else in the system environment.

Because runtime configuration can be set in several ways, configuration settings have levels of precedence. Here's the order of precedence for verbose mode:

1. The default value for config->verbose is hardcoded to -1 in the source code.

2. The environment variable PYTHONVERBOSE is used to set the value of config->verbose.

3. If the environment variable does not exist, then the default value of -1 will remain.

---

[16]https://docs.python.org/3/using/cmdline.html

4. In `config_parse_cmdline()` within `Python` ▸ `initconfig.c`, the command-line flag is used to set the value, if provided.

5. This value is copied to a global variable, `Py_VerboseFlag` by `_Py_GetGlobalVariablesAsDict()`.

All `PyConfig` values follow the same sequence and order of precedence:

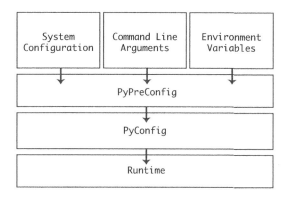

Viewing Runtime Flags

CPython interpreters have a set of **runtime flags**. These flags are advanced features used for toggling CPython-specific behaviors. Within a Python session, you can access the runtime flags, like verbose mode and quiet mode, by using the `sys.flags` named tuple.

All -x flags are available inside the `sys._xoptions` dictionary:

```
$ ./python -X dev -q
```

```
>>> import sys
>>> sys.flags
sys.flags(debug=0, inspect=0, interactive=0, optimize=0,
  dont_write_bytecode=0, no_user_site=0, no_site=0,
  ignore_environment=0, verbose=0, bytes_warning=0,
  quiet=1, hash_randomization=1, isolated=0,
  dev_mode=True, utf8_mode=0)
```

```
>>> sys._xoptions
{'dev': True}
```

Build Configuration

Along with the runtime configuration in Include ▸ cpython ▸ initconfig.h, there's also a build configuration located inside pyconfig.h in the root folder. This file is created dynamically in the ./configure step in the build process for macOS and Linux, or by build.bat in Windows.

You can see the build configuration by running the following:

```
$ ./python -m sysconfig

Platform: "macosx-10.15-x86_64"
Python version: "3.9"
Current installation scheme: "posix_prefix"

Paths:
    data = "/usr/local"
    include = "/Users/anthonyshaw/CLionProjects/cpython/Include"
    platinclude = "/Users/anthonyshaw/CLionProjects/cpython"
...
```

Build configuration properties are compile-time values used to select additional modules to be linked into the binary. For example, debuggers, instrumentation libraries, and memory allocators are all set at compile time.

With the three configuration stages, the CPython interpreter can now take input and process text into executable code.

Building a Module From Input

Before any code can be executed, it must be compiled into a module from an input. As discussed before, inputs can vary in type:

- Local files and packages
- I/O streams, such as `stdin` or a memory pipe
- Strings

Inputs are read, passed to the parser, and then passed to the compiler:

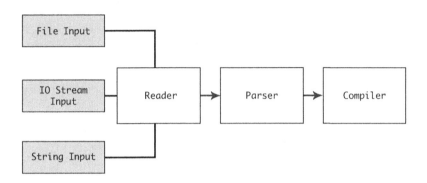

Due to this flexibility, a large portion of the CPython source code is dedicated to processing inputs to the CPython parser.

Related Source Files

There are four main files that deal with the command-line interface:

File	Purpose
Lib ▸ runpy.py	Standard library module for importing Python modules and executing them
Modules ▸ main.c	Functions wrapping the execution of external code, such as from a file, module, or input stream
Programs ▸ python.c	The entry point for the python executable for Windows, Linux, and macOS Serves only as a wrapper for Modules/main.c
Python ▸ pythonrun.c	Functions wrapping the internal C APIs for processing inputs from the command line

Reading Files and Input

Once CPython has the runtime configuration and the command-line arguments, it can load the code it needs to execute. This task is handled by `pymain_main()` inside `Modules ▶ main.c`.

CPython will now execute the provided code with any options specified in the newly created `PyConfig` instance.

Input String From the Command Line

CPython can execute a small Python application at the command line with the `-c` option. For example, consider what happens when you execute `print(2 ** 2)`:

```
$ ./python -c "print(2 ** 2)"

4
```

First, `pymain_run_command()` is executed inside `Modules ▶ main.c`, taking the command passed in `-c` as an argument in the C type `wchar_t*`.

> **Note**
>
> The `wchar_t*` type is often used as a low-level storage type for Unicode data across CPython since the size of the type can store UTF-8 characters.
>
> When converting the `wchar_t*` to a Python string, the `Objects ▶ unicodeobject.c` file has a helper function, `PyUnicode_FromWideChar()`, that returns a Unicode string. The encoding to UTF-8 is then done by `PyUnicode_AsUTF8String()`.
>
> Python Unicode strings are covered in depth in the "Unicode String Type" section of the "Objects and Types" chapter.

Once this is complete, `pymain_run_command()` passes the Python bytes object to `PyRun_SimpleStringFlags()` for execution.

`PyRun_SimpleStringFlags()` is part of `Python ▸ pythonrun.c`. Its purpose is to turn a string into a Python module and then send it on to be executed.

A Python module needs to have an entry point, `__main__`, to be executed as a standalone module, and `PyRun_SimpleStringFlags()` creates this entry point implicitly.

Once `PyRun_SimpleStringFlags()` has created a module and a dictionary, it calls `PyRun_StringFlags()`. `PyRun_SimpleStringFlags()` creates a fake filename and then calls the Python parser to create an abstract syntax tree (AST) from the string and return a module. You'll learn more about ASTs in the next chapter.

> **Note**
>
> Python modules are the data structure used to hand parsed code on to the compiler. The C structure for a Python module is `mod_ty` and is defined in `Include ▸ Python-ast.h`.

Input With a Local Module

Another way to execute Python commands is to use the `-m` option with the name of a module. A typical example is `python -m unittest`, which runs the `unittest` module in the standard library.

The ability to execute modules as scripts was initially proposed in PEP 338. The standard for explicit relative imports was defined in PEP366.

The `-m` flag implies that, within the module package, you want to execute whatever is inside the entry point (`__main__`).[17] It also implies that you want to search `sys.path` for the named module.

This search mechanism in the import library (`importlib`) is why you don't need to remember where the `unittest` module is stored on your file system.

---

[17]https://realpython.com/python-main-function/

CPython imports a standard library module, `runpy`, and executes it using `PyObject_Call()`. The import is done using the C API function `Py-Import_ImportModule()`, found within the `Python ▸ import.c` file.

> **Note**
>
> In Python, if you have an object and want to get an attribute, then you can call `getattr()`. In the C API, this call is `PyObject_GetAttrString()`, which is found in `Objects ▸ object.c`.
>
> If you want to run a callable, then you can give it parentheses, or you can run the `__call__()` property on any Python object. `__call__()` is implemented inside `Objects ▸ object.c`:
>
> ```
> >>> my_str = "hello, world"
> >>> my_str.upper()
> 'HELLO, WORLD'
> >>> my_str.upper.__call__()
> 'HELLO, WORLD'
> ```

The `runpy` module is written in pure Python and is located in `Lib ▸ runpy.py`.

Executing `python -m <module>` is equivalent to running `python -m runpy <module>`. The `runpy` module was created to abstract the process of locating and executing modules on an operating system.

`runpy` does three things to run the target module:

1. Calls `__import__()` for the module name you provided
2. Sets `__name__` (the module name) to a namespace called `__main__`
3. Executes the module within the `__main__` namespace

The `runpy` module also supports executing directories and ZIP files.

Input From a Script File or Standard Input

If the first argument to `python` is a filename, such as `python test.py`, then CPython will open a file handle and pass the handle to `PyRun_SimpleFileExFlags()` inside Python▸`pythonrun.c`.

There are three paths this function can take:

1. If the file path is a `.pyc` file, then it will call `run_pyc_file()`.
2. If the file path is a script file (`.py`), then it will run `PyRun_FileExFlags()`.
3. If the file path is `stdin` because the user ran `<command> | python`, then treat `stdin` as a file handle and run `PyRun_FileExFlags()`.

For `stdin` and basic script files, CPython will pass the file handle to `PyRun_FileExFlags()` located in the Python▸`pythonrun.c` file.

The purpose of `PyRun_FileExFlags()` is similar to `PyRun_SimpleStringFlags()`. CPython will load the file handle into `PyParser_ASTFromFileObject()`.

Identical to `PyRun_SimpleStringFlags()`, once `PyRun_FileExFlags()` has created a Python module from the file, it sends the module to `run_mod()` to be executed.

Input From Compiled Bytecode

If the user runs `python` with a path to a `.pyc` file, then instead of loading the file as a plain text file and parsing it, CPython will assume that the `.pyc` file contains a code object written to disk.

In `PyRun_SimpleFileExFlags()`, there's a clause for the user providing a file path to a `.pyc` file.

`run_pyc_file()` inside Python ▸ `pythonrun.c` marshals the code object from the `.pyc` file using a file handle.

The code object data structure on the disk is the CPython compiler's way to cache compiled code so that it doesn't need to parse it every time the script is called.

> **Note**
>
> **Marshaling** is a term for copying the contents of a file into memory and converting them to a specific data structure.

Once the code object has been marshaled to memory, it's sent to `run_eval_code_obj()`, which calls `Python ▸ ceval.c` to execute the code.

Conclusion

In this chapter, you've uncovered how Python's many configuration options are loaded and how code is inputted into the interpreter.

Python's flexibility with input makes it a great tool for a range of applications, such as:

- Command-line utilities
- Long-running network applications, like web servers
- Short, composable scripts

Python's ability to set configuration properties in many ways introduces complexity. For example, if you tested a Python application on Python 3.8 and it executed correctly, but then it failed in a different environment, then you would need to understand which settings were different in that environment.

This means you'd need to inspect environment variables, runtime flags, and even the sys config properties.

The compile-time properties found in sys config can differ between Python distributions. For example, Python 3.8 downloaded from Python.org for macOS has different default values than the Python 3.8 distribution found on Homebrew or the one found on the Anaconda distribution.

All these input methods output a Python module. In the next chapter, you'll look at how modules are created from input.

Lexing and Parsing With Syntax Trees

In the previous chapter, you explored how Python text is read from various sources. Next, it needs to be converted into a structure that the compiler can use.

This stage is called **parsing**:

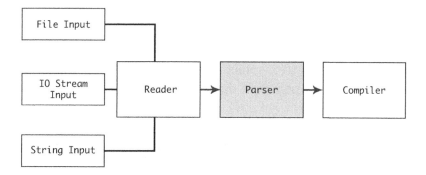

In this chapter, you'll explore how the text is parsed into logical structures that can be compiled.

There are two structures used to parse code in CPython, the **concrete syntax tree (CST)** and the **abstract syntax tree (AST)**:

The parsing process has two parts:

1. Creating a concrete syntax tree using a **parser-tokenizer**, or **lexer**
2. Creating an abstract syntax tree from a concrete syntax tree using a **parser**

These two steps are common paradigms used in many programming languages.

Concrete Syntax Tree Generation

The concrete syntax tree, sometimes known as a **parse tree**, is an ordered, rooted tree structure that represents code in a context-free grammar.

The CST is created from a **tokenizer** and a **parser**. You explored the parser generator in the chapter "The Python Language and Grammar." The output from the parser generator is a deterministic finite automaton (DFA) parsing table describing the possible states of a context-free grammar.

See Also

The original author of Python, Guido van Rossum, developed a contextual grammar for use in CPython 3.9 as an alternative to LL(1), the grammar used in previous versions of CPython. The new grammar is called **parser expression grammar (PEG)**.

The PEG parser was made available in Python 3.9. In Python 3.10, the old LL(1) grammar will be removed completely.

In the "Python Language and Grammar" chapter, you explored some expression types, such as if_stmt and with_stmt. The CST represents grammar symbols like if_stmt as branches, with tokens and terminals as leaf nodes.

For example, the arithmetic expression a + 1 becomes the following CST:

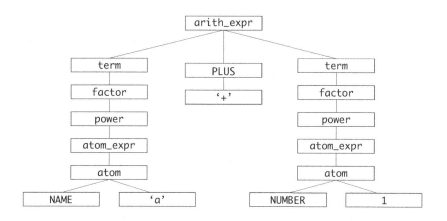

An arithmetic expression is represented here with three major branches: the left branch, the operator branch, and the right branch.

The parser iterates through tokens from an input stream and matches them against the possible states and tokens in the grammar to build a CST.

All the symbols shown in the CST above are defined in Grammar ▸ Grammar:

```
arith_expr: term (('+'|'-') term)*
term: factor (('*'|'@'|'/'|'%'|'//') factor)*
factor: ('+'|'-'|'~') factor | power
power: atom_expr ['**' factor]
atom_expr: [AWAIT] atom trailer*
atom: ('(' [yield_expr|testlist_comp] ')' |
       '[' [testlist_comp] ']' |
       '{' [dictorsetmaker] '}' |
       NAME | NUMBER | STRING+ | '...' | 'None' | 'True' | 'False')
```

The tokens are defined in Grammar ▸ Tokens:

```
ENDMARKER
NAME
NUMBER
STRING
NEWLINE
INDENT
DEDENT

LPAR                    '('
RPAR                    ')'
LSQB                    '['
RSQB                    ']'
COLON                   ':'
COMMA                   ','
SEMI                    ';'
PLUS                    '+'
MINUS                   '-'
STAR                    '*'
...
```

A NAME token represents the name of a variable, function, class, or module. Python's syntax doesn't allow a NAME to be one of the reserved keywords, like await and async, or a numeric or other literal type.

For example, if you tried to define a function named 1, then Python would raise a SyntaxError:

```
>>> def 1():
  File "<stdin>", line 1
    def 1():
        ^
SyntaxError: invalid syntax
```

A NUMBER is a particular token type to represent one of Python's many numeric values. Python has a special grammar for numbers, including the following:

- **Octal values**, such as 0o20

- **Hexadecimal values**, such as 0x10

- **Binary values**, such as 0b10000

- **Complex numbers**, such as 10j

- **Floating-point numbers**, such as 1.01

- **Underscores as commas**, such as 1_000_000

You can see compiled symbols and tokens using the symbol and token modules in Python:

```
$ ./python
>>> import symbol
>>> dir(symbol)
['__builtins__', '__cached__', '__doc__', '__file__', '__loader__',
 '__name__', '__package__', '__spec__', '_main', '_name', '_value',
 'and_expr', 'and_test', 'annassign', 'arglist', 'argument',
 'arith_expr', 'assert_stmt', 'async_funcdef', 'async_stmt',
 'atom', 'atom_expr',
...
>>> import token
>>> dir(token)
['AMPER', 'AMPEREQUAL', 'AT', 'ATEQUAL', 'CIRCUMFLEX',
 'CIRCUMFLEXEQUAL', 'COLON', 'COMMA', 'COMMENT', 'DEDENT', 'DOT',
 'DOUBLESLASH', 'DOUBLESLASHEQUAL', 'DOUBLESTAR', 'DOUBLESTAREQUAL',
...
```

The CPython Parser-Tokenizer

Programming languages have different implementations of the lexer. Some use a lexer generator as a complement to the parser generator.

CPython has a parser-tokenizer module, written in C.

Related Source Files

Here are the source files relating to the parser-tokenizer:

File	Purpose
Python ▶ pythonrun.c	Executes the parser and the compiler from an input
Parser ▶ parsetok.c	The parser and tokenizer implementation
Parser ▶ tokenizer.c	Tokenizer implementation
Parser ▶ tokenizer.h	Header file for the tokenizer implementation that describes data models like token state
Include ▶ token.h	Declaration of token types, generated by Tools ▶ scripts ▶ generate_token.py
Include ▶ node.h	Parse tree node interface and macros for the tokenizer

Inputting Data Into the Parser From a File

The entry point for the parser-tokenizer, PyParser_ASTFromFileObject(), takes a file handle, compiler flags, and a PyArena instance and converts the file object into a module.

There are two steps:

1. Convert to a CST using PyParser_ParseFileObject().
2. Convert to an AST or module using the AST function PyAST_FromNodeObject().

The PyParser_ParseFileObject() function has two important tasks:

1. Instantiating a tokenizer state, tok_state, using PyTokenizer_FromFile()
2. Converting the tokens into a CST (a list of nodes) using parsetok()

Parser-Tokenizer Flow

The parser-tokenizer takes text input and executes the tokenizer and parser in a loop until the cursor is at the end of the text (or a syntax error occurs).

Before execution, the parser-tokenizer establishes `tok_state`, a temporary data structure to store all states used by the tokenizer. The tokenizer state contains information such as the current cursor position and line.

The parser-tokenizer calls `tok_get()` to get the next token. The parser-tokenizer passes the resulting token ID to the parser, which uses the parser generator DFA to create a node on the concrete syntax tree.

`tok_get()` is one of the most complex functions in the whole CPython codebase. It has over 640 lines and includes decades of heritage with edge cases, new language features, and syntax.

The process of calling the tokenizer and parser in a loop can be illustrated like this:

101

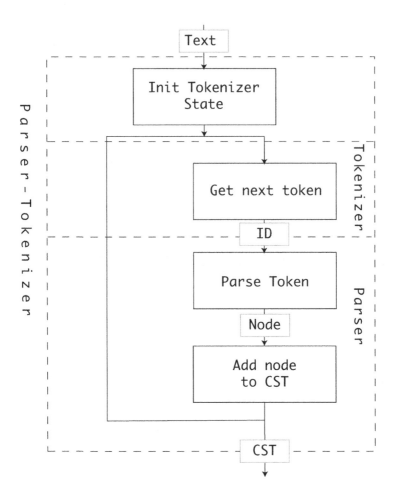

The CST root `node` returned by `PyParser_ParseFileObject()` is essential for the next stage, converting a CST into an abstract syntax tree (AST).

The node type is defined in Include ▸ node.h:

```
typedef struct _node {
    short           n_type;
    char            *n_str;
    int             n_lineno;
    int             n_col_offset;
```

```
    int              n_nchildren;
    struct _node     *n_child;
    int              n_end_lineno;
    int              n_end_col_offset;
} node;
```

Since the CST is a tree of syntax, token IDs, and symbols, it would be difficult for the compiler to make quick, Python-based decisions.

Before you jump into the AST, there's a way to access the output from the parser stage. CPython has a standard library module, parser, which exposes the C functions with a Python API.

The output will be numeric, using the token and symbol numbers generated by the make regen-grammar stage and stored in Include ▸ token.h:

```
>>> from pprint import pprint
>>> import parser
>>> st = parser.expr('a + 1')
>>> pprint(parser.st2list(st))
[258,
 [332,
  [306,
   [310,
    [311,
     [312,
      [313,
       [316,
        [317,
         [318,
          [319,
           [320,
            [321, [322, [323, [324, [325, [1, 'a']]]]]],
            [14, '+'],
            [321, [322, [323, [324, [325, [2, '1']]]]]]]]]]]]]]]]],
 [4, ''],
 [0, '']]
```

To make it easier to understand, you can take all the numbers in the symbol and token modules, put them into a dictionary, and recursively replace the values in the output of parser.st2list() with the names of the tokens:

cpython-book-samples ▸ 21 ▸ lex.py

```python
import symbol
import token
import parser


def lex(expression):
    symbols = {v: k for k, v in symbol.__dict__.items()
               if isinstance(v, int)}
    tokens = {v: k for k, v in token.__dict__.items()
              if isinstance(v, int)}
    lexicon = {**symbols, **tokens}
    st = parser.expr(expression)
    st_list = parser.st2list(st)

    def replace(l: list):
        r = []
        for i in l:
            if isinstance(i, list):
                r.append(replace(i))
            else:
                if i in lexicon:
                    r.append(lexicon[i])
                else:
                    r.append(i)
        return r

    return replace(st_list)
```

You can run `lex()` with a simple expression like `a + 1` to see how this is represented as a parser tree:

```
>>> from pprint import pprint
>>> pprint(lex('a + 1'))

['eval_input',
 ['testlist',
  ['test',
   ['or_test',
    ['and_test',
     ['not_test',
      ['comparison',
       ['expr',
        ['xor_expr',
         ['and_expr',
          ['shift_expr',
           ['arith_expr',
            ['term',
             ['factor', ['power', ['atom_expr', ['atom',
['NAME', 'a']]]]]],
            ['PLUS', '+'],
            ['term',
             ['factor',
              ['power', ['atom_expr', ['atom', ['NUMBER',
'1']]]]]]]]]]]]]]]]],
 ['NEWLINE', ''],
 ['ENDMARKER', '']]
```

In the output, you can see the symbols in lowercase, such as `'arith_expr'`, and the tokens in uppercase, such as `'NUMBER'`.

Abstract Syntax Trees

The next stage in the CPython interpreter is to convert the CST generated by the parser into something more logical that can be executed.

Concrete syntax trees are a very literal representation of the text in the code file. At this stage, it could be a number of languages. Python's basic grammatical structure has been interpreted, but you couldn't use the CST to establish functions, scopes, loops or any of the core Python language features.

Before code is compiled, the CST needs to be converted into a higher-level structure that represents actual Python constructs. The structure is a representation of the CST called an abstract syntax tree (AST).

As an example, a binary operation in the AST is called a `BinOp` and is defined as a type of expression. It has three components:

1. `left`: The left-hand part of the operation

2. `op`: The operator, such as +, -, or *

3. `right`: The right-hand part of the expression

The AST for a + 1 can be represented like this:

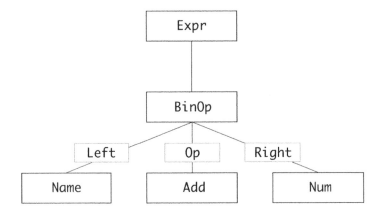

ASTs are produced by the CPython parser process, but you can also generate them from Python code using the `ast` module in the standard library.

Before diving into the implementation of the AST, it would be useful to understand what an AST looks like for a basic piece of Python code.

Related Source Files

Below are the source files relating to abstract syntax trees:

File	Purpose
Include ▸ Python-ast.h	Declaration of AST node types, generated by Parser ▸ asdl_c.py
Parser ▸ Python.asdl	A list of AST node types and properties in a domain-specific-language, **ASDL 5**
Python ▸ ast.c	The AST implementation

Using Instaviz to View Abstract Syntax Trees

Instaviz is a Python package written for use with this book. It displays ASTs and compiled code in a web interface.

To install Instaviz, install the `instaviz` package from `pip`:

```
$ pip install instaviz
```

Then open up a REPL by running `python` at the command line with no arguments.

The function `instaviz.show()` takes a single argument of type `code object`. You'll cover code objects in the next chapter. For this example, define a function and use the name of the function as the argument value:

```
$ python
>>> import instaviz
>>> def example():
        a = 1
        b = a + 1
        return b

>>> instaviz.show(example)
```

You'll see a notification on the command line that a web server has started on port 8080. If you were using that port for something else, then you could change it by calling `instaviz.show(example, port=9090)` or another port number.

In the web browser, you can see a detailed breakdown of your function:

Code Object Properties

Field	Value
co_argcount	0
co_cellvars	()
co_code	64017d007c00640117007d017c015300
co_consts	(None, 1)
co_filename	test.py
co_firstlineno	4
co_freevars	()
co_kwonlyargcount	0
co_lnotab	b'\x00\x01\x04\x01\x08\x01'
co_name	foo
co_names	()
co_nlocals	2
co_stacksize	2
co_varnames	('a', 'b')

```
4 def foo():
5     a = 1
6     b = a + 1
7     return b
```

Graph direction: Up-Down Down-Up Left-Right Right-Left

108

The bottom-left graph is the function you declared in the REPL, represented as an abstract syntax tree. Each node in the tree is an AST type. They're found in the `ast` module and all inherit from `_ast.AST`.

Some of the nodes have properties that link them to child nodes, unlike the CST, which has a generic child node property.

For example, if you click on the `Assign` node in the center, then it links to the line `b = a + 1`:

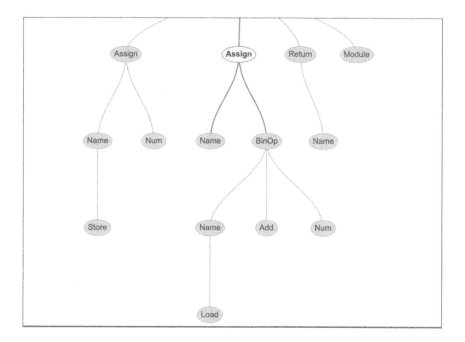

The `Assign` node has two properties:

1. **targets** is a list of names to assign. It's a list because you can assign to multiple variables with a single expression using unpacking.

2. **value** is the value to assign, which in this case is a `BinOp` statement, `a + 1`.

If you click on the `BinOp` statement, then it shows the relevant properties:

- **left:** The node to the left of the operator
- **op:** The operator, in this case an `Add` node (+) for addition
- **right:** The node to the right of the operator

Node Properties

Select a node on the AST graph to see properties.

json	object
left	object
id : 'a'	string
ctx	object
op	object
right	object
n : 1	number
lineno : 3	number

AST Compilation

Compiling an AST in C is not a straightforward task. The Python ▸ ast.c module has over 5,000 lines of code.

There are a few entry points, forming part of the AST's public API. The AST API takes a node tree (CST), a filename, the compiler flags, and a memory storage area.

The result type is `mod_ty`, representing a Python module defined in In-clude ▶ Python-ast.h.

`mod_ty` is a container structure for one of the four module types in Python:

1. Module

2. Interactive

3. Expression

4. FunctionType

The module types are all listed in Parser ▶ Python.asdl. You'll see the module types, statement types, expression types, operators, and comprehensions all defined in this file.

The names of the types in Parser ▶ Python.asdl relate to the classes generated by the AST and the same classes named in the ast standard module library:

```
-- ASDL's 4 builtin types are:
-- identifier, int, string, constant

module Python
{
    mod = Module(stmt* body, type_ignore *type_ignores)
        | Interactive(stmt* body)
        | Expression(expr body)
        | FunctionType(expr* argtypes, expr returns)
```

The ast module imports Include ▶ Python-ast.h, a file created automatically from Parser ▶ Python.asdl when regenerating grammar. The parameters and names in Include ▶ Python-ast.h correlate directly to those specified in Parser ▶ Python.asdl.

The `mod_ty` type is generated into `Include ▸ Python-ast.h` from the `Module` definition in `Parser ▸ Python.asdl`:

```
enum _mod_kind {Module_kind=1, Interactive_kind=2, Expression_kind=3,
                FunctionType_kind=4};
struct _mod {
    enum _mod_kind kind;
    union {
        struct {
            asdl_seq *body;
            asdl_seq *type_ignores;
        } Module;

        struct {
            asdl_seq *body;
        } Interactive;

        struct {
            expr_ty body;
        } Expression;

        struct {
            asdl_seq *argtypes;
            expr_ty returns;
        } FunctionType;

    } v;
};
```

The C header file and structures are there so that the `Python ▸ ast.c` program can quickly generate the structures with pointers to the relevant data.

The AST entry point, `PyAST_FromNodeObject()`, is essentially a `switch` statement around the result from `TYPE(n)`. `TYPE()` is a macro used by the AST to determine the type of nodes in the concrete syntax tree. The result of `TYPE()` will be either a symbol or a token type.

By starting at the root node, it can be only one of the module types defined as Module, Interactive, Expression, or FunctionType:

- For file_input, the type should be Module.

- For eval_input, such as from a REPL, the type should be Expression.

For each type of statement, there's a corresponding ast_for_xxx C function in Python ▸ ast.c, which will look at the CST nodes to complete the properties for that statement.

One of the simpler examples is the power expression, such as 2 ** 4, or 2 to the power of 4. ast_for_power() will return a BinOp with the operator as Pow (power), the left hand as e (2), and the right hand as f (4):

Python ▸ ast.c line 2717

```
static expr_ty
ast_for_power(struct compiling *c, const node *n)
{
    /* power: atom trailer* ('**' factor)*
     */
    expr_ty e;
    REQ(n, power);
    e = ast_for_atom_expr(c, CHILD(n, 0));
    if (!e)
        return NULL;
    if (NCH(n) == 1)
        return e;
    if (TYPE(CHILD(n, NCH(n) - 1)) == factor) {
        expr_ty f = ast_for_expr(c, CHILD(n, NCH(n) - 1));
        if (!f)
            return NULL;
        e = BinOp(e, Pow, f, LINENO(n), n->n_col_offset,
                    n->n_end_lineno, n->n_end_col_offset, c->c_arena);
    }
    return e;
}
```

You can see the result of this if you send a short function to the `instaviz` module:

```
>>> def foo():
        2**4
>>> import instaviz
>>> instaviz.show(foo)
```

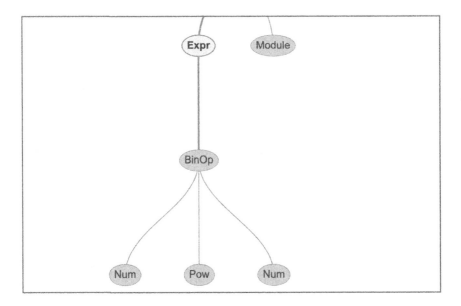

You can also see the corresponding properties in the UI:

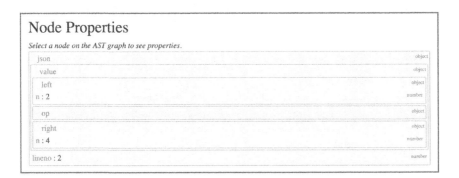

In summary, each statement type and expression has a corresponding `ast_for_*()` function to create it. The arguments are defined in `Parser` ▸ `Python.asdl` and exposed via the `ast` module in the standard library.

If an expression or statement has children, then it will call the corresponding `ast_for_*()` child function in a depth-first traversal.

Important Terms to Remember

Below are some key terms from this chapter:

- **Abstract syntax tree (AST):** A contextual tree representation of Python's grammar and statements
- **Concrete syntax tree (CST):** A non-contextual tree representation of tokens and symbols
- **Parse tree:** Another term for concrete syntax tree
- **Token:** A type of symbol, such as +
- **Tokenization:** The process of converting text into tokens
- **Parsing:** The process of converting text into a CST or AST

Example: Adding an Almost-Equal Comparison Operator

To bring all this together, you can add a new piece of syntax to the Python language and recompile CPython to understand it.

A **comparison expression** compares two or more values:

```
>>> a = 1
>>> b = 2
>>> a == b
False
```

Operators used in comparison expressions are called **comparison operators**. Here are some you may recognize:

- **Less than:** <
- **Greater than:** >
- **Equal to:** ==
- **Not equal to:** !=

> **See Also**
>
> Rich comparisons in the data model were proposed for Python 2.1 in PEP 207. The PEP contains context, history, and justification for custom Python types to implement comparison methods.

Now let's add another comparison operator called **almost equal** that will be represented by ~=. It will have the following behaviors:

- If you compare a float and an integer, then it will cast the float into an integer and compare the result.
- If you compare two integers, then it will use the normal equality operators.

This new operator should return the following in a REPL:

```
>>> 1 ~= 1
True
>>> 1 ~= 1.0
True
>>> 1 ~= 1.01
True
>>> 1 ~= 1.9
False
```

To add the new operator, you first need to update the CPython grammar. In Grammar ▸ python.gram, the comparison operators are defined as a symbol, comp_op:

```
comparison[expr_ty]:
    | a=bitwise_or b=compare_op_bitwise_or_pair+ ...
    | bitwise_or
compare_op_bitwise_or_pair[CmpopExprPair*]:
    | eq_bitwise_or
    | noteq_bitwise_or
    | lte_bitwise_or
    | lt_bitwise_or
    | gte_bitwise_or
    | gt_bitwise_or
    | notin_bitwise_or
    | in_bitwise_or
    | isnot_bitwise_or
    | is_bitwise_or
eq_bitwise_or[CmpopExprPair*]: '==' a=bitwise_or ...
noteq_bitwise_or[CmpopExprPair*]:
    | (tok='!=' {_PyPegen_check_barry_as_flufl(p) ? NULL : tok}) ...
lte_bitwise_or[CmpopExprPair*]: '<=' a=bitwise_or ...
lt_bitwise_or[CmpopExprPair*]: '<' a=bitwise_or ...
gte_bitwise_or[CmpopExprPair*]: '>=' a=bitwise_or ...
gt_bitwise_or[CmpopExprPair*]: '>' a=bitwise_or ...
notin_bitwise_or[CmpopExprPair*]: 'not' 'in' a=bitwise_or ...
in_bitwise_or[CmpopExprPair*]: 'in' a=bitwise_or ...
isnot_bitwise_or[CmpopExprPair*]: 'is' 'not' a=bitwise_or ...
is_bitwise_or[CmpopExprPair*]: 'is' a=bitwise_or ...
```

Change the `compare_op_bitwise_or_pair` expression to also allow a new `ale_bitwise_or` pair:

```
compare_op_bitwise_or_pair[CmpopExprPair*]:
    | eq_bitwise_or
...
    | ale_bitwise_or
```

Define the new `ale_bitwise_or` expression beneath the existing `is_bitwise_or` expression:

```
...
is_bitwise_or[CmpopExprPair*]: 'is' a=bitwise_or ...
ale_bitwise_or[CmpopExprPair*]: '~=' a=bitwise_or
    { _PyPegen_cmpop_expr_pair(p, AlE, a) }
```

This new type defines a named expression, `ale_bitwise_or`, that contains the `'~='` terminal.

The function call `_PyPegen_cmpop_expr_pair(p, AlE, a)` is an expression to get a `cmpop` node from the AST. The type is `AlE`, for **Al**most **E**qual.

Next, add a token to `Grammar ▶ Tokens`:

```
ATEQUAL               '@='
RARROW                '->'
ELLIPSIS              '...'
COLONEQUAL            ':='
# Add this line
ALMOSTEQUAL           '~='
```

To update the grammar and tokens in C, you need to regenerate the headers.

Use the following command on macOS or Linux:

```
$ make regen-token regen-pegen
```

Use the following command on Windows, within the `PCBuild` directory:

```
> build.bat --regen
```

These steps will automatically update the tokenizer. For example, open the `Parser/token.c` source and see how a case in the `PyToken_TwoChars()` function has changed:

```
case '~':
    switch (c2) {
    case '=': return ALMOSTEQUAL;
    }
    break;
}
```

If you recompile CPython at this stage and open a REPL, then you'll see that the tokenizer can successfully recognize the token, but the AST doesn't know how to handle it:

```
$ ./python
>>> 1 ~= 2
SystemError: invalid comp_op: ~=
```

This exception is raised by `ast_for_comp_op()` inside `Python ▸ ast.c` because it doesn't recognize ALMOSTEQUAL as a valid operator for a comparison statement.

`Compare` is an expression type defined in `Parser ▸ Python.asdl`. It has properties for the left expression; a list of operators called `ops`, and a list of expressions to compare to called `comparators`:

```
| Compare(expr left, cmpop* ops, expr* comparators)
```

Inside the `Compare` definition is a reference to the `cmpop` enumeration:

```
cmpop = Eq | NotEq | Lt | LtE | Gt | GtE | Is | IsNot | In | NotIn
```

This is a list of possible AST leaf nodes that can act as comparison operators. Ours is missing and needs to be added. Update the list of options to include a new type, `AlE`:

```
cmpop = Eq | NotEq | Lt | LtE | Gt | GtE | Is | IsNot | In | NotIn | AlE
```

Next, regenerate the AST again to update the AST C header files:

```
$ make regen-ast
```

This will update the comparison operator (_cmpop) enumeration inside
Include/Python-ast.h to include the AlE option:

```
typedef enum _cmpop { Eq=1, NotEq=2, Lt=3, LtE=4, Gt=5, GtE=6, Is=7,
                      IsNot=8, In=9, NotIn=10, AlE=11 } cmpop_ty;
```

The AST has no knowledge that the ALMOSTEQUAL token is equivalent to
the AlE comparison operator. So you need to update the C code for the
AST.

Navigate to ast_for_comp_op() in Python▸ast.c. Find the switch statement for the operator tokens. This returns one of the _cmpop enumeration values.

Add two lines to catch the ALMOSTEQUAL token and return the AlE comparison operator:

Python▸ast.c line 1222

```
static cmpop_ty
ast_for_comp_op(struct compiling *c, const node *n)
{
    /* comp_op: '<'|'>'|'=='|'>='|'<='|'!='|'in'|'not' 'in'|'is'
               |'is' 'not'
    */
    REQ(n, comp_op);
    if (NCH(n) == 1) {
        n = CHILD(n, 0);
        switch (TYPE(n)) {
            case LESS:
                return Lt;
            case GREATER:
                return Gt;
            case ALMOSTEQUAL: // Add this line to catch the token
                return AlE;    // And this one to return the AST node
```

At this stage, the tokenizer and the AST can parse this code, but the compiler won't know how to handle the operator. To test the AST representation, use `ast.parse()` and explore the first operator in the expression:

```
>>> import ast
>>> m = ast.parse('1 ~= 2')
>>> m.body[0].value.ops[0]
<_ast.AlE object at 0x10a8d7ee0>
```

This is an instance of our `AlE` comparison operator type, so the AST has correctly parsed the code.

In the next chapter, you'll learn how the CPython compiler works and revisit the almost-equal operator to build out its behavior.

Conclusion

CPython's versatility and low-level execution API make it the ideal candidate for an embedded scripting engine. You'll see CPython used in many UI applications, such as game design, 3D graphics, and system automation.

The interpreter process is flexible and efficient. Now that you have an understanding of how it works, you're ready to understand the compiler.

The Compiler

After completing the task of parsing, the interpreter has an AST with the operations, functions, classes, and namespaces of the Python code.

The job of the **compiler** is to turn the AST into instructions the CPU can understand:

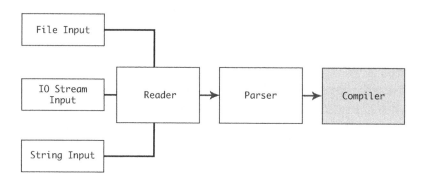

This compilation task is split into two components:

1. **Compiler:** Traverse the AST and create a **control flow graph** (CFG), which represents the logical sequence for execution.

2. **Assembler:** Convert the nodes in the CFG to sequential, executable statements known as **bytecode.**

Here's a visual representation of the compilation process:

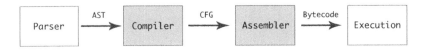

Important

Throughout this chapter, it's important to remember that the unit of compilation for CPython is a **module**. The compilation steps and process indicated in this chapter will happen once for each module in your project.

In this chapter, you'll focus on the compilation of an AST module into a code object.

`PyAST_CompileObject()` is the main entry point to the CPython compiler. It takes a Python AST module as its primary argument, along with the name of the file and the globals, locals, and `PyArena` all created earlier in the interpreter process.

Note

You're starting to get into the guts of the CPython compiler now, with decades of development and computer science theory behind it. Don't be put off by the size and complexity. Once you break down the compiler into logical steps, it's less difficult to understand.

Related Source Files

Here are the source files related to the compiler:

File	Purpose
Python▸compile.c	Compiler implementation
Include▸compile.h	Compiler API and type definitions

Important Terms

This chapter refers to many terms that may be new to you:

- The **compiler state** is implemented as a container type, which contains one **symbol table**.
- The symbol table contains many **variable names** and can optionally contain child symbol tables.
- The compiler type contains many **compiler units**.
- Each compiler unit can contain many names, variable names, constants, and cell variables.
- A compiler unit contains many **basic frame blocks**.
- Basic frame blocks contain many **bytecode instructions**.

The compiler state container and its components can be illustrated like this:

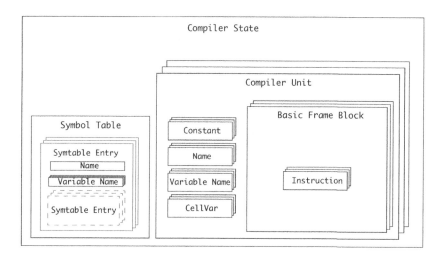

Instantiating a Compiler

Before the compiler starts, a **global compiler state** is created. The compiler state (compiler type) structure contains properties used by the compiler, such as compiler flags, the stack, and the PyArena. It also contains links to other data structures, like the symbol table.

Here are the fields in the compiler state:

Field	Type	Purpose
c_arena	PyArena *	Pointer to the memory allocation arena
c_const_cache	PyObject * (dict)	Python dict holding all constants, including names tuple
c_do_not_emit_bytecode	int	Flag for disabling bytecode compilation
c_filename	PyObject * (str)	Filename being compiled
c_flags	PyCompilerFlags *	Inherited compiler flags (see the "Compiler Flags" section)
c_future	PyFutureFeatures *	Pointer to module's __future__
c_interactive	int	Flag for interactive mode
c_nestlevel	int	Current nesting level
c_optimize	int	Optimization level
c_st	symtable *	Compiler's symbol table
c_stack	PyObject * (list)	Python list holding compiler_unit pointers
u	compiler_unit*	Compiler state for the current block

The compiler state is instantiated inside PyAST_CompileObject():

- If the module doesn't have a docstring (__doc__) property, then an empty one is created here, as with the __annotations__ property.

- PyAST_CompileObject() sets the passed value as the compiler state filename, which is used for stack traces and exception handling.

- The memory allocation arena for the compiler is set to the one used by the interpreter. See "Custom Memory Allocators" in the "Memory Management" chapter for more on memory allocators.

- Any future flags are configured before the code is compiled.

Future Flags and Compiler Flags

There are two types of flags to toggle the features inside the compiler, **future flags** and **compiler flags**. These flags can be set in two places:

1. The configuration state, which contains environment variables and command-line flags

2. Inside the source code of the module through the use of __future__ statements

For more information on the configuration state, see the "Configuration State" section in the "Configuration and Input" chapter.

Future Flags

Future flags are required because of the syntax or features in that specific module. For example, Python 3.7 introduced delayed evaluation of type hints through the annotations future flag:

```
from __future__ import annotations
```

The code after this statement might use unresolved type hints, so the __future__ statement is required. Otherwise, the module wouldn't import.

Reference of Future Flags in 3.9

As of 3.9, all but two of the future flags (annotations and barry_as_FLUFL) are mandatory and are automatically enabled:

Import	Purpose
absolute_import	Enable absolute imports (PEP 328)
annotations	Postpone evaluation of type annotations (PEP 563)
barry_as_FLUFL	Include Easter egg (PEP 401)
division	Use the true division operator (PEP 238)
generator_stop	Enable StopIteration inside generators (PEP 479)
generators	Introduce simple generators (PEP 255)
nested_scopes	Add statically nested scoping (PEP 227)
print_function	Make print a function (PEP 3105)
unicode_literals	Make str literals Unicode instead of bytes (PEP 3112)
with_statement	Enable the with statement (PEP 343)

> **Note**
>
> The majority of the __future__ flags were used to aid portability between Python 2 and 3. As Python 4.0 approaches, you may see more future flags added.

Compiler Flags

Compiler flags are specific to the environment, so they might change the way the code executes or the way the compiler runs, but they shouldn't link to the source like __future__ statements do.

One example of a compiler flag would be the -o flag[18] for optimizing the use of assert statements. This flag disables any assert statements that may have been put in the code for debugging purposes.[19] It can also be enabled with the PYTHONOPTIMIZE=1 environment variable setting.

---

[18]https://docs.python.org/3/using/cmdline.html#cmdoption-o
[19]https://realpython.com/python-debugging-pdb/

Symbol Tables

Before the code is compiled, a **symbol table** is created by the
`PySymtable_BuildObject()` API.

The purpose of the symbol table is to provide a list of namespaces,
globals, and locals for the compiler to use for referencing and resolving scopes.

Related Source Files

Here are the source files related to the symbol table:

File	Purpose
Python ▸ symtable.c	Symbol table implementation
Include ▸ symtable.h	Symbol table API definition and type definitions
Lib ▸ symtable.py	symtable standard library module

Symbol Table Data Structure

The symtable structure should be one symtable instance for the compiler, so namespacing becomes essential.

For example, if you create a method called resolve_names() in one class
and declare another method with the same name in another class,
then you would want to be sure which one is called inside the module.

The symtable serves this purpose, as well as ensuring that variables
declared within a narrow scope don't automatically become globals.

The symbol table structure, `symtable`, has the following fields:

Field	Type	Purpose
recursion_depth	int	Current recursion depth
recursion_limit	int	Recursion limit before `RecursionError` is raised
st_blocks	PyObject * (dict)	Map of AST node addresses to symbol table entries
st_cur	_symtable_entry	Current symbol table entry
st_filename	PyObject * (str)	Name of the file being compiled
st_future	PyFutureFeatures	Module's future features that affect the symbol table
st_global	PyObject * (dict)	Reference to the symbols in st_top
st_nblocks	int	Number of blocks used
st_private	PyObject * (str)	Name of current class (optional)
st_stack	PyObject * (list)	Stack of namespace info
st_top	_symtable_entry	Symbol table entry for the module

Using the `symtable` Standard Library Module

Some of the symbol table C API is exposed in Python through the `symtable` module in the standard library.

Using another module called `tabulate` (available on PyPI), you can create a script to print a symbol table.

Symbol tables can be nested, so if a module contains a function or class, then that will have a symbol table.

Create a script called `symviz.py` with a recursive `show()` function:

cpython-book-samples ▸ 30 ▸ symviz.py

```python
import tabulate
import symtable

code = """
def calc_pow(a, b):
    return a ** b
a = 1
b = 2
c = calc_pow(a,b)
"""


_st = symtable.symtable(code, "example.py", "exec")


def show(table):
    print("Symtable {0} ({1})".format(table.get_name(),
                                      table.get_type()))
    print(
        tabulate.tabulate(
            [
                (
                    symbol.get_name(),
                    symbol.is_global(),
                    symbol.is_local(),
                    symbol.get_namespaces(),
                )
                for symbol in table.get_symbols()
            ],
            headers=["name", "global", "local", "namespaces"],
            tablefmt="grid",
        )
    )
    if table.has_children():
        [show(child) for child in table.get_children()]


show(_st)
```

Run `symviz.py` at the command line to see the symbol tables for the example code:

```
(venv) → instaviz git:(master) ✗ python symviz.py
Symtable top (module)
+-----------+-----------+----------+------------------------------------------------------+
| name      | global    | local    | namespaces                                           |
+===========+===========+==========+======================================================+
| calc_pow  | False     | True     | [<Function SymbolTable for calc_pow in example.py>]  |
+-----------+-----------+----------+------------------------------------------------------+
| a         | False     | True     | ()                                                   |
+-----------+-----------+----------+------------------------------------------------------+
| b         | False     | True     | ()                                                   |
+-----------+-----------+----------+------------------------------------------------------+
| c         | False     | True     | ()                                                   |
+-----------+-----------+----------+------------------------------------------------------+
Symtable calc_pow (function)
+--------+-----------+----------+---------------+
| name   | global    | local    | namespaces    |
+========+===========+==========+===============+
| a      | False     | True     | ()            |
+--------+-----------+----------+---------------+
| b      | False     | True     | ()            |
+--------+-----------+----------+---------------+
```

Symbol Table Implementation

The implementation of symbol tables is in Python ▸ `symtable.c` and the primary interface is `PySymtable_BuildObject()`.

Similarly to the AST compilation covered in the last chapter, `PySymtable_BuildObject()` switches between the `mod_ty` possible types (`Module`, `Interactive`, `Expression`, and `FunctionType`) and visits each of the statements inside them.

The symbol table recursively explores the nodes and branches of the AST (of type `mod_ty`) and adds entries to the `symtable`:

Python ▸ symtable.c line 261

```
struct symtable *
PySymtable_BuildObject(mod_ty mod, PyObject *filename,
                       PyFutureFeatures *future)
{
    struct symtable *st = symtable_new();
    asdl_seq *seq;
    int i;
    PyThreadState *tstate;
    int recursion_limit = Py_GetRecursionLimit();
...
    st->st_top = st->st_cur;
    switch (mod->kind) {
    case Module_kind:
        seq = mod->v.Module.body;
        for (i = 0; i < asdl_seq_LEN(seq); i++)
            if (!symtable_visit_stmt(st,
                        (stmt_ty)asdl_seq_GET(seq, i)))
                goto error;
        break;
    case Expression_kind:
        ...
    case Interactive_kind:
        ...
    case FunctionType_kind:
        ...
    }
    ...
}
```

For a module, PySymtable_BuildObject() loops through each statement in the module and calls symtable_visit_stmt(), which is a huge switch statement with a case for each statement type (defined in Parser ▸ Python.asdl).

Each statement type has a corresponding function to resolve symbols. For example, a function definition (FunctionDef_kind) statement type has particular logic for the following actions:

- Checking the current recursion depth against the recursion limit
- Adding the name of the function to the symbol table so that it can be called or passed as a function object
- Resolving non-literal default arguments from the symbol table
- Resolving type annotations
- Resolving function decorators

Finally, symtable_enter_block() visits the block with the contents of the function. Then the arguments are visited and resolved, and the body of the function is visited and resolved.

> **Important**
>
> If you've ever wondered why Python's default arguments are mutable, the reason is in symtable_visit_stmt(). Argument defaults are a reference to the variable in the symtable.
>
> No extra work is done to copy any values to an immutable type.

As a preview, here's the C code for those steps in building a symtable for a function in symtable_visit_stmt():

Python ▸ symtable.c line 1171

```c
static int
symtable_visit_stmt(struct symtable *st, stmt_ty s)
{
    if (++st->recursion_depth > st->recursion_limit) {
        PyErr_SetString(PyExc_RecursionError,
            "maximum recursion depth exceeded during compilation");
        VISIT_QUIT(st, 0);
    }
```

```
switch (s->kind) {
case FunctionDef_kind:
    if (!symtable_add_def(st, s->v.FunctionDef.name, DEF_LOCAL))
        VISIT_QUIT(st, 0);
    if (s->v.FunctionDef.args->defaults)
        VISIT_SEQ(st, expr, s->v.FunctionDef.args->defaults);
    if (s->v.FunctionDef.args->kw_defaults)
        VISIT_SEQ_WITH_NULL(st, expr,
          s->v.FunctionDef.args->kw_defaults);
    if (!symtable_visit_annotations(st, s, s->v.FunctionDef.args,
                            s->v.FunctionDef.returns))
        VISIT_QUIT(st, 0);
    if (s->v.FunctionDef.decorator_list)
        VISIT_SEQ(st, expr, s->v.FunctionDef.decorator_list);
    if (!symtable_enter_block(st, s->v.FunctionDef.name,
                        FunctionBlock, (void *)s, s->lineno,
                        s->col_offset))
        VISIT_QUIT(st, 0);
    VISIT(st, arguments, s->v.FunctionDef.args);
    VISIT_SEQ(st, stmt, s->v.FunctionDef.body);
    if (!symtable_exit_block(st, s))
        VISIT_QUIT(st, 0);
    break;
case ClassDef_kind: {
    ...
}
case Return_kind:
    ...
case Delete_kind:
    ...
case Assign_kind:
    ...
case AnnAssign_kind:
    ...
```

Once the resulting symbol table has been created, it's passed on to the compiler.

Core Compilation Process

Now that the PyAST_CompileObject() has a compiler state, a symtable, and a module in the form of the AST, the actual compilation can begin.

The core compiler has two purposes:

1. To convert the state, symtable, and AST into a control flow graph (CFG)

2. To protect the execution stage from runtime exceptions by catching any logic or code errors

Accessing the Compiler From Python

You can call the compiler in Python by calling the built-in function compile(). It returns a code object:

```
>>> co = compile("b+1", "test.py", mode="eval")
>>> co
<code object <module> at 0x10f222780, file "test.py", line 1>
```

As with the symtable() API, a simple expression should have a mode of "eval", and a module, function, or class should have a mode of "exec".

The compiled code can be found in the co_code property of the code object:

```
>>> co.co_code
b'e\x00d\x00\x17\x00S\x00'
```

The standard library also includes a dis module, which disassembles the bytecode instructions. You can print them on the screen or get a list of Instruction instances.

> **Note**
>
> The Instruction type in the dis module is a reflection of the instr type in the C API.

If you import `dis` and give `dis()` the code object's `co_code` property, then the function disassembles it and prints the instructions on the REPL:

```
>>> import dis
>>> dis.dis(co.co_code)
          0 LOAD_NAME              0 (0)
          2 LOAD_CONST             0 (0)
          4 BINARY_ADD
          6 RETURN_VALUE
```

`LOAD_NAME`, `LOAD_CONST`, `BINARY_ADD`, and `RETURN_VALUE` are all bytecode instructions. They're called bytecode because, in binary form, they're one byte long. However, since Python 3.6, the storage format has been changed to a `word`, so now they're technically "wordcode," not bytecode.

The full list of bytecode instructions[20] is available for each version of Python, and it does change between versions. For example, some new bytecode instructions were introduced in Python 3.7 to speed up the execution of specific method calls.

In earlier chapters, you explored the `instaviz` package. This included a visualization of the code object type by running the compiler. `instaviz` also displays the bytecode operations inside the code objects.

Execute `instaviz` again to see the code object and bytecode for a function defined on the REPL:

```
>>> import instaviz
>>> def example():
        a = 1
        b = a + 1
        return b
>>> instaviz.show(example)
```

---

[20]https://docs.python.org/3/library/dis.html#python-bytecode-instructions

Compiler C API

The entry point for AST module compilation, compiler_mod(), switches to different compiler functions depending on the module type. If you assume that mod is a Module, then the module is compiled into the c_stack property as compiler units. Then assemble() is run to create a PyCodeObject from the compiler unit stack.

The new code object is returned and sent on for execution by the interpreter or cached and stored on disk as a .pyc file:

Python ▸ compile.c line 1820

```c
static PyCodeObject *
compiler_mod(struct compiler *c, mod_ty mod)
{
    PyCodeObject *co;
    int addNone = 1;
    static PyObject *module;
    ...
    switch (mod->kind) {
    case Module_kind:
        if (!compiler_body(c, mod->v.Module.body)) {
            compiler_exit_scope(c);
            return 0;
        }
        break;
    case Interactive_kind:
        ...
    case Expression_kind:
        ...
    ...
    co = assemble(c, addNone);
    compiler_exit_scope(c);
    return co;
}
```

compiler_body() loops over each statement in the module and visits it:

Python ▸ compile.c line 1782

```
static int
compiler_body(struct compiler *c, asdl_seq *stmts)
{
    int i = 0;
    stmt_ty st;
    PyObject *docstring;
    ...
    for (; i < asdl_seq_LEN(stmts); i++)
        VISIT(c, stmt, (stmt_ty)asdl_seq_GET(stmts, i));
    return 1;
}
```

The statement type is determined through a call to asdl_seq_GET(), which looks at the AST node type.

Through a macro, VISIT calls a function in Python ▸ compile.c for each statement type:

```
#define VISIT(C, TYPE, V) {\
    if (!compiler_visit_ ## TYPE((C), (V))) \
        return 0; \
}
```

For a stmt (the generic type for a statement), the compiler will then call compiler_visit_stmt() and switch through all the potential statement types found in Parser ▸ Python.asdl:

Python ▸ compile.c line 3375

```
static int
compiler_visit_stmt(struct compiler *c, stmt_ty s)
{
    Py_ssize_t i, n;

    /* Always assign a lineno to the next instruction for a stmt. */
    SET_LOC(c, s);
```

```
switch (s->kind) {
case FunctionDef_kind:
    return compiler_function(c, s, 0);
case ClassDef_kind:
    return compiler_class(c, s);
...
case For_kind:
    return compiler_for(c, s);
...
}

return 1;
}
```

As an example, here's the `for` statement in Python:

```python
for i in iterable:
    # block
else:   # optional if iterable is False
    # block
```

You can visualize the `for` statement in a railroad diagram:

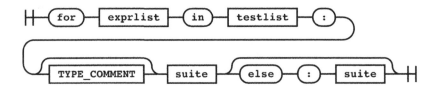

If the statement is a `for` type, then `compiler_visit_stmt()` calls `compiler_for()`. There's an equivalent `compiler_*()` function for all the statement and expression types. The more straightforward types create the bytecode instructions inline, while some of the more complex statement types call other functions.

Instructions

Many of the statements can have substatements. A `for` loop has a body, but you can also have complex expressions in the assignment and the iterator.

The compiler emits **blocks** to the compiler state. These blocks contain sequences of instructions. The instruction data structure has an opcode, arguments, the target block (if this is a jump instruction, which you'll learn about below), and the line number of the statement.

Instruction Type

The instruction type, `instr`, has the following fields:

Field	Type	Purpose
i_jabs	unsigned	Flag to specify this is a absolute jump instruction
i_jrel	unsigned	Flag to specify this is a relative jump instruction
i_lineno	int	Line number for which this instruction was created
i_opcode	unsigned char	Opcode number this instruction represents (see Include ▸ Opcode.h)
i_oparg	int	Opcode argument
i_target	basicblock*	Pointer to the `basicblock` target when `i_jrel` is true

Jump Instructions

Jump instructions are used to jump from one instruction to another. They can be either absolute or relative.

Absolute jump instructions specify the exact instruction number in the compiled code object, whereas **relative jump instructions** specify the jump target relative to another instruction.

141

Basic Frame Blocks

A basic frame block (of type `basicblock`) contains the following fields:

Field	Type	Purpose
b_ialloc	int	Length of instruction array (b_instr)
b_instr	instr *	Pointer to an array of instructions
b_iused	int	Number of instructions used (b_instr)
b_list	basicblock *	List of blocks in this compilation unit (in reverse order)
b_next	basicblock*	Pointer to the next block reached by normal control flow
b_offset	int	Instruction offset for the block, computed by assemble_jump_offsets()
b_return	unsigned	Is true if a RETURN_VALUE opcode is inserted
b_seen	unsigned	Used to perform a DFS of basicblocks (see "Assembly")
b_startdepth	int	Depth of the stack upon entry of the block, computed by stackdepth()

Operations and Arguments

Different types of operations require different arguments. For example, ADDOP_JREL and ADDOP_JABS refer to "**add o**peration with **j**ump to a **rel**ative position" and "**add o**peration with **j**ump to an **abs**olute position," respectively.

There are other macros: ADDOP_I calls compiler_addop_i(), which adds an operation with an integer argument. ADDOP_O calls compiler_addop_o(), which adds an operation with a PyObject argument.

Assembly

Once these compilation stages have completed, the compiler has a list of frame blocks, each containing a list of instructions and a pointer to the next block. The assembler performs a depth-first search (DFS) of the basic frame blocks and merges the instructions into a single bytecode sequence.

Assembler Data Structure

The assembler state structure, `assembler`, is declared in `Python ▸ compile.c` and has the following fields:

Field	Type	Purpose
a_bytecode	PyObject * (str)	String containing bytecode
a_lineno	int	Last lineno of emitted instruction
a_lineno_off	int	Bytecode offset of last lineno
a_lnotab	PyObject * (str)	String containing lnotab
a_lnotab_off	int	Offset into lnotab
a_nblocks	int	Number of reachable blocks
a_offset	int	Offset into bytecode
a_postorder	basicblock **	List of blocks in DFS postorder

Assembler Depth-First Search Algorithm

The assembler uses a depth-first search (DFS) to traverse the nodes in the basic frame block graph. The DFS algorithm isn't specific to CPython, but it's commonly used in graph traversal.

Whereas the CST and AST are both tree structures, the compiler state is a graph structure in which the nodes are basic frame blocks containing instructions.

The basic frame blocks are linked by two graphs. One is in reverse order of creation based on the `b_list` property of each block. A series of basic frame blocks named alphabetically from A to O would look like this:

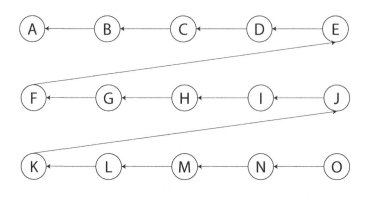

The graph created from the b_list is used to sequentially visit every block in a compiler unit

The second graph uses the b_next property of each block. This list represents the control flow. Vertices in this graph are created by calls to compiler_use_next_block(c, next), where next is the next block to draw a vertex to from the current block (c->u->u_curblock).

The for loop node graph might look something like this:

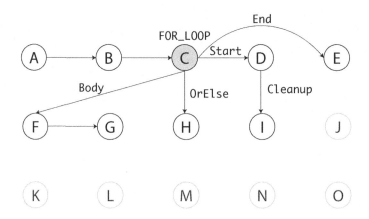

Both the sequential and control flow graphs are used, but the control flow graph is the one used by the DFS implementation.

Assembler C API

The assembler API has an entry point, `assemble()`, which has the following responsibilities:

- Calculate the number of blocks for memory allocation.
- Ensure that every block that falls off the end returns None.
- Resolve any jump statements offsets that were marked as relative.
- Call `dfs()` to perform a depth-first-search of the blocks.
- Emit all the instructions to the compiler.
- Call `makecode()` with the compiler state to generate the `PyCodeObject`.

Python ▸ `compile.c` line 6010

```c
static PyCodeObject *
assemble(struct compiler *c, int addNone)
{
    ...
    if (!c->u->u_curblock->b_return) {
        NEXT_BLOCK(c);
        if (addNone)
            ADDOP_LOAD_CONST(c, Py_None);
        ADDOP(c, RETURN_VALUE);
    }
    ...
    dfs(c, entryblock, &a, nblocks);

    /* Can't modify the bytecode after computing jump offsets. */
    assemble_jump_offsets(&a, c);

    /* Emit code in reverse postorder from dfs. */
    for (i = a.a_nblocks - 1; i >= 0; i--) {
        b = a.a_postorder[i];
```

```
        for (j = 0; j < b->b_iused; j++)
            if (!assemble_emit(&a, &b->b_instr[j]))
                goto error;
    }
    ...

    co = makecode(c, &a);
  error:
    assemble_free(&a);
    return co;
}
```

Depth-First Search

The depth-first search is performed by dfs() in Python ▶ compile.c, which follows the b_next pointers in each of the blocks, marks them as seen by toggling b_seen and then adds them to the assemblers' a_postorder list in reverse order.

The function loops back over the assembler's post-order list and for each block, if it has a jump operation, recursively call dfs() for that jump:

Python ▶ compile.c line 5441

```
static void
dfs(struct compiler *c, basicblock *b, struct assembler *a, int end)
{
    int i, j;

    /* Get rid of recursion for normal control flow.
       Since the number of blocks is limited, unused space in a_postorder
       (from a_nblocks to end) can be used as a stack for still not ordered
       blocks. */
    for (j = end; b && !b->b_seen; b = b->b_next) {
        b->b_seen = 1;
        assert(a->a_nblocks < j);
        a->a_postorder[--j] = b;
```

```
    }
    while (j < end) {
        b = a->a_postorder[j++];
        for (i = 0; i < b->b_iused; i++) {
            struct instr *instr = &b->b_instr[i];
            if (instr->i_jrel || instr->i_jabs)
                dfs(c, instr->i_target, a, j);
        }
        assert(a->a_nblocks < j);
        a->a_postorder[a->a_nblocks++] = b;
    }
}
```

Once the assembler has assembled the graph into a CFG using DFS, the code object can be created.

Creating a Code Object

The task of makecode() is to go through the compiler state and some of the assembler's properties and to put these into a PyCodeObject by calling PyCode_New().

The variable names and constants are put as properties to the code object:

Python ▸ compile.c line 5893

```
static PyCodeObject *
makecode(struct compiler *c, struct assembler *a)
{
...

    consts = consts_dict_keys_inorder(c->u->u_consts);
    names = dict_keys_inorder(c->u->u_names, 0);
    varnames = dict_keys_inorder(c->u->u_varnames, 0);
...
    cellvars = dict_keys_inorder(c->u->u_cellvars, 0);
...
```

```
        freevars = dict_keys_inorder(c->u->u_freevars,
                            PyTuple_GET_SIZE(cellvars));
...
        flags = compute_code_flags(c);
        if (flags < 0)
            goto error;

        bytecode = PyCode_Optimize(a->a_bytecode, consts,
                            names, a->a_lnotab);
...
        co = PyCode_NewWithPosOnlyArgs(
            posonlyargcount+posorkeywordargcount,
            posonlyargcount, kwonlyargcount, nlocals_int,
            maxdepth, flags, bytecode, consts, names,
            varnames, freevars, cellvars, c->c_filename,
            c->u->u_name, c->u->u_firstlineno, a->a_lnotab);
...
        return co;
}
```

You may also notice that the bytecode is sent to `PyCode_Optimize()` before it's sent to `PyCode_NewWithPosOnlyArgs()`. This function is part of the bytecode optimization process in `Python` ▸ `peephole.c`.

The peephole optimizer goes through the bytecode instructions and, in certain scenarios, replaces them with other instructions. For example, there's an optimizer that removes any unreachable instructions that follow a `return` statement.

Using Instaviz to Show a Code Object

You can pull together all the compiler stages with the `instaviz` module:

```
import instaviz

def foo():
    a = 2**4
    b = 1 + 5
    c = [1, 4, 6]
    for i in c:
        print(i)
    else:
        print(a)
    return c


instaviz.show(foo)
```

This will produce a large and complex AST graph tree. You can see the bytecode instructions in sequence:

Disassembled Code

OpCode	Operation Name	Numeric Arg	Resolved Arg Value	Argument description
100	LOAD_CONST	1	16	16
125	STORE_FAST	0	a	a
100	LOAD_CONST	2	6	6
125	STORE_FAST	1	b	b
100	LOAD_CONST	3	1	1
100	LOAD_CONST	4	4	4
100	LOAD_CONST	2	6	6
103	BUILD_LIST	3	3	

Here's the code object with the variable names, constants, and binary co_code:

Code Object Properties

Field	Value
co_argcount	0
co_cellvars	()
co_code	64017d0064027d0164036404640267037d02781c7c0244005d0c7d
co_consts	(None, 16, 6, 1, 4)
co_filename	test.py
co_firstlineno	4
co_freevars	()
co_kwonlyargcount	0
co_lnotab	b'\x00\x01\x04\x01\x04\x01\n\x01\n\x01\x0c\x02\x08\x01'

Try it out with some other, more complex code to learn more about CPython's compiler and code objects.

Example: Implementing the Almost-Equal Operator

After covering the compiler, the bytecode instructions, and the assembler, you can now modify CPython to support the almost-equal operator that you compiled into the grammar in the last chapter.

First, you have to add an internal #define for the Py_AlE operator so it can be referenced inside the rich comparison functions for PyObject.

Open Include ▸ object.h and locate the following #define statements:

```
/* Rich comparison opcodes */
#define Py_LT 0
#define Py_LE 1
#define Py_EQ 2
#define Py_NE 3
#define Py_GT 4
#define Py_GE 5
```

Add an additional value, PyAlE, with a value of 6:

```
/* New almost-equal comparator */
#define Py_AlE 6
```

Just underneath this expression is a macro, `Py_RETURN_RICHCOMPARE`. Update this macro with a case statement for `Py_AlE`:

```
/*
 * Macro for implementing rich comparisons
 *
 * Needs to be a macro because any C-comparable type can be used
 */
#define Py_RETURN_RICHCOMPARE(val1, val2, op)                          \
    do {                                                               \
        switch (op) {                                                  \
        case Py_EQ: if ((val1) == (val2)) Py_RETURN_TRUE; Py_RETURN_FALSE; \
        case Py_NE: if ((val1) != (val2)) Py_RETURN_TRUE; Py_RETURN_FALSE; \
        case Py_LT: if ((val1) < (val2)) Py_RETURN_TRUE; Py_RETURN_FALSE; \
        case Py_GT: if ((val1) > (val2)) Py_RETURN_TRUE; Py_RETURN_FALSE; \
        case Py_LE: if ((val1) <= (val2)) Py_RETURN_TRUE; Py_RETURN_FALSE; \
        case Py_GE: if ((val1) >= (val2)) Py_RETURN_TRUE; Py_RETURN_FALSE; \
/* + */ case Py_AlE: if ((val1) == (val2)) Py_RETURN_TRUE; Py_RETURN_FALSE;\
        default:                                                       \
            Py_UNREACHABLE();                                          \
        }                                                              \
    } while (0)
```

Inside Objects ▸ object.c, there's a guard to check that the operator is between 0 and 5. Because you added the value 6, you have to update that assertion:

Objects ▸ object.c line 709

```
PyObject *
PyObject_RichCompare(PyObject *v, PyObject *w, int op)
{
    PyThreadState *tstate = _PyThreadState_GET();

    assert(Py_LT <= op && op <= Py_GE);
```

Change that last line to the following:

```
assert(Py_LT <= op && op <= Py_AlE);
```

Next, you need to update the COMPARE_OP opcode to support Py_AlE as a value for the operator type.

First, edit Objects ▸ object.c and add Py_AlE into the _Py_SwappedOp list. This list is used for matching whether a custom class has one operator dunder method but not the other.

For example, if you defined a class, Coordinate, you could define an equality operator by implementing the __eq__ magic method:

```python
class Coordinate:
    def __init__(self, x, y):
        self.x = x
        self.y = y

    def __eq__(self, other):
        if isinstance(other, Coordinate):
            return (self.x == other.x and self.y == other.y)
        return super(self, other).__eq__(other)
```

Even though you haven't implemented __ne__ (not equal) for Coordinate, CPython assumes that the opposite of __eq__ can be used.

```
>>> Coordinate(1, 100) != Coordinate(2, 400)
True
```

Inside Objects ▸ object.c, locate the _Py_SwappedOp list and add Py_AlE to the end. Then add "~=" to the end of the opstrings list:

```c
int _Py_SwappedOp[] = {Py_GT, Py_GE, Py_EQ, Py_NE, Py_LT, Py_LE, Py_AlE};

static const char * const opstrings[]
    = {"<", "<=", "==", "!=", ">", ">=", "~="};
```

Open Lib/opcode.py and edit the list of rich comparison operators:

```
cmp_op = ('<', '<=', '==', '!=', '>', '>=')
```

Include the new operator at the end of the tuple:

```
cmp_op = ('<', '<=', '==', '!=', '>', '>=', '~=')
```

The opstrings list is used for error messages if rich comparison operators aren't implemented on a class.

Next, you can update the compiler to handle the case of a Py-Cmp_A1E property in a BinOp node. Open Python ▸ compile.c and find compiler_addcompare():

Python ▸ compile.c line 2479

```
static int compiler_addcompare(struct compiler *c, cmpop_ty op)
{
    int cmp;
    switch (op) {
    case Eq:
        cmp = Py_EQ;
        break;
    case NotEq:
        cmp = Py_NE;
        break;
    case Lt:
        cmp = Py_LT;
        break;
    case LtE:
        cmp = Py_LE;
        break;
    case Gt:
        cmp = Py_GT;
        break;
    case GtE:
        cmp = Py_GE;
        break;
```

Next, add another `case` to this switch statement to pair the AlE AST `comp_op` enumeration with the `PyCmp_AlE` opcode comparison enumeration:

```
...
case AlE:
    cmp = Py_AlE;
    break;
```

You can now program the behavior of the almost-equal operator to match the following scenario:

- `1 ~= 2` is `False`.

- `1 ~= 1.01` is `True` using floor rounding.

You can achieve this with some additional code. For now, you'll cast both floats into integers and compare them.

CPython's API has many functions for dealing with `PyLong` (`int`) and `PyFloat` (`float`) types. This will be covered in the chapter "Objects and Types."

Locate `float_richcompare()` in Objects ▸ `floatobject.c` and, under the `Compare:` goto definition, add the following case:

Objects ▸ `floatobject.c` line 358

```
static PyObject*
float_richcompare(PyObject *v, PyObject *w, int op)
{
  ...
    case Py_GT:
        r = i > j;
        break;
    /* New Code START */
    case Py_AlE: {
        double diff = fabs(i - j);
        double rel_tol = 1e-9; // relative tolerance
        double abs_tol = 0.1;  // absolute tolerance
```

```
            r = (((diff <= fabs(rel_tol * j))  ||
                  (diff <= fabs(rel_tol * i))) ||
                  (diff <= abs_tol));
        }
        break;
    }
    /* New Code END */
    return PyBool_FromLong(r);
```

This code will handle the comparison of floating point numbers when the almost-equal operator has been used. It uses logic similar to `math.isclose()`, defined in PEP 485, but with a hardcoded absolute tolerance of 0.1.

Another safeguard that you need to change is in the evaluation loop, Python▸ceval.c. You'll cover the evaluation loop in the next chapter.

Search for this code snippet:

```
...
        case TARGET(COMPARE_OP): {
            assert(oparg <= Py_GE);
```

Change the assertion to the following:

```
assert(oparg <= Py_AlE);
```

After recompiling CPython, open a REPL and test it out:

```
$ ./python
>>> 1.0 ~= 1.01
True
>>> 1.02 ~= 1.01
True
>>> 1.02 ~= 2.01
False
>>> 1 ~= 1.01
True
>>> 1 ~= 1
```

```
True
>>> 1 ~= 2
False
>>> 1 ~= 1.9
False
>>> 1 ~= 2.0
False
>>> 1.1 ~= 1.101
True
```

In later chapters, you'll extend this implementation across other types.

Conclusion

In this chapter, you've explored how a parsed Python module is converted into a symbol table, a compilation state, and then a series of bytecode operations:

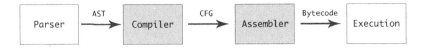

It's now the job of the CPython interpreter's core evaluation loop to execute those modules. In the next chapter, you'll explore how code objects are executed.

The Evaluation Loop

So far, you've seen how Python code is parsed into an abstract syntax tree and compiled into code objects. These code objects contain lists of discrete operations in the form of bytecode.

There's one major thing missing for these code objects to be executed and come to life: They need input. In Python, these inputs take the form of local and global variables.

In this chapter, you'll be introduced to a concept called a **value stack**, which is where variables are created, modified, and used by the bytecode operations in your compiled code objects.

Execution of code in CPython happens within a central loop called the **evaluation loop**. The CPython interpreter will evaluate and execute a code object fetched from either the marshaled .pyc file or the compiler:

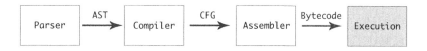

In the evaluation loop, each of the bytecode instructions is taken and executed using a stack frame–based system[21].

---

[21]https://realpython.com/cpython-stack-frame

> **Note**
>
> **Stack frames** are a data type used by many runtimes, not just Python. Stack frames allow functions to be called and variables to be returned between functions. Stack frames also contain arguments, local variables, and other stateful information.
>
> A stack frame exists for every function call, and they're stacked in sequence. You can see CPython's frame stack anytime an exception is unhandled:
>
> ```
> Traceback (most recent call last):
>   File "example_stack.py", line 8, in <module>  <--- Frame
>     function1()
>   File "example_stack.py", line 5, in function1 <--- Frame
>     function2()
>   File "example_stack.py", line 2, in function2 <--- Frame
>     raise RuntimeError
> RuntimeError
> ```

Related Source Files

Here are the source files related to the evaluation loop:

File	Purpose
Python ▸ ceval.c	The core evaluation loop implementation
Python ▸ ceval-gil.h	The GIL definition and control algorithm

Important Terms

Here are a few important terms that you'll use in this chapter:

- The evaluation loop will take a **code object** and convert it into a series of **frame objects**.
- The interpreter has at least one **thread**.

- Each thread has a **thread state**.
- Frame objects are executed in a stack, called the **frame stack**.
- Variables are referenced in a **value stack**.

Constructing Thread State

Before a frame can be executed, it needs to be linked to a thread. CPython can have many threads running at any one time within a single interpreter. The **interpreter state** includes a linked list of those threads.

CPython always has at least one thread, and each thread has its own state.

> **See Also**
>
> Threading is covered in more detail in the "Parallelism and Concurrency" chapter.

Thread State Type

The thread state type, PyThreadState, has over thirty properties, including the following:

- A unique identifier
- A linked list to the other thread states
- The interpreter state it was spawned by
- The currently executing frame
- The current recursion depth
- Optional tracing functions
- The exception currently being handled
- Any async exception currently being handled

- A stack of exceptions raised when multiple exceptions have been raised (within an `except` block, for example)

- A GIL counter

- Async generator counters

Related Source Files

The source files related to the thread state are spread across many files:

File	Purpose
Python ▸ thread.c	The thread API implementation
Include ▸ threadstate.h	Some of the thread state API and types definition
Include ▸ pystate.h	The interpreter state API and types definition
Include ▸ pythread.h	The threading API
Include ▸ cpython ▸ pystate.h	Some of the thread and interpreter state API

Constructing Frame Objects

Compiled code objects are inserted into frame objects. Frame objects are a Python type, so they can be referenced from both C and Python.

Frame objects also contain other runtime data required for executing the instructions in the code objects. This data includes the local variables, global variables, and built-in modules.

Frame Object Type

The frame object type is a `PyObject` with the following additional properties:

Field	Type	Purpose
f_back	PyFrameObject *	Pointer to the previous in the stack, or NULL if first frame
f_blockstack	PyTryBlock[]	Sequence of for, try, and loop blocks
f_builtins	PyObject * (dict)	Symbol table for the builtin module
f_code	PyCodeObject *	Code object to be executed
f_executing	char	Flag whether the frame is still executing
f_gen	PyObject *	Borrowed reference to a generator, or NULL
f_globals	PyObject * (dict)	Global symbol table (PyDictObject)
f_iblock	int	Index of this frame in f_blockstack
f_lasti	int	Last instruction, if called
f_lineno	int	Current line number
f_locals	PyObject *	Local symbol table (any mapping)
f_localsplus	PyObject *[]	Union of locals plus stack
f_stacktop	PyObject **	Next free slot in f_valuestack
f_trace	PyObject *	Pointer to a custom tracing function (see "Frame Execution Tracing")
f_trace_lines	char	Toggle for the custom tracing function to trace at line level
f_trace_opcodes	char	Toggle for the custom tracing function to trace at an opcode level
f_valuestack	PyObject **	Pointer to the last local

Related Source Files

Here are the source files related to frame objects:

File	Purpose
Objects ▸ frameobject.c	The frame object implementation and Python API
Include ▸ frameobject.h	The frame object API and type definition

Frame Object Initialization API

The API for frame object initialization, PyEval_EvalCode(), is the entry point for evaluating a code object. PyEval_EvalCode() is a wrapper around the internal function _PyEval_EvalCode().

> **Note**
>
> `_PyEval_EvalCode()` is a complex function that defines many be-
> haviors of both frame objects and the interpreter loop. It's an
> important function to understand as it can also teach you some
> principles of the CPython interpreter design.

In this section, you'll step through the logic in `_PyEval\_EvalCode()`.

`_PyEval_EvalCode()` specifies many arguments:

- **tstate:** A `PyThreadState` * pointing to the thread state of the thread
  this code will be evaluated on
- **_co:** A `PyCodeObject*` containing the code to be put into the frame
  object
- **globals:** A `PyObject*` (`dict`) with variable names as keys and their
  values
- **locals:** A `PyObject*` (`dict`) with variable names as keys and their
  values

> **Note**
>
> In Python, local and global variables are stored as a dictionary.
> You can access this dictionary with the built-in functions `lo-`
> `cals()` and `globals()`:
>
> ```
> >>> a = 1
> >>> print(locals()["a"])
> 1
> ```

The other arguments are optional and aren't used for the basic API:

- **argcount:** The number of positional arguments
- **args:** A `PyObject*` (`tuple`) with positional argument values in order
- **closure:** A tuple with strings to merge into the code object's
  `co_freevars` field

- **defcount:** The length of default values for positional arguments

- **defs:** A list of default values for positional arguments

- **kwargs:** A list of keyword argument values

- **kwcount:** The number of keyword arguments

- **kwdefs:** A dictionary with the default values for keyword arguments

- **kwnames:** A list of keyword argument names

- **name:** The name for this evaluation statement as a string

- **qualname:** The qualified name for this evaluation statement as a string

The call to `_PyFrame_New_NoTrack()` creates a new frame. This API is also available from the C API using `PyFrame_New()`. `_PyFrame_New_NoTrack()` will create a new `PyFrameObject` by following these steps:

1. Set the frame `f_back` property to the thread state's last frame.

2. Load the current built-in functions by setting the `f_builtins` property and loading the `builtins` module using `PyModule_GetDict()`.

3. Set the `f_code` property to the code object being evaluated.

4. Set the `f_valuestack` property to an empty value stack.

5. Set the `f_stacktop` pointer to `f_valuestack`.

6. Set the global property, `f_globals`, to the `globals` argument.

7. Set the locals property, `f_locals`, to a new dictionary.

8. Set the `f_lineno` to the code object's `co_firstlineno` property so that tracebacks contain line numbers.

9. Set all the remaining properties to their default values.

With the new `PyFrameObject` instance, the arguments to the frame object can be constructed:

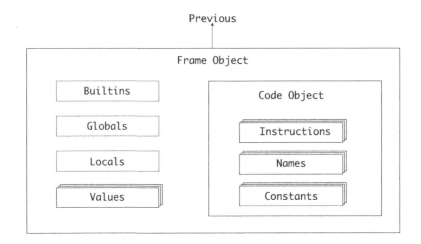

Converting Keyword Parameters to a Dictionary

Function definitions can contain a **kwargs catch-all for keyword-arguments:

```
def example(arg, arg2=None, **kwargs):
    print(kwargs["x"], kwargs["y"])  # resolves to a dictionary key
example(1, x=2, y=3)  # 2 3
```

In this scenario, a new dictionary is created, and the unresolved arguments are copied across. The kwargs name is then set as a variable in the local scope of the frame.

Converting Positional Arguments into Variables

Each of the positional arguments (if provided) are set as local variables. In Python, function arguments are already local variables within the function body. When a positional argument is defined with a value, it's available within the function scope:

```
def example(arg1, arg2):
    print(arg1, arg2)
example(1, 2)  # 1 2
```

The reference counter for those variables is incremented, so the garbage collector won't remove them until the frame has evaluated, such as when the function has finished and returned.

Packing Positional Arguments into *args

As with **kwargs, a function argument prepended with * can be set to catch all remaining positional arguments. This argument is a tuple, and the *args name is set as a local variable:

```
def example(arg, *args):
    print(arg, args[0], args[1])


example(1, 2, 3)  # 1 2 3
```

Loading Keyword Arguments

If the function is called with keyword arguments and values, then a dictionary is filled with any remaining keyword arguments passed by the caller that don't resolve to named arguments or positional arguments.

For example, the e argument is neither positional nor named, so it's added to **remaining:

```
>>> def my_function(a, b, c=None, d=None, **remaining):
        print(a, b, c, d, remaining)

>>> my_function(a=1, b=2, c=3, d=4, e=5)
(1, 2, 3, 4, {"e": 5})
```

> **Note**
>
> **Positional-only arguments** are a new feature in Python 3.8. Introduced in PEP 570, positional-only arguments are a way of stopping users of your API from using positional arguments with a keyword syntax.
>
> For example, this simple function converts Fahrenheit to Celsius. Note the use of the forward slash (/) as a special argument that separates positional-only arguments from the other arguments:
>
> ```
> def to_celsius(fahrenheit, /, options=None):
>     return (fahrenheit-32)*5/9
> ```
>
> All arguments to the left of / must be called only as positional arguments. Arguments to the right can be called as either positional or keyword arguments:
>
> ```
> >>> to_celsius(110)
> ```
>
> Calling the function using a keyword argument to a positional-only argument will raise a `TypeError`:
>
> ```
> >>> to_celsius(fahrenheit=110)
> Traceback (most recent call last):
>   File "<stdin>", line 1, in <module>
> TypeError: to_celsius() got some positional-only arguments
>  passed as keyword arguments: 'fahrenheit'
> ```

The resolution of the keyword argument dictionary values comes after all other arguments are unpacked. The PEP 570 positional-only arguments are shown by starting the keyword argument loop at co_posonlyargcount. If the / symbol was used on the third argument, then the value of co_posonlyargcount would be 2.

PyDict_SetItem() is called for each remaining argument for adding it to the locals dictionary. When executing, each of the keyword arguments become scoped local variables.

If a keyword argument is defined with a value, then it's available within this scope:

```
def example(arg1, arg2, example_kwarg=None):
    print(example_kwarg)  # example_kwarg is already a local variable.
```

Adding Missing Positional Arguments

Any positional arguments provided to a function call that aren't in the list of positional arguments are added to an *args tuple. If this tuple doesn't exist, then an exception is raised.

Adding Missing Keyword Arguments

Any keyword arguments provided to a function call that aren't in the list of named keyword arguments are added to a **kwargs dictionary. If this dictionary doesn't exist, then an exception is raised.

Collapsing Closures

Any closure names are added to the code object's list of free variable names.

Creating Generators, Coroutines, and Asynchronous Generators

If the evaluated code object has a flag that it's a generator, coroutine, or async generator, then a new frame is created using one of the unique methods in the generator, coroutine, or async libraries, and the current frame is added as a property.

> **See Also**
>
> The APIs and implementations of generators, coroutines, and async frames are covered in the chapter "Parallelism and Concurrency."

The new frame is then returned, and the original frame isn't evaluated. The frame is evaluated only when the generator, coroutine, or async method is called to execute its target.

Lastly, `_PyEval_EvalFrame()` is called with the new frame.

Frame Execution

As covered earlier in the chapters "Lexing and Parsing With Syntax Trees" and "The Compiler," the code object contains a binary encoding of the bytecode to be executed. It also contains a list of variables and a symbol table.

The local and global variables are determined at runtime based on how the function, module, or block was called. This information is added to the frame by `_PyEval_EvalCode()`.

There are other uses of frames, like the coroutine decorator, which dynamically generates a frame with the target as a variable.

The public API, `PyEval_EvalFrameEx()`, calls the interpreter's configured frame evaluation function in the `eval_frame` property. Frame evaluation was made pluggable in Python 3.7 with PEP 523.

`_PyEval_EvalFrameDefault()` is the default frame evaluation function and the only option bundled with CPython.

This central function brings everything together and brings your code to life. It contains decades of optimization since even a single line of code can have a significant impact on performance for the whole of CPython.

Everything that gets executed in CPython goes through the frame evaluation function.

Note

Something you might notice when reading Python ▸ ceval.c is how many times C macros have been used.

C macros are a way of having reusable code without the overhead of making function calls. The compiler converts the macros into C code and then compiles the generated code.

In Visual Studio Code, inline macro expansion shows once you've installed the official C/C++ extension:

```
1122        dtrace_function_entry(f);
1123
1124    co = f->f_code;
1125    names = co->co_names;
1126    consts = co->co_consts;
1127    fastlocals = f->f_localsplus;
1128    freevars = f->f_localsplus + co->co_nlocals;
1129    assert(
1130    assert(   #define _Py_IS_ALIGNED(p,a) (!((uintptr_t)(p) & (uintptr_t)((a) - 1)))
1131    assert(  Check if pointer "p" is aligned to "a"-bytes boundary.
1132    assert(_Py_IS_ALIGNED(PyBytes_AS_STRING(co->co_code), sizeof(_Py_CODEUNIT)));
1133    first_instr = (_Py_CODEUNIT *) PyBytes_AS_STRING(co->co_code);
1134    /*
1135       f->f_lasti refers to the index of the last instruction,
1136       unless it's -1 in which case next_instr should be first_instr.
1137
1138       YIELD_FROM sets f_lasti to itself, in order to repeatedly yield
1139       multiple values.
1140
1141       When the PREDICT() macros are enabled, some opcode pairs follow in
```

In CLion, select a macro and press ⌥Alt + ⌥Space to peek into its definition.

Frame Execution Tracing

You can step through frame execution in Python 3.7 and beyond by enabling the tracing attribute on the current thread. The PyFrameObject type contains an f_trace property of type PyObject *. The value is expected to point to a Python function.

This code example sets the global tracing function to a function called my_trace() that gets the stack from the current frame, prints the disassembled opcodes to the screen, and adds some extra information for debugging:

cpython-book-samples ▶ 31 ▶ my_trace.py

```python
import sys
import dis
import traceback
import io


def my_trace(frame, event, args):
    frame.f_trace_opcodes = True
    stack = traceback.extract_stack(frame)
    pad = "   "*len(stack) + "|"
    if event == "opcode":
        with io.StringIO() as out:
            dis.disco(frame.f_code, frame.f_lasti, file=out)
            lines = out.getvalue().split("\n")
            [print(f"{pad}{l}") for l in lines]
    elif event == "call":
        print(f"{pad}Calling {frame.f_code}")
    elif event == "return":
        print(f"{pad}Returning {args}")
    elif event == "line":
        print(f"{pad}Changing line to {frame.f_lineno}")
    else:
        print(f"{pad}{frame} ({event} - {args})")
    print(f"{pad}--------------------------------")
    return my_trace
sys.settrace(my_trace)

# Run some code for a demo
eval('"-".join([letter for letter in "hello"])')
```

sys.settrace() will set the current thread state default tracing function
to the one provided. Any new frames created after this call will have
f_trace set to this function.

This code snippet prints the code within each stack and points to the
next operation before it's executed. When a frame returns a value, the
return statement is printed:

```
→ cpython git:(master) ✗ ./python.exe my_trace.py
  |Calling <code object <module> at 0x104cdc110, file "<string>", line 1>
  |-----------------------------------------------------
  |Changing line to 1
  |-----------------------------------------------------
  |  1 -->      0 LOAD_CONST           0 ('-')
             2 LOAD_METHOD          0 (join)
             4 LOAD_CONST           1 (<code object <listcomp> at 0x104cdcee0, file "<string>", line 1>)
             6 LOAD_CONST           2 ('<listcomp>')
             8 MAKE_FUNCTION        0
            10 LOAD_CONST           3 ('hello')
            12 GET_ITER
            14 CALL_FUNCTION        1
            16 CALL_METHOD          1
            18 RETURN_VALUE

  |-----------------------------------------------------
  |  1        0 LOAD_CONST           0 ('-')
  -->        2 LOAD_METHOD          0 (join)
             4 LOAD_CONST           1 (<code object <listcomp> at 0x104cdcee0, file "<string>", line 1>)
             6 LOAD_CONST           2 ('<listcomp>')
             8 MAKE_FUNCTION        0
            10 LOAD_CONST           3 ('hello')
            12 GET_ITER
            14 CALL_FUNCTION        1
            16 CALL_METHOD          1
            18 RETURN_VALUE
```

The full list of possible bytecode instructions is available on the `dis`
module documentation.[22]

The Value Stack

Inside the core evaluation loop, a value stack is created. This stack
is a list of pointers to `PyObject` instances. These could be values like
variables, references to functions (which are objects in Python), or
any other Python object.

Bytecode instructions in the evaluation loop will take input from the
value stack.

Example Bytecode Operation: BINARY_OR

The binary operations that you've been exploring in previous chapters
compile into a single instruction.

For example, let's say you inserted an `or` statement in Python:

```
if left or right:
    pass
```

The compiler would compile this `or` operation into a `BINARY_OR` instruction:

---

[22]https://docs.python.org/3/library/dis.html#python-bytecode-instructions

171

```
static int
binop(struct compiler *c, operator_ty op)
{
    switch (op) {
    case Add:
        return BINARY_ADD;
    ...
    case BitOr:
        return BINARY_OR;
```

In the evaluation loop, the case for a BINARY_OR will take two values from the value stack, the left and right operations, then call PyNumber_Or against those two objects:

```
    ...
    case TARGET(BINARY_OR): {
        PyObject *right = POP();
        PyObject *left = TOP();
        PyObject *res = PyNumber_Or(left, right);
        Py_DECREF(left);
        Py_DECREF(right);
        SET_TOP(res);
        if (res == NULL)
            goto error;
        DISPATCH();
    }
```

The result, res, is then set as the top of the stack, overriding the current top value.

Value Stack Simulations

To understand the evaluation loop, you have to understand the value stack.

One way to think of the value stack is as a wooden peg on which you can stack cylinders. In this scenario, you would add or remove only one cylinder at a time, and always to or from the top of the stack.

In CPython, you add objects to the value stack with the PUSH(a) macro, where a is a pointer to a PyObject.

For example, assume you created a PyLong with the value 10 and pushed it onto the value stack:

```
PyObject *a = PyLong_FromLong(10);
PUSH(a);
```

This action would have the following effect:

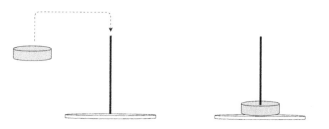

In the next operation, to fetch that value, you would use the POP() macro to take the top value from the stack:

```
PyObject *a = POP();  // a is PyLongObject with a value of 10
```

This action would return the top value and end up with an empty value stack:

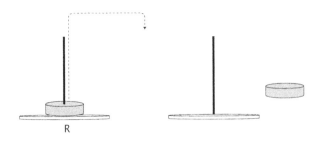

R

Now let's say you added two values to the stack:

```
PyObject *a = PyLong_FromLong(10);
PyObject *b = PyLong_FromLong(20);
PUSH(a);
PUSH(b);
```

These would end up in the order in which they were added, so a would be pushed to the second position in the stack:

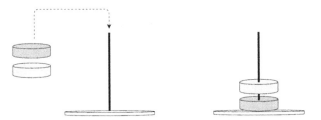

If you were to fetch the top value in the stack, then you would get a pointer to b because it's at the top:

```
PyObject *val = POP(); // returns ptr to b
```

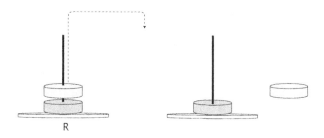

If you need to fetch the pointer to the top value in the stack without popping it, then you can use the PEEK(v) operation, where v is the stack position:

```
PyObject *first = PEEK(0);
```

0 represents the top of the stack, and 1 would represent the second position:

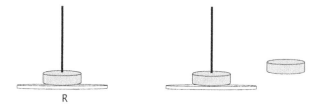

You can use the DUP_TOP() macro to clone the value at the top of the stack:

```
DUP_TOP();
```

This action would copy the value at the top to form two pointers to the same object:

The rotation macro ROT_TWO swaps the first and second values:

```
ROT_TWO();
```

This action would switch the order of the first and second values:

Stack Effects

Each of the opcodes has a predefined **stack effect** calculated by stack_effect() inside Python ▸ compile.c. This function returns the delta in the number of values inside the stack for each opcode.

Stack effects can have a positive, negative, or zero value. Once the operation has been executed, if the stack effect (such as +1) doesn't match the delta in the value stack, then an exception is raised.

Example: Adding an Item to a List

In Python, when you create a list, the `append()` method is available on the list object:

```
my_list = []
my_list.append(obj)
```

In this example, `obj` is an object that you want to append to the end of the list.

There are two operations involved in this operation:

1. **LOAD_FAST** to load `obj` to the top of the value stack from the list of `locals` in the frame

2. **LIST_APPEND** to add the object

LOAD_FAST involves five steps:

1. The pointer to `obj` is loaded from GETLOCAL(), where the variable to load is the operation argument. The list of variable pointers is stored in `fastlocals`, which is a copy of the `PyFrame` attribute `f_localsplus`. The operation argument is a number pointing to the index in the `fastlocals` array pointer. This means that Python loads a local as a copy of the pointer rather than having to look up the variable name.

2. If the variable no longer exists, then an unbound local variable error is raised.

3. The reference counter for `value` (in our case, `obj`) is increased by one.

4. The pointer to `obj` is pushed to the top of the value stack.

5. The FAST_DISPATCH macro is called. If tracing is enabled, then the loop runs again with all the tracing. If tracing isn't enabled, then a `goto` is called to `fast_next_opcode`. The `goto` jumps back to the top of the loop for the next instruction.

Here are are the five steps in LOAD_FAST:

```
    . . .
    case TARGET(LOAD_FAST): {
        PyObject *value = GETLOCAL(oparg);                  // 1.
        if (value == NULL) {
            format_exc_check_arg(
                PyExc_UnboundLocalError,
                UNBOUNDLOCAL_ERROR_MSG,
                PyTuple_GetItem(co->co_varnames, oparg));
            goto error;                                     // 2.
        }
        Py_INCREF(value);                                   // 3.
        PUSH(value);                                        // 4.
        FAST_DISPATCH();                                    // 5.
    }
    . . .
```

The pointer to obj is now at the top of the value stack, and the next instruction, LIST_APPEND, is executed.

Many of the bytecode operations reference base types, like PyUnicode or PyNumber. For example, LIST_APPEND appends an object to the end of a list. To achieve this, it pops the pointer from the value stack and returns the pointer to the last object in the stack.

The macro is a shortcut for the following:

```
PyObject *v = (*--stack_pointer);
```

Now the pointer to obj is stored as v. The list pointer is loaded from PEEK(oparg).

Then the C API for Python lists is called for list and v. The code for this is inside Objects ▸ listobject.c, which you'll explore in the chapter "Objects and Types."

Next, a call to PREDICT is made, which guesses that the next operation will be JUMP_ABSOLUTE. The PREDICT macro has compiler-generated goto statements for each of the potential operations' case statements.

This means the CPU can jump to that instruction and not have to go through the loop again:

```
...
        case TARGET(LIST_APPEND): {
            PyObject *v = POP();
            PyObject *list = PEEK(oparg);
            int err;
            err = PyList_Append(list, v);
            Py_DECREF(v);
            if (err != 0)
                goto error;
            PREDICT(JUMP_ABSOLUTE);
            DISPATCH();
        }
...
```

Note

Some opcodes come in pairs, making it possible to predict the second code when the first is run. For example, COMPARE_OP is often followed by POP_JUMP_IF_FALSE or POP_JUMP_IF_TRUE.

If you're collecting opcode statistics, then you have two choices:

1. Keep the predictions turned on and interpret the results as if some opcodes had been combined.

2. Turn off predictions so that the opcode frequency counter updates for both opcodes.

Opcode prediction is disabled with threaded code since the latter allows the CPU to record separate branch prediction information for each opcode.

Some of the operations, such as CALL_FUNCTION and CALL_METHOD, have an operation argument referencing another compiled function. In this case, another frame is pushed to the frame stack in the thread, and the evaluation loop runs for that function until the function completes.

Each time a new frame is created and pushed onto the stack, the value of the frame's f_back is set to the current frame before the new one is created. This nesting of frames is clear when you see a stack trace:

cpython-book-samples ▸ 31 ▸ example_stack.py

```
def function2():
  raise RuntimeError

def function1():
  function2()

if __name__ == "__main__":
  function1()
```

Calling this on the command line will give you the following:

```
$ ./python example_stack.py

Traceback (most recent call last):
  File "example_stack.py", line 8, in <module>
    function1()
  File "example_stack.py", line 5, in function1
    function2()
  File "example_stack.py", line 2, in function2
    raise RuntimeError
RuntimeError
```

In Lib ▸ traceback.py, you can use walk_stack() to get tracebacks:

```
def walk_stack(f):
    """Walk a stack yielding the frame and line number for each frame.

    This will follow f.f_back from the given frame. If no frame is given,
    the current stack is used. Usually used with StackSummary.extract.
    """
    if f is None:
        f = sys._getframe().f_back.f_back
    while f is not None:
```

```
yield f, f.f_lineno
f = f.f_back
```

The parent's parent (sys._getframe().f_back.f_back) is set as the frame because you don't want to see the call to walk_stack() or print_trace() in the traceback. The f_back pointer is followed to the top of the call stack.

sys._getframe() is the Python API to get the frame attribute of the current thread.

Here's how that frame stack would look with three frames, each with its code object, and a thread state pointing to the current frame:

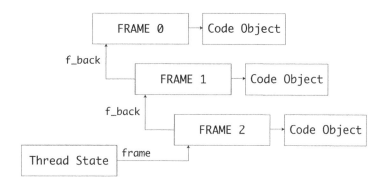

Conclusion

In this chapter, you've been introduced to the *brain* of CPython. The core evaluation loop is the interface between compiled Python code and the underlying C extension modules, libraries, and system calls.

Some topics in this chapter have been glossed over since you'll go into them in upcoming chapters. For example, the CPython interpreter has a core evaluation loop, but you can have multiple loops running at the same time, whether that be in parallel or concurrently.

CPython can have multiple evaluation loops running multiple frames on a system. In the upcoming chapter "Parallelism and Concurrency," you'll see how the frame stack system is used for CPython to run on multiple cores or CPUs. Also, CPython's frame object API enables frames to be paused and resumed in the form of asynchronous programming.

Loading variables using a value stack requires memory allocation and management. For CPython to run effectively, it has to have a solid memory management process. In the next chapter, you'll explore that memory management process and how it relates to the PyObject pointers used by the evaluation loop.

Memory Management

The two most important parts of your computer are the memory and the CPU. One can't work without the other. They must be utilized well, and they must be efficient.

When designing a programming language, the authors need to decide how the user should manage computer memory. There are many options depending on how simple the authors want the interface to be, whether they want the language to be cross-platform, and whether they value performance over stability.

The authors of Python have made these decisions for you and have also left you with some additional decisions to make yourself.

In this chapter, you'll explore how C manages memory since CPython is written in C. You'll look at two critical aspects to managing memory in Python:

1. Reference counting
2. Garbage collection

By the end of this chapter, you'll understand how CPython allocates memory on the operating system, how object memory is allocated and freed, and how CPython manages memory leaks.

Memory Allocation in C

In C, variables must have their memory allocated from the operating system before they can be used. There are three memory allocation mechanisms in C:

1. **Static memory allocation**: Memory requirements are calculated at compile time and allocated by the executable when it starts.

2. **Automatic memory allocation**: Memory requirements for a scope are allocated within the call stack when a frame is entered and are freed once the frame is terminated.

3. **Dynamic memory allocation**: Memory can be requested and allocated dynamically at runtime by calls to the memory allocation API.

Static Memory Allocation in C

Types in C have a fixed size. The compiler calculates the memory requirements for all static and global variables and then compiles that requirement into the application:

```
static int number = 0;
```

You can see the size of a type in C by using `sizeof()`. On my system, a 64-bit macOS running GCC, an `int` is 4 bytes. Basic types in C can have different sizes depending on the architecture and compiler.

Arrays are statically defined. Consider this array of 10 integers:

```
static int numbers[10] = {0,1,2,3,4,5,6,7,8,9};
```

The C compiler converts this statement into an allocation of `sizeof(int)` * 10 bytes of memory.

The C compiler uses system calls to allocate memory. These system calls depend on the operating system and are low-level functions to the kernel to allocate memory from the system memory pages.

184

Automatic Memory Allocation in C

Similarly to static memory allocation, automatic memory allocation calculates memory allocation requirements at compile time.

This example application converts 100 degrees Fahrenheit to Celsius:

cpython-book-samples ▸ 32 ▸ automatic.c

```
#include <stdio.h>

static const double five_ninths = 5.0/9.0;

double celsius(double fahrenheit) {
    double c = (fahrenheit - 32) * five_ninths;
    return c;
}

int main() {
    double f = 100;
    printf("%f F is %f C\n", f, celsius(f));
    return 0;
}
```

This example uses both static and automatic memory allocation:

- The const value five_ninths is allocated statically because it has the static keyword.

- The variable c within celsius() is allocated automatically when celsius() is called and freed when celsius() is completed.

- The variable f within main() is allocated automatically when main() is called and freed when main() is completed.

- The result of celsius(f) is implicitly allocated automatically.

- The automatic memory requirements of main() are freed when the function completes.

Dynamic Memory Allocation in C

In many cases, neither static nor automatic memory allocation is sufficient. For example, a program might not be able to calculate memory requirements at compile time because they're determined by user input.

In such cases, memory is allocated **dynamically**. Dynamic memory allocation works by calls to the C memory allocation APIs. Operating systems reserve a section of the system memory for dynamic allocation to processes. This section of memory is called a **heap**.

In the following example, you'll allocate memory dynamically to an array of Fahrenheit and Celsius values. The application calculates the Celsius values corresponding to a user-specified number of Fahrenheit values:

cpython-book-samples ▸ 32 ▸ dynamic.c

```c
#include <stdio.h>
#include <stdlib.h>

static const double five_ninths = 5.0/9.0;

double celsius(double fahrenheit) {
    double c = (fahrenheit - 32) * five_ninths;
    return c;
}

int main(int argc, char** argv) {
    if (argc != 2)
        return -1;
    int number = atoi(argv[1]);
    double* c_values = (double*)calloc(number, sizeof(double));
    double* f_values = (double*)calloc(number, sizeof(double));
    for (int i = 0 ; i < number ; i++ ){
        f_values[i] = (i + 10) * 10.0 ;
        c_values[i] = celsius((double)f_values[i]);
    }
```

186

```
for (int i = 0 ; i < number ; i++ ){
    printf("%f F is %f C\n", f_values[i], c_values[i]);
}
free(c_values);
free(f_values);

return 0;
}
```

If you execute this program with the argument 4, then it will print the resulting values:

```
100.000000 F is 37.777778 C
110.000000 F is 43.333334 C
120.000000 F is 48.888888 C
130.000000 F is 54.444444 C
```

This example uses dynamic memory allocation to allocate a block of memory from the heap that is then returned when it's no longer needed. If any dynamically allocated memory isn't freed, then it will cause a **memory leak**.

Design of the Python Memory Management System

Being built on top of C, CPython has to use the constraints of static, dynamic, and automatic memory allocation. Some design aspects of the Python language make those constraints even more challenging:

1. Python is a dynamically typed language. The size of variables can't be calculated at compile time.

2. Most of Python's core types are dynamically sized. The list type can be of any size, dict can have any number of keys, and even int is dynamic. The user never has to specify the size of these types.

187

3. Names in Python can be reused for values of different types:

```
>>> a_value = 1
>>> a_value = "Now I'm a string"
>>> a_value = ["Now" , "I'm", "a", "list"]
```

To overcome these constraints, CPython relies heavily on dynamic memory allocation but adds safety rails to automate the freeing of memory using the garbage collection and reference counting algorithms.

Instead of the Python developer having to allocate memory, Python object memory is allocated automatically by a single, unified API. This design requires that the entire CPython standard library and core modules (written in C) use this API.

Allocation Domains

CPython comes with three dynamic memory allocation domains:

1. The **raw domain** is used for allocation from the system heap and large, or non-object related memory.

2. The **object domain** is used for allocation of all Python object-related memory.

3. The **PyMem domain** is the same as PYMEM_DOMAIN_OBJ. It exists for legacy API purposes.

Each domain implements the same interface of functions:

- _Alloc(size_t size) allocates memory of size bytes and returns a pointer.

- _Calloc(size_t nelem, size_t elsize) allocates nelem elements, each of size elsize, and returns a pointer.

- _Realloc(void *ptr, size_t new_size) reallocates memory of size new_size.

- _Free(void *ptr) frees memory at ptr back to the heap.

The `PyMemAllocatorDomain` enumeration represents the three domains in CPython as PYMEM_DOMAIN_RAW, PYMEM_DOMAIN_OBJ, and PYMEM_DOMAIN_MEM.

Memory Allocators

CPython uses two memory allocators:

1. `malloc`: The operating system allocator for the **raw** memory domain

2. `pymalloc`: The CPython allocator for the **PyMem** and **object memory** domains

> **Note**
>
> The CPython allocator, `pymalloc`, is compiled into CPython by default. You can remove it by recompiling CPython after setting `WITH_PYMALLOC = 0` in `pyconfig.h`. If you remove it, then the PyMem and object memory domain APIs will use the system allocator.

If you compiled CPython with debugging (using `--with-pydebug` on macOS or Linux or the `Debug` target on Windows), then each of the memory allocation functions will go to a Debug implementation. For example, with debugging enabled, your memory allocation calls would execute `_PyMem_DebugAlloc()` instead of `_PyMem_Alloc()`.

The CPython Memory Allocator

The CPython memory allocator sits on top of the system memory allocator and has its algorithm for allocation. This algorithm is similar to the system allocator except that it's customized to CPython:

- Most of the memory allocation requests are small and of a fixed size because `PyObject` is 16 bytes, `PyASCIIObject` is 42 bytes, `PyCompactUnicodeObject` is 72 bytes, and `PyLongObject` is 32 bytes.

- The `pymalloc` allocator allocates memory blocks only up to 256 KB. Anything larger is sent to the system allocator.

- The `pymalloc` allocator uses the GIL instead of the system thread-safety check.

To help clarify this situation, you can imagine a sports stadium, home of CPython FC, as an analogy. To help manage crowds, CPython FC has implemented a system breaking the stadium up into sections A to E, each with seating in rows 1 to 40:

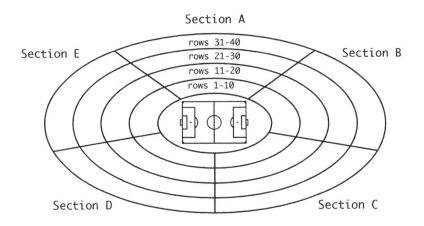

At the front of the stadium, rows 1 to 10 are the roomier premium seats, with 80 seats in each row. At the back, rows 31 to 40 are the economy seats, with 150 seats per row.

The Python memory allocation algorithm has similar characteristics:

- Just like the stadium has seats, the pymalloc algorithm has memory **blocks**.

- Just like seats can either be premium, regular, or economy, memory blocks are all of a range of fixed sizes. You can't bring your deck chair!

- Just like seats of the same size are put into rows, blocks of the same size are put into **pools**.

A central register keeps a record of where blocks are and the number of blocks available in a pool, just as the stadium allocates seating. When a row in the stadium is full, the next row is used. When a pool of blocks is full, the next pool is used. Pools are grouped into **arenas**, just like the stadium groups the rows into sections.

There are several advantages to this strategy:

1. The algorithm is more performant for CPython's main use case: small, short-lived objects.
2. The algorithm uses the GIL instead of system thread-lock detection.
3. The algorithm uses memory mapping (`mmap()`) instead of heap allocation.

Related Source Files

Here are the source files related to the memory allocator:

File	Purpose
Include ▸ pymem.h	PyMem allocator API
Include ▸ cpython ▸ pymem.h	PyMem memory allocator configuration API
Include ▸ internal ▸ pycore_mem.h	Garbage collector data structure and internal APIs
Objects ▸ obmalloc.c	Domain allocator implementations and the `pymalloc` implementation

Important Terms

Below are some important terms that you'll encounter in this chapter:

- Requested memory is matched to a **block** size.
- Blocks of the same size are all put into the same **pool** of memory.
- Pools are grouped into **arenas**.

Blocks, Pools, and Arenas

The largest group of memory is an arena. CPython creates arenas of 256 KB to align with the system page size. A system page boundary is a fixed-length contiguous chunk of memory.

Even with modern high-speed memory, contiguous memory will load faster than fragmented memory. It's beneficial to have contiguous memory.

Arenas

Arenas are allocated against the system heap and with `mmap()`[23] on systems supporting anonymous memory mappings. Memory mapping helps reduce heap fragmentation of the arenas.

Here's a visual representation of four arenas within the system heap:

```
                              System Heap
  ┌─────────────┐ ┌─────────────┐ ┌─────────────┐ ┌─────────────┐
  │   Arena     │ │   Arena     │ │   Arena     │ │   Arena     │
  │             │ │             │ │             │ │             │
  │   256KB     │ │   256KB     │ │   256KB     │ │   256KB     │
  │             │ │             │ │             │ │             │
  └─────────────┘ └─────────────┘ └─────────────┘ └─────────────┘
```

---

[23]http://man7.org/linux/man-pages/man2/mmap.2.html

Arenas have the data struct `arenaobject`:

Field	Type	Purpose
address	uintptr_t	Memory address of the arena
pool_address	block *	Pointer to the next pool to be carved off for allocation
nfreepools	uint	The number of available pools in the arena (free pools plus never-allocated pools)
ntotalpools	uint	The total number of pools in the arena, whether or not available
freepools	pool_header*	Singly linked list of available pools
nextarena	arena_object*	Next arena (see note)
prevarena	arena_object*	Previous arena (see note)

> **Note**
>
> Arenas are linked together in a doubly linked list inside the arena data structure using the `nextarena` and `prevarena` pointers.
>
> If this arena is **unallocated**, then the `nextarena` member is used. The `nextarena` member links all unassociated arenas in the singly linked `unused_arena_objects` global variable.
>
> When this arena is associated with an allocated arena with at least one available pool, both `nextarena` and `prevarena` are used in the doubly linked `usable_arenas` list. This list is maintained in increasing order of `nfreepools` values.

Pools

Within an arena, pools are created for block sizes up to 512 bytes. For 32-bit systems, the step is 8 bytes, so there are 64 classes:

Request in bytes	Size of allocated block	Size class index
1–8	8	0
9–16	16	1
17–24	24	2
25–32	32	3
...	...	...
497–504	504	62
505–512	512	63

For 64-bit systems, the step is 16 bytes, so there are 32 classes:

Request in bytes	Size of allocated block	Size class index
1–16	16	0
17–32	32	1
33–48	48	2
49–64	64	3
...	...	...
480–496	496	30
496–512	512	31

Pools are all 4096 bytes (4 KB), so there are always 64 pools in an arena:

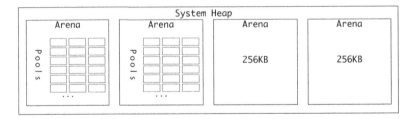

Pools are allocated on demand. When no available pools are available for the requested size class index, a new one is provisioned. Arenas have a **high-water mark** to index how many pools have been provisioned.

Pools have three possible states:

1. **Full**: All available blocks in that pool are allocated.

2. **Used**: The pool is allocated, and some blocks have been set, but it still has space.

3. **Empty**: The pool is allocated, but no blocks have been set.

Within an arena, the high-water mark sits at the last allocated pool:

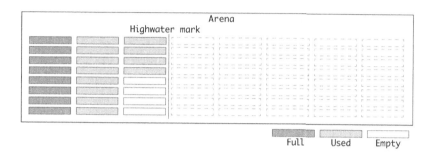

Pools have the data structure `poolp`, which is a static allocation of the struct `pool_header`. The `pool_header` type has the following properties:

Field	Type	Purpose
ref	uint	Number of currently allocated blocks in this pool
freeblock	block *	Pointer to this pool's free list head
nextpool	pool_header*	Pointer to the next pool of this size class
prevpool	pool_header*	Pointer to the previous pool of this size class
arenaindex	uint	Singly-linked list of available pools
szidx	uint	Size class index of this pool
nextoffset	uint	Number of bytes to unused block
maxnextoffset	uint	Maximum number that `nextoffset` can be until pool is full

Each pool of a certain size class will keep a doubly linked list to the next and previous pools of that class. When the allocation task happens, it's easy to jump between pools of the same size class within an arena by following this list.

Pool Tables

A register of the pools within an arena is called a **pool table**. A pool table is a headed, circular, doubly linked list of partially used pools.

The pool table is segmented by size class index, `i`. For an index of `i`, `usedpools[i + i]` points to the header of a list of all partially used pools that have the size index for that size class.

Pool tables have some essential characteristics:

- When a pool becomes full, it's unlinked from its `usedpools[]` list.

- If a full pool has a block freed, then the pool back is put back in the used state. The newly freed pool is linked in at the front of the appropriate `usedpools[]` list so that the next allocation for its size class will use the freed block.

- On transition to empty, a pool is unlinked from its `usedpools[]` list and linked to the front of its arena's singly linked `freepools` list.

Blocks

Within a pool, memory is allocated into blocks. Blocks have the following characteristics:

- Within a pool, blocks of fixed size class can be allocated and freed.

- Available blocks within a pool are listed in the singly linked list `freeblock`.

- When a block is freed, it's inserted at the front of the `freeblock` list.

- When a pool is initialized, only the first two blocks are linked within the `freeblock` list.

- As long a pool is in the used state, there will be a block available for allocating.

Here's what a partially allocated pool looks like with a combination of used, freed, and available blocks:

Block Allocation API

When a block of memory is requested by a memory domain that uses pymalloc, pymalloc_alloc() is called. This function is a good place to insert a breakpoint and step through the code to test your knowledge of blocks, pools, and arenas:

Objects ▸ obmalloc.c line 1590

```
static inline void*
pymalloc_alloc(void *ctx, size_t nbytes)
{
...
```

A request of nbytes = 30 is neither zero nor above the SMALL_REQUEST_THRESHOLD of 512:

```
if (UNLIKELY(nbytes == 0)) {
    return NULL;
}
if (UNLIKELY(nbytes > SMALL_REQUEST_THRESHOLD)) {
    return NULL;
}
```

For a 64-bit system, the size class index is calculated as 1. This correlates to the second size class index (17–32 bytes).

The target pool is then usedpools[1 + 1] (usedpools[2]):

```
uint size = (uint)(nbytes - 1) >> ALIGNMENT_SHIFT;
poolp pool = usedpools[size + size];
block *bp;
```

Next, a check is done to see if there's an available ('used') pool for the size class index. If the freeblock list is at the end of the pool, then there are still clean blocks available in that pool.

pymalloc_pool_extend() is called to extend the freeblock list:

```
if (LIKELY(pool != pool->nextpool)) {
    /*
     * There is a used pool for this size class.
     * Pick up the head block of its free list.
     */
    ++pool->ref.count;
    bp = pool->freeblock;
    assert(bp != NULL);

    if (UNLIKELY((pool->freeblock = *(block **)bp) == NULL)) {
        // Reached the end of the free list. Try to extend it.
        pymalloc_pool_extend(pool, size);
    }
}
```

If there are no available pools, then a new pool is created and the first block is returned. allocate_from_new_pool() automatically adds the new pool to the usedpools list:

```
else {
    /* There isn't a pool of the right size class immediately
     * available. Use a free pool.
     */
    bp = allocate_from_new_pool(size);
}

return (void *)bp;
}
```

Finally, the new block address is returned.

Using the Python Debug API

The `sys` module contains an internal function, `_debugmallocstats()`, to get the number of blocks in use for each of the size class pools. It will also print the number of arenas allocated and reclaimed along with the total number of blocks used.

You can use this function to see the running memory usage:

```
$ ./python -c "import sys; sys._debugmallocstats()"

Small block threshold = 512, in 32 size classes.

class   size   num pools   blocks in use   avail blocks
-----   ----   ---------   -------------   ------------
    0     16           1             181             72
    1     32           6             675             81
    2     48          18            1441             71
...
2 free 18-sized PyTupleObjects * 168 bytes each =              336
3 free 19-sized PyTupleObjects * 176 bytes each =              528
```

The output shows the size class index table, the allocations, and some additional statistics.

The Object and PyMem Memory Allocation Domains

CPython's object memory allocator is the first of the three domains that you'll explore. The purpose of the object memory allocator is to allocate memory related to Python objects, such as new object headers and object data, like dictionary keys and values or list items.

The allocator is also used for the compiler, AST, parser, and evaluation loop. An excellent example of the object memory allocator in use is the PyLongObject (int) type constructor, PyLong_New():

- When a new int is constructed, memory is allocated from the object allocator.
- The size of the request is the size of the PyLongObject struct plus the amount of memory required to store the digits.

Python longs aren't equivalent to C's long type. They're a *list* of digits. The number 12378562834 in Python would be represented as the list of digits [1,2,3,7,8,5,6,2,8,3,4]. This memory structure is how Python can deal with huge numbers without having to worry about 32- or 64-bit integer constraints.

Take a look at the PyLong constructor to see an example of object memory allocation:

```
PyLongObject *
_PyLong_New(Py_ssize_t size)
{
    PyLongObject *result;
    ...
    if (size > (Py_ssize_t)MAX_LONG_DIGITS) {
        PyErr_SetString(PyExc_OverflowError,
                        "too many digits in integer");
        return NULL;
    }
    result = PyObject_MALLOC(offsetof(PyLongObject, ob_digit) +
                            size*sizeof(digit));
    if (!result) {
        PyErr_NoMemory();
        return NULL;
    }
    return (PyLongObject*)PyObject_INIT_VAR(result, &PyLong_Type, size);
}
```

If you were to call _PyLong_New(2), it would calculate the size_t value like this:

Value	Bytes
sizeof(digit)	4
size	2
header offset	26
Total	**32**

A call to `PyObject_MALLOC()` would be made with a `size_t` value of 32.

On my system, the maximum number of digits in a long, `MAX_LONG_DIGITS`, is 2305843009213693945 (a very, very big number). If you ran `_Py-Long_New(2305843009213693945)`, then it would call `PyObject_MALLOC()` with a `size_t` of 9223372036854775804 bytes, or 8,589,934,592 gigabytes (more RAM than I have available).

Using the `tracemalloc` Module

The `tracemalloc` module in the standard library can be used to debug memory allocation through the object allocator. It provides information on where an object was allocated and the number of memory blocks allocated. As a debug tool, `tracemalloc` can help you calculate the amount of memory consumed by running your code and detect memory leaks.

To enable memory tracing, you can start Python with `-X tracemalloc=1`, where 1 is the number of frames deep you want to trace. Alternatively, you can enable memory tracing using the `PYTHONTRACEMALLOC=1` environment variable. You can specify how many frames deep to trace by replacing the 1 with any integer.

You can use `take_snapshot()` to create a snapshot instance, then compare multiple snapshots using `compare_to()`. Create an example `tracedemo.py` file to see this in action:

cpython-book-samples ▸ 32 ▸ tracedemo.py

```python
import tracemalloc

tracemalloc.start()

def to_celsius(fahrenheit, /, options=None):
    return (fahrenheit-32)*5/9

values = range(0, 100, 10)   # values 0, 10, 20, ... 90

for v in values:
    c = to_celsius(v)

after = tracemalloc.take_snapshot()

tracemalloc.stop()
after = after.filter_traces([tracemalloc.Filter(True, '**/tracedemo.py')])
stats = after.statistics('lineno')

for stat in stats:
    print(stat)
```

Executing this will print a list of the memory used by line, from highest to lowest:

```
$ ./python -X tracemalloc=2 tracedemo.py

/Users/.../tracedemo.py:5: size=712 B, count=2, average=356 B
/Users/.../tracedemo.py:13: size=512 B, count=1, average=512 B
/Users/.../tracedemo.py:11: size=480 B, count=1, average=480 B
/Users/.../tracedemo.py:8: size=112 B, count=2, average=56 B
/Users/.../tracedemo.py:6: size=24 B, count=1, average=24 B
```

The line with the highest memory consumption was `return (fahrenheit-32)*5/9`, which performs the actual calculation.

The Raw Memory Allocation Domain

The raw memory allocation domain is used either directly or when the other two domains are called with a request size over 512 KB. It takes the request size, in bytes, and calls `malloc(size)`. If the size argument is 0, then some systems will return NULL for `malloc(0)`, which would be treated as an error. Some platforms would return a pointer with no memory behind it, which would break `pymalloc`.

To solve these problems, `_PyMem_RawMalloc()` adds an extra byte before calling `malloc()`.

> **Important**
>
> By default, the PyMem domain allocators use the object allocators. `PyMem_Malloc()` and `PyObject_Malloc()` have the same execution path.

Custom Domain Allocators

CPython also allows you to override the allocation implementation for any of the three domains. If your system environment requires bespoke memory checks or algorithms for memory allocation, then you can plug a new set of allocation functions into the runtime.

`PyMemAllocatorEx` is a `typedef` `struct` with members for all the methods you would need to implement to override the allocator:

```
typedef struct {
    /* User context passed as the first argument to the four functions */
    void *ctx;

    /* Allocate a memory block */
    void* (*malloc) (void *ctx, size_t size);

    /* Allocate a memory block initialized by zeros */
    void* (*calloc) (void *ctx, size_t nelem, size_t elsize);
```

```
/* Allocate or resize a memory block */
void* (*realloc) (void *ctx, void *ptr, size_t new_size);

/* Release a memory block */
void (*free) (void *ctx, void *ptr);
} PyMemAllocatorEx;
```

The API method `PyMem_GetAllocator()` is available to get the existing implementation:

```
PyMemAllocatorEx * existing_obj;
PyMem_GetAllocator(PYMEM_DOMAIN_OBJ, existing_obj);
```

> **Important**
>
> There are some important design tests for custom allocators:
>
> - The new allocator must return a distinct non-NULL pointer when requesting zero bytes.
>
> - For the PYMEM_DOMAIN_RAW domain, the allocator must be thread-safe.

If you implemented the functions `My_Malloc()`, `My_Calloc()`, `My_Realloc()`, and `My_Free()` using the signatures in `PyMemAllocatorEx`, then you could override the allocator for any domain, such as the PYMEM_DOMAIN_OBJ domain:

```
PyMemAllocatorEx my_allocators =
    {NULL, My_Malloc, My_Calloc, My_Realloc, My_Free};
PyMem_SetAllocator(PYMEM_DOMAIN_OBJ, &my_allocators);
```

Custom Memory Allocation Sanitizers

Memory allocation sanitizers are additional algorithms placed between the system call to allocate memory and the kernel function to allocate the memory on the system. They're used for environments that require specific stability constraints or very high security or for debugging memory allocation bugs.

CPython can be compiled using several memory sanitizers. These are part of the compiler libraries, not something developed for CPython. They typically slow down CPython significantly and can't be combined. They're generally for use in debugging scenarios or systems in which preventing corrupt memory access is critical.

AddressSanitizer

AddressSanitizer is a fast memory error detector. It can detect many runtime memory–related bugs:

- Out-of-bounds accesses to heap, stack, and globals
- Memory being used after it has been freed
- Double free and invalid free

You can enable AddressSanitizer by running the following:

```
$ ./configure --with-address-sanitizer ...
```

> **Important**
>
> AddressSanitizer can slow down applications by up to two times and consume up to three times more memory.

AddressSanitizer is supported on the following operating systems:

- Linux
- macOS
- NetBSD
- FreeBSD

See the official documentation[24] for more information.

---

[24]https://clang.llvm.org/docs/AddressSanitizer.html

MemorySanitizer

MemorySanitizer is a detector of uninitialized reads. If an address space is addressed before it's been initialized (allocated), then the process is stopped before the memory can be read.

You can enable the memory sanitizer by running the following:

```
$ ./configure --with-memory-sanitizer ...
```

> **Important**
>
> MemorySanitizer can slow down applications by up to two times and consume up to two times more memory.

MemorySanitizer is supported on the following operating systems:

- Linux
- NetBSD
- FreeBSD

See the official documentation[25] for more information.

UndefinedBehaviorSanitizer

UndefinedBehaviorSanitizer (UBSan) is a fast undefined behavior detector. It can catch various kinds of undefined behavior during execution:

- A misaligned or null pointer
- A signed integer overflow
- Conversion to, from, or between floating-point types

---

[25]https://clang.llvm.org/docs/MemorySanitizer.html

You can enable UBSan by running the following:

```
$ ./configure --with-undefined-behavior-sanitizer ...
```

UBSan is supported on the following operating systems:

- Linux
- macOS
- NetBSD
- FreeBSD

See the official documentation[26] for more information.

UBSan has many configurations. Using
`--with-undefined-behavior-sanitizer` will set the `undefined` profile. To
use another profile like `nullability`, run `./configure` with the custom
CFLAGS:

```
$ ./configure CFLAGS="-fsanitize=nullability" \
    LDFLAGS="-fsanitize=nullability"
```

After you recompile CPython, this configuration will produce a
CPython binary using the UndefinedBehaviorSanitizer.

The PyArena Memory Arena

Throughout this book, you'll see references to a `PyArena` object. The
`PyArena` is a separate arena allocation API used for the compiler, frame
evaluation, and other parts of the system not run from Python's object
allocation API.

The `PyArena` also has its own list of allocated objects within the arena
structure. Memory allocated by the `PyArena` is not a target of the
garbage collector.

---

[26]https://clang.llvm.org/docs/UndefinedBehaviorSanitizer.html

When memory is allocated in a `PyArena` instance, it will capture a running total of the number of blocks allocated, then call `PyMem_Alloc`. Allocation requests to the `PyArena` use the object allocator for blocks smaller than or equal to 512 KB and the raw allocator for larger blocks.

Related Files

Here are the files related to the `PyArena`:

File	Purpose
Include ▸ pyarena.h	The PyArena API and type definitions
Python ▸ pyarena.c	The PyArena implementation

Reference Counting

As you've seen so far in this chapter, CPython is built on C's dynamic memory allocation system. Memory requirements are determined at runtime, and memory is allocated on the system using the `PyMem` APIs.

For the Python developer, this system has been abstracted and simplified. Developers don't have to worry much about allocating and freeing memory.

To simplify memory management, Python adopts two strategies for managing the memory allocated by objects:

1. Reference counting
2. Garbage collection

You'll look at each in more detail below.

Creating Variables in Python

To create a variable in Python, you have to assign a value to a *uniquely* named variable:

```
my_variable = ["a", "b", "c"]
```

When a value is assigned to a variable in Python, the name of the variable is checked within the locals and globals scope to see if it already exists.

In the above example, my_variable isn't already within any locals() or globals() dictionary. A new list object is created, and a pointer is stored in the locals() dictionary.

Now there's one **reference** to my_variable. A list object's memory shouldn't be freed while there are valid references to it. If its memory were freed, then the my_variable pointer would point to invalid memory space, and CPython would crash.

Throughout the C source code for CPython, you'll see calls to Py_INCREF() and Py_DECREF(). These macros are the primary API for incrementing and decrementing references to Python objects. Whenever something depends on a value, the reference count is incremented. When that dependency is no longer valid, the reference count is decremented.

If a reference count reaches zero, then it's assumed that the memory is no longer needed, and it's automatically freed.

Incrementing References

Every instance of PyObject has an ob_refcnt property. This property is a counter of the number of references to that object.

References to an object are incremented under many scenarios. In the CPython code base, there are over 3,000 calls to Py_INCREF(). The most frequent calls are when an object is:

• Assigned to a variable name

• Referenced as a function or method argument

• Returned, or yielded, from a function

The logic behind the Py_INCREF macro has only one step. It increments the ob_refcnt value by one:

```
static inline void _Py_INCREF(PyObject *op)
{
    _Py_INC_REFTOTAL;
    op->ob_refcnt++;
}
```

If CPython is compiled in debug mode, then _Py_INC_REFTOTAL will increment a global reference counter, _Py_RefTotal.

> **Note**
>
> You can see the global reference counter by adding the -X showrefcount flag when running a debug build of CPython:
>
> ```
> $ ./python -X showrefcount -c "x=1; x+=1; print(f'x is {x}')"
> x is 2
> [18497 refs, 6470 blocks]
> ```
>
> The first number in brackets is the number of references made during the process, and the second is the number of allocated blocks.

Decrementing References

References to an object are decremented when a variable falls outside the scope in which it was declared. Scope in Python can refer to a function or method, a comprehension, or a lambda. These are some of the more literal scopes, but there are many other implicit scopes, like passing variables to a function call.

Py_DECREF() is more complex than Py_INCREF() because it also handles the logic of a reference count reaching 0, requiring the object memory to be freed:

```
static inline void _Py_DECREF(
#ifdef Py_REF_DEBUG
    const char *filename, int lineno,
#endif
    PyObject *op)
{
    _Py_DEC_REFTOTAL;
    if (--op->ob_refcnt != 0) {
#ifdef Py_REF_DEBUG
        if (op->ob_refcnt < 0) {
            _Py_NegativeRefcount(filename, lineno, op);
        }
#endif
    }
    else {
        _Py_Dealloc(op);
    }
}
```

Inside Py_DECREF(), when the reference counter (ob_refcnt) value becomes 0, the object destructor is called through _Py_Dealloc(op), and any allocated memory is freed.

As with Py_INCREF(), there are some additional functions when CPython has been compiled in debug mode.

For an increment, there should be an equivalent decrement operation. If a reference count becomes a negative number, then this indicates an imbalance in the C code. An attempt to decrement references to an object that has no references will give this error message:

```
<file>:<line>: _Py_NegativeRefcount: Assertion failed:
    object has negative ref count
Enable tracemalloc to get the memory block allocation traceback

object address  : 0x109eaac50
object refcount : -1
object type     : 0x109cadf60
```

```
object type name: <type>
object repr      : <refcnt -1 at 0x109eaac50>
```

When making changes to the behavior of an operation, the Python language, or the compiler, you must carefully consider the impact on object references.

Reference Counting in Bytecode Operations

A large portion of the reference counting in Python happens within the bytecode operations in Python ▸ ceval.c.

Count the references to the y variable in this example:

```
y = "hello"

def greet(message=y):
    print(message.capitalize() + " " + y)

messages = [y]

greet(*messages)
```

At first glance, there are four references to y:

1. As a variable in the top-level scope
2. As a default value for the keyword argument message
3. Inside greet()
4. As an item in the messages list

Run this code with the following additional snippet:

```
import sys
print(sys.getrefcount(y))
```

There are in fact six total references to y.

Instead of sitting within a central function that has to cater to all these cases and more, the logic for incrementing and decrementing references is split into small parts.

A bytecode operation should have a determining impact on the reference counter for the objects that it takes as arguments.

For example, in the frame evaluation loop, the LOAD_FAST operation loads the object with a given name and pushes it to the top of the value stack. Once the variable name, which is provided in the oparg, has been resolved using GETLOCAL(), the reference counter is incremented:

```
...
    case TARGET(LOAD_FAST): {
        PyObject *value = GETLOCAL(oparg);
        if (value == NULL) {
            format_exc_check_arg(tstate, PyExc_UnboundLocalError,
                                 UNBOUNDLOCAL_ERROR_MSG,
                                 PyTuple_GetItem(co->co_varnames, oparg));
            goto error;
        }
        Py_INCREF(value);
        PUSH(value);
        FAST_DISPATCH();
    }
```

A LOAD_FAST operation is compiled by many AST nodes that have operations.

For example, let's say you assign two variables, a and b, then create third, c, based on the product of a and b:

```
a = 10
b = 20
c = a * b
```

In the third operation, c = a * b, the right-hand side expression, a * b, would be assembled into three operations:

1. LOAD_FAST, resolving the variable a and pushing it to the value stack, then incrementing the references to a by one

2. LOAD_FAST, resolving the variable b and pushing it to the value stack, then incrementing the references to b by one

3. BINARY_MULTIPLY, multiplying the variables to the left and right and pushing the result to the value stack

The binary multiply operator, BINARY_MULTIPLY, knows that references to the left and right variables in the operation have been loaded to the first and second positions in the value stack. It's also implied that the LOAD_FAST operation increments its reference counters.

In the implementation of the BINARY_MULTIPLY operation, the references to both a (left) and b (right) are decremented once the result has been calculated:

```
case TARGET(BINARY_MULTIPLY): {
    PyObject *right = POP();
    PyObject *left = TOP();
    PyObject *res = PyNumber_Multiply(left, right);
    Py_DECREF(left);
    Py_DECREF(right);
    SET_TOP(res);
    if (res == NULL)
        goto error;
    DISPATCH();
}
```

The resulting number, res, will have a reference count of 1 before it's set as the top of the value stack.

The Benefits of the CPython Reference Counter

CPython's reference counter has the benefits of being simple, fast, and efficient. The biggest drawback of the reference counter is that it needs to account for, and carefully balance, the effect of every operation.

As you just saw, a bytecode operation increments the counter, and it's assumed that an equivalent operation will decrement it properly. What happens if there's an unexpected error? Have all possible scenarios been tested?

Everything discussed so far is within the realm of the CPython runtime. The Python developer has little to no control over this behavior.

There's also a significant flaw in the reference counting approach: **cyclical references**.

Take this Python example:

```
x = []
x.append(x)
del x
```

The reference count for x is still 1 because it referred to itself.

To cater to this complexity and resolve these types of memory leaks, CPython has a second memory management mechanism called **garbage collection**.

Garbage Collection

How often does your garbage get collected? Weekly or fortnightly?

When you're finished with something, you discard it and throw it in the trash. But that trash doesn't get collected right away. You need to wait for the garbage trucks to come and pick it up.

CPython uses the same principle for the garbage collection algorithm. CPython's garbage collector works to deallocate memory that's been used for objects that no longer exist. It's enabled by default and operates in the background.

Because the garbage collection algorithm is a lot more complicated than the reference counter, it doesn't happen all the time. If it did, then it would consume a vast amount of CPU resources. The garbage collection runs periodically after a set number of operations.

Related Source Files

Here are the source files related to the garbage collector:

File	Purpose
Modules ▸ gcmodule.c	The garbage collection module and algorithm implementation
Include ▸ internal ▸ pycore_mem.h	The garbage collection data structure and internal APIs

The Garbage Collector Design

As you discovered in the previous section, every Python object retains a counter of the number of references to it. Once that counter reaches zero, the object is finalized, and the memory is freed.

Many of the Python **container types**, like lists, tuples, dictionaries, and sets, could result in cyclical references. The reference counter is an insufficient mechanism to ensure that objects that are no longer required are freed.

While creating cyclical references in containers should be avoided, there are many examples within the standard library and the core interpreter. Here's another common example in which a container type (class) can refer to itself:

```
cpython-book-samples ▸ 32 ▸ user.py

__all__ = ["User"]

class User(BaseUser):
    name: 'str' = ""
    login: 'str' = ""

    def __init__(self, name, login):
        self.name = name
        self.login = login
        super(User).__init__()

    def __repr__(self):
        return ""

class BaseUser:
    def __repr__(self):
        # This creates a cyclical reference
        return User.__repr__(self)
```

In this example, the instance of User links to the BaseUser type, which references back to the instance of User. The goal of the garbage collector is to find **unreachable** objects and mark them as garbage.

Some garbage collector algorithms, like **mark and sweep** or **stop and copy**, start at the root of the system and explore all *reachable* objects. This is hard to do in CPython because C extension modules can define and store their own objects. You couldn't easily determine all objects by simply looking at locals() and globals().

For long-running processes or large data processing tasks, running out of memory would cause a significant issue.

Instead, the CPython garbage collector leverages the existing reference counter and a custom garbage collector algorithm to find all unreachable objects. Because the reference counter is already in place, the role of the CPython garbage collector is to look for cyclical references in certain container types.

Container Types Included in the Garbage Collector

The garbage collector will look for types that have the flag Py_TPFLAGS_HAVE_GC set in their type definition. You'll cover type definitions in the chapter "Objects and Types."

Here are the types that are marked for garbage collection:

- Class, method, and function objects
- Cell objects
- Byte arrays, byte, and Unicode strings
- Dictionaries
- Descriptor objects, used in attributes
- Enumeration objects
- Exceptions
- Frame objects
- Lists, tuples, named tuples, and sets
- Memory objects
- Modules and namespaces
- Type and weak reference objects
- Iterators and generators
- Pickle buffers

Wondering what's missing? Floats, integers, Booleans, and NoneType aren't marked for garbage collection.

Custom types written with C extension models can be marked as requiring garbage collection using the garbage collector C API.[27]

---

[27]https://docs.python.org/3.8/c-api/gcsupport.html

Untrackable Objects and Mutability

The garbage collector will track certain types for changes in their properties to determine which are unreachable.

Some container instances aren't subject to change because they're immutable, so the API provides a mechanism for **untracking.** The fewer objects there are to be tracked by the garbage collector, the faster and more efficient the garbage collection is.

An excellent example of untrackable objects is tuples. Tuples are immutable. Once you create them, they can't be changed. However, tuples can contain mutable types, like lists and dictionaries.

This design in Python creates many side effects, one of which is the garbage collection algorithm. When a tuple is created, unless it's empty, it's marked for tracking.

When the garbage collector runs, every tuple looks at its contents to see if it contains only immutable (untracked) instances. This step is completed in `_PyTuple_MaybeUntrack()`. If the tuple determines that it contains only immutable types, like Booleans and integers, then it will remove itself from the garbage collection tracking by calling `_PyObject_GC_UNTRACK()`.

Dictionaries are empty and untracked when they're created. When an item is added to a dictionary, if it's a tracked object, then the dictionary requests to be tracked by the garbage collector.

You can see if any object is being tracked by calling `gc.is_tracked(obj)`.

Garbage Collection Algorithm

Next, you'll explore the garbage collection algorithm. The CPython core development team has written a detailed guide[28] that you can refer to for more information.

---

[28]https://devguide.python.org/garbage_collector/

Initialization

The PyGC_Collect() entry point follows a five-step process to start and stop the garbage collector:

1. Get the garbage collection state, GCState, from the interpreter.

2. Check to see if the garbage collector is enabled.

3. Check to see if the garbage collector is already running.

4. Run the collection function, collect(), with progress callbacks.

5. Mark the garbage collection as completed.

When the collection stage is run and completed, you can specify callback methods using the gc.callbacks list. Callbacks should have the method signature f(stage: str, info: dict):

```
Python 3.9 (tags/v3.9:9cf67522, Oct 5 2020, 10:00:00)
[Clang 6.0 (clang-600.0.57)] on darwin
Type "help", "copyright", "credits" or "license" for more information.
>>> import gc
>>> def gc_callback(phase, info):
...     print(f"GC phase:{phase} with info:{info}")
...
>>> gc.callbacks.append(gc_callback)
>>> x = []
>>> x.append(x)
>>> del x
>>> gc.collect()
GC phase:start with info:{'generation': 2,'collected': 0,'uncollectable': 0}
GC phase:stop with info:{'generation': 2,'collected': 1,'uncollectable': 0}
1
```

The Collection Stage

In the main garbage collection function, collect() targets one of three generations in CPython. Before you learn about the generations, it's important to first understand the collection algorithm.

For each collection, the garbage collector uses a doubly linked list of type PyGC_HEAD. So that the garbage collector doesn't have to find all container types, those that are targets for the garbage collector have an additional header that links them all in a doubly linked list.

When one of these container types is created, it adds itself to the list, and when it's destroyed, it removes itself. You can see an example in the cellobject.c type:

Objects ▸ cellobject.c line 7

```
PyObject *
PyCell_New(PyObject *obj)
{
    PyCellObject *op;

    op = (PyCellObject *)PyObject_GC_New(PyCellObject, &PyCell_Type);
    if (op == NULL)
        return NULL;
    op->ob_ref = obj;
    Py_XINCREF(obj);

>>  _PyObject_GC_TRACK(op);
    return (PyObject *)op;
}
```

Because cells are mutable, the object is marked to be tracked by a call to _PyObject_GC_TRACK().

When cell objects are deleted, cell_dealloc() is called. This function takes three steps:

1. The destructor tells the garbage collector to stop tracking this instance by calling _PyObject_GC_UNTRACK(). Because it's been destroyed, its contents don't need to be checked for changes in subsequent collections.

2. `Py_XDECREF` is a standard call in any destructor to decrement the reference counter. The reference counter for an object is initialized to 1, so this counters that operation.

3. `PyObject_GC_Del()` removes the object from the garbage collection linked list by calling `gc_list_remove()` and then frees the memory with `PyObject_FREE()`.

Here's the source of `cell_dealloc()`:

Objects ▸ cellobject.c line 79

```
static void
cell_dealloc(PyCellObject *op)
{
    _PyObject_GC_UNTRACK(op);
    Py_XDECREF(op->ob_ref);
    PyObject_GC_Del(op);
}
```

When a collection starts, it merges younger generations into the current generation. For example, if you're collecting the second generation, then when it starts collecting, it will merge the first generation's objects into the garbage collection list using `gc_list_merge()`. The garbage collector will then determine unreachable objects in the young (currently targeted) generation.

The logic for determining unreachable objects is located in `deduce_unreachable()`. It follows these stages:

1. For every object in the generation, copy the reference count value `ob->ob_refcnt` to `ob->gc_ref`.

2. For every object, subtract internal (cyclical) references from `gc_refs` to determine how many objects can be collected by the garbage collector. If `gc_refs` ends up equal to 0, then the object is unreachable.

3. Create a list of unreachable objects and add every object that meets the criteria in step 2 to it.

4. Remove every object that meets the criteria in step 2 from the generation list.

There's no single method for determining cyclical references. Each type must define a custom function with signature traverseproc in the tp_traverse slot. To complete step 2 above, deduce_unreachable() calls the traversal function for every object within subtract_refs(). The traversal function should run the callback visit_decref() for every item it contains:

Modules ▸ gcmodule.c line 462

```
static void
subtract_refs(PyGC_Head *containers)
{
    traverseproc traverse;
    PyGC_Head *gc = GC_NEXT(containers);
    for (; gc != containers; gc = GC_NEXT(gc)) {
        PyObject *op = FROM_GC(gc);
        traverse = Py_TYPE(op)->tp_traverse;
        (void) traverse(FROM_GC(gc),
                    (visitproc)visit_decref,
                    op);
    }
}
```

The traversal functions are kept within each object's source code in Objects. For example, the tuple type's traversal, tupletraverse(), calls visit_decref() on all of its items. The dictionary type will call visit_decref() on all keys and values.

Any object that doesn't end up being moved to the unreachable list graduates to the next generation.

Freeing Objects

Once unreachable objects have been determined, they can be (carefully) freed following the steps below. The approach depends on whether the type implements the old or the new finalizer slot:

1. If an object has defined a finalizer in the legacy `tp_del` slot, then it can't safely be deleted and is marked as uncollectable. These are added to the `gc.garbage` list for the developer to destroy manually.

2. If an object has defined a finalizer in the `tp_finalize` slot, then it's marked as finalized to avoid calling it twice.

3. If an object in step 2 has been resurrected by being initialized again, then the garbage collector reruns the collection cycle.

4. For all objects, the `tp_clear` slot is called. This slot changes the reference count, `ob_refcnt`, to 0, triggering the freeing of memory.

Generational Garbage Collection

Generational garbage collection is a technique based on the observation that most objects (80 percent or more) are destroyed shortly after being created.

CPython's garbage collector uses three generations that have thresholds to trigger their collections. The youngest generation (0) has a high threshold to avoid the collection loop being run too frequently. If an object survives garbage collection, then it'll move to the second generation and then to the third.

In the collection function, a single generation is targeted, and it merges younger generations into it before execution. For this reason, if you run `collect()` on generation 1, then it will collect generation 0. Likewise, running `collect()` on generation 2 will collect generations 0 and 1.

When objects are instantiated, the generational counters are incremented. When the counter reaches a user-defined threshold, `collect()` runs automatically.

Using the Garbage Collection API From Python

CPython's standard library comes with a `gc` Python module to interface with the arena and the garbage collector. Here's how to use the gc module in debug mode:

```
>>> import gc
>>> gc.set_debug(gc.DEBUG_STATS)
```

This will print the statistics whenever the garbage collector is run:

```
gc: collecting generation 2...
gc: objects in each generation: 3 0 4477
gc: objects in permanent generation: 0
gc: done, 0 unreachable, 0 uncollectable, 0.0008s elapsed
```

You use gc.DEBUG_COLLECTABLE to discover when items are collected for garbage. When you combine this with the gc.DEBUG_SAVEALL debug flag, it will move items to a gc.garbage list once they've been collected:

```
>>> import gc
>>> gc.set_debug(gc.DEBUG_COLLECTABLE | gc.DEBUG_SAVEALL)
>>> z = [0, 1, 2, 3]
>>> z.append(z)
>>> del z
>>> gc.collect()
gc: collectable <list 0x10d594a00>
>>> gc.garbage
[[0, 1, 2, 3, [...]]]
```

You can get the threshold after which the garbage collector is run by calling get_threshold():

```
>>> gc.get_threshold()
(700, 10, 10)
```

You can also get the current threshold counts:

```
>>> gc.get_count()
(688, 1, 1)
```

Lastly, you can run the collection algorithm manually for a generation, and it will return the collected total:

```
>>> gc.collect(0)
24
```

If you don't specify a generation, then it will default to 2, which merges generations 0 and 1:

```
>>> gc.collect()
20
```

Conclusion

In this chapter, you've seen how CPython allocates, manages, and frees memory. These operations happen thousands of times during the life cycle of even the simplest Python script. The reliability and scalability of CPython's memory management system are what enable it to scale from a two-line script all the way to running some of the world's most popular websites.

The object and raw memory allocation systems you've been shown in this chapter will come in useful if you develop C extension modules. C extension modules require an intimate knowledge of CPython's memory management system. Even a single missing Py_INCREF() can cause a memory leak or system crash.

When you're working with pure Python code, knowledge of the garbage collector is useful for designing long-running Python code. For example, if you designed a single function that executes over hours, days, or even longer, then this function would need to carefully manage its memory within the constraints of the system on which it was executing.

You can now use some of the techniques you learned in this chapter to control and tweak the garbage collection generations to better optimize your code and its memory footprint.

Parallelism and Concurrency

The first computers were designed to do one thing at a time. A lot of their work was in the field of computational mathematics. As time went on, computers were needed to process inputs from a variety of sources, some as far away as distant galaxies.

The consequence of this is that computer applications now spend a lot of time idly waiting for responses, whether they be from a bus, an input, a memory location, a computation, an API, or a remote resource.

Another progression in computing was the move away from a single-user terminal to a multitasking operating system. Applications needed to run in the background to listen and respond on the network and process inputs such as the mouse cursor.

Multitasking was required well before the advent of modern multi-core CPUs, so operating systems have long been able to share system resources between multiple processes.

At the core of any operating system is a registry of running processes. Each process has an owner, and it can request resources, like memory or CPU. In the last chapter, you explored memory allocation.

For a CPU, the process will request **CPU time** in the form of operations to be executed. The operating system controls which process uses the CPU. It does this by allocating CPU time and scheduling processes by priority:

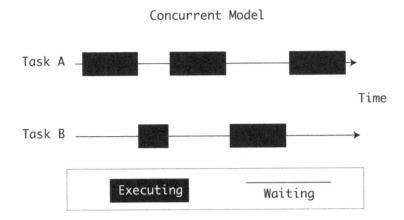

A single process may need to do multiple things at once. For example, if you use a word processor, it needs to check your spelling while you're typing. Modern applications accomplish this by running multiple threads concurrently and handling their own resources.

Concurrency is an excellent solution to dealing with multitasking, but CPUs have their limits. Some high-performance computers deploy either multiple CPUs or multiple cores to spread tasks. Operating systems provide a way of scheduling processes across multiple CPUs:

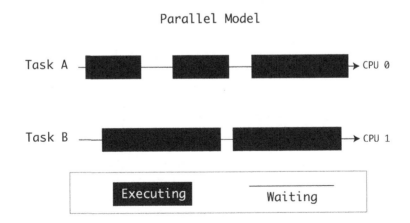

In summary, computers use parallelism and concurrency to handle the problem of multitasking:

- To have **parallelism**, you need multiple computational units. Computational units can be CPUs or cores.

- To have **concurrency**, you need a way of scheduling tasks so that idle ones don't lock the resources.

Many parts of CPython's design abstract the complexity of operating systems to provide a simple API for developers. CPython's approach to parallelism and concurrency is no exception.

Models of Parallelism and Concurrency

CPython offers many approaches to parallelism and concurrency. Your choice depends on several factors. There are also overlapping use cases across models as CPython has evolved.

You may find that for a particular problem, there are multiple concurrency implementations to choose from, each with their own pros and cons.

There are four models bundled with CPython:

Approach	Module	Concurrent	Parallel
Threading	threading	Yes	No
Multiprocessing	multiprocessing	Yes	Yes
Async	asyncio	Yes	No
Subinterpreters	subinterpreters	Yes	Yes

The Structure of a Process

One of the tasks for an operating system like Windows, macOS, or Linux is to control running processes. These processes could be UI applications like a browser or an IDE. They could also be background processes like network services or operating system services.

To control these processes, the operating system provides an API for starting a new process. When a process is created, it's registered by the operating system so that it knows which processes are running. Processes are given a unique ID (PID). Depending on the operating system, they can have several other properties.

POSIX processes have a minimum set of properties that are registered in the operating system:

- Controlling terminal
- Current working directory
- Effective group ID and effective user ID
- File descriptors and file mode creation mask
- Process group ID and process ID
- Real group ID and real user ID
- Root directory

You can see these attributes for running processes in macOS or Linux by running the ps command.

> **See Also**
>
> The IEEE POSIX Standard (1003.1-2017) defines the interface and standard behaviors for processes and threads.

Windows has a similar list of properties but sets its own standard. The Windows file permissions, directory structures, and process registry are very different from POSIX.

Windows processes, represented by Win32_Process, can be queried in WMI, the Windows Management Instrumentation runtime, or by using the Task Manager.

Once a process is started on an operating system, it is given:

- A **stack** of memory for calling subroutines

- A **heap** (see "Dynamic Memory Allocation in C")

- Access to **files**, **locks**, and **sockets** on the operating system

The CPU on your computer also keeps additional data when the process is executing, such as:

- A **register** holding the current instruction being executed or any other data needed by the process for that instruction

- An **instruction pointer**, or **program counter**, indicating which instruction in the program sequence is being executed

The CPython process comprises the compiled CPython interpreter and the compiled modules. These modules are loaded at runtime and converted into instructions by the CPython evaluation loop:

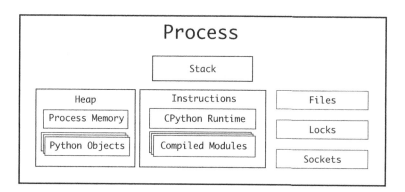

The program register and program counter point to a **single** instruction in the process. This means that only one instruction can be executing at any one time. For CPython, this means that only one Python bytecode instruction can be executing at a given time.

There are two main approaches to allowing parallel execution of instructions in a process:

1. Fork another process.

2. Spawn a thread.

Now that you've reviewed what makes up a process, you can explore forking and spawning child processes.

Multiprocess Parallelism

POSIX systems provide an API for any process to **fork** a child process. Forking processes is a low-level API call to the operating system that can be made by any running process.

When this call is made, the operating system will clone all the attributes of the currently running process and create a new process. This clone operation includes the heap, register, and counter position of the parent process. The child process can read any variables from the parent process at the time of forking.

Forking a Process in POSIX

As an example, take the Fahrenheit-to-Celsius example application used at the beginning of "Dynamic Memory Allocation in C." You can adapt it to spawn a child process for each Fahrenheit value instead of calculating them in sequence by using fork(). Each child process will continue operating from that point:

cpython-book-samples ▸ 33 ▸ thread_celsius.c

```
#include <stdio.h>
#include <stdlib.h>
#include <unistd.h>

static const double five_ninths = 5.0/9.0;

double celsius(double fahrenheit){
    return (fahrenheit - 32) * five_ninths;
}
```

```
int main(int argc, char** argv) {
    if (argc != 2)
        return -1;
    int number = atoi(argv[1]);
    for (int i = 1 ; i <= number ; i++ ) {
        double f_value = 100 + (i*10);
        pid_t child = fork();
        if (child == 0) { // Is child process
            double c_value = celsius(f_value);
            printf("%f F is %f C (pid %d)\n", f_value, c_value, getpid());
            exit(0);
        }
    }
    printf("Spawned %d processes from %d\n", number, getpid());
    return 0;
}
```

Running the above program on the command line would give an output similar to this:

```
$ ./thread_celsius 4
110.000000 F is 43.333333 C (pid 57179)
120.000000 F is 48.888889 C (pid 57180)
Spawned 4 processes from 57178
130.000000 F is 54.444444 C (pid 57181)
140.000000 F is 60.000000 C (pid 57182)
```

The parent process (57178) spawned four processes. For each child process, the program continues at the line child = fork(), where the resulting value of child is 0. It then completes the calculation, prints the value, and exits the process. Finally, the parent process outputs how many processes it spawned and its own PID.

The time it took for the third and fourth child processes to complete was longer than it took for the parent process to complete. This is why the parent process prints the final output before the third and fourth print their own.

A parent process can exit with its own exit code before a child process. Child processes are added to a process group by the operating system, making it easier to control all related processes:

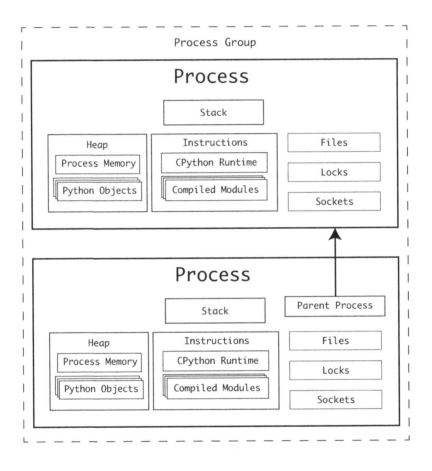

The biggest downside to this approach to parallelism is that the child process is a complete copy of the parent process.

In the case of CPython, this means you would have two CPython interpreters running, and both would have to load the modules and all the libraries. This creates significant overhead. Using multiple processes makes sense when the overhead of forking a process is outweighed by the size of the task being completed.

Another major downside of forked processes is that they have a separate, isolated heap from the parent process. This means that the child process cannot write to the memory space of the parent process.

When the child process is created, the parent's heap becomes available to the child process. To send information back to the parent, some form of interprocess communication (IPC) must be used.

> **Note**
>
> The `os` module offers a wrapper around `fork()`.

Multiprocessing in Windows

So far, you've been learning about the POSIX model. Windows doesn't provide an equivalent to `fork()`, and Python *should* (as best as possible) have the same API across Linux, macOS, and Windows.

To overcome this, the `CreateProcessW()` API is used to spawn another `python.exe` process with a `-c` command-line argument. This step is known as **spawning** a process and is also available on POSIX. You'll see references to it throughout this chapter.

The `multiprocessing` Package

CPython provides an API on top of the operating system process-forking API that makes it straightforward to create multiprocess parallelism in Python.

This API is available from the `multiprocessing` package, which provides expansive capabilities for pooling processes, queues, forking, creating shared memory heaps, connecting processes together, and more.

Related Source Files

Here are the source files related to multiprocessing:

File	Purpose
Lib▸multiprocessing	Python source for the multiprocessing package
Modules▸_posixsubprocess.c	C extension module wrapping the POSIX fork() syscall
Modules▸_winapi.c	C extension module wrapping the Windows kernel APIs
Modules▸_multiprocessing	C extension module used by the multiprocessing package
PC▸msvcrtmodule.c	A Python interface to the Microsoft Visual C runtime library

Spawning and Forking Processes

The multiprocessing package offers three methods to start a new parallel process:

1. Forking an interpreter (POSIX only)

2. Spawning a new interpreter process (POSIX and Windows)

3. Running a fork server in which a new process is created that then forks any number of processes (POSIX only)

> **Note**
>
> For Windows and macOS, the default start method is spawning. For Linux, the default is forking. You can override the default method using multiprocessing.set_start_method().

The Python API for starting a new process takes a callable, target, and a tuple of arguments, args.

Take this example of spawning a new process to convert Fahrenheit to Celsius:

cpython-book-samples ▶ 33 ▶ spawn_process_celsius.py

```python
import multiprocessing as mp
import os

def to_celsius(f):
    c = (f - 32) * (5/9)
    pid = os.getpid()
    print(f"{f}F is {c}C (pid {pid})")

if __name__ == '__main__':
    mp.set_start_method('spawn')
    p = mp.Process(target=to_celsius, args=(110,))
    p.start()
```

While you can start a single process, the multiprocessing API assumes you want to start multiple. There are convenience methods for spawning multiple processes and feeding them sets of data. One of those methods is the Pool class.

The previous example can be expanded to calculate a range of values in separate Python interpreters:

cpython-book-samples ▶ 33 ▶ pool_process_celsius.py

```python
import multiprocessing as mp
import os

def to_celsius(f):
    c = (f - 32) * (5/9)
    pid = os.getpid()
    print(f"{f}F is {c}C (pid {pid})")

if __name__ == '__main__':
    mp.set_start_method('spawn')
    with mp.Pool(4) as pool:
        pool.map(to_celsius, range(110, 150, 10))
```

Note that the output shows the same PID. Because the CPython interpreter process has a significant overhead, the `Pool` will consider each process in the pool a **worker**. If a worker has completed, it will be reused.

You can change that setting by replacing this line:

```
with mp.Pool(4) as pool:
```

Replace it with the following code:

```
with mp.Pool(4, maxtasksperchild=1) as pool:
```

Now the previous multiprocessing example will print something similar to this:

```
$ python pool_process_celsius.py
110F is 43.333333333333336C (pid 5654)
120F is 48.88888888888889C (pid 5653)
130F is 54.44444444444445C (pid 5652)
140F is 60.0C (pid 5655)
```

The output shows the process IDs of the newly spawned processes and the calculated values.

Creation of Child Processes

Both of these scripts will create a new Python interpreter process and pass data to it using `pickle`.

> **See Also**
>
> The `pickle` module is a serialization package used for serializing Python objects. For more info, check out *Real Python*'s "The Python pickle Module: How to Persist Objects in Python."[a]
>
> ---
> [a]https://realpython.com/python-pickle-module/

For POSIX systems, the creation of the subprocess by the `multipro-cessing` module is equivalent to this command, where `<i>` is the file handle descriptor, and `<j>` is the pipe handle descriptor:

```
$ python -c 'from multiprocessing.spawn import spawn_main; \
    spawn_main(tracker_fd=<i>, pipe_handle=<j>)' --multiprocessing-fork
```

For Windows systems, the parent PID is used instead of a tracker file descriptor as in this command, where`<k>` is the parent PID and `<j>` is the pipe handle descriptor:

```
> python.exe -c 'from multiprocessing.spawn import spawn_main; \
    spawn_main(parent_pid=<k>, pipe_handle=<j>)' --multiprocessing-fork
```

Piping Data to the Child Process

When the new child process has been instantiated on the operating system, it will wait for initialization data from the parent process.

The parent process writes two objects to a pipe file stream. The pipe file stream is a special I/O stream used to send data between processes on the command line.

The first object written by the parent process is the **preparation data** object. This object is a dictionary containing some information about the parent, such as the executing directory, the start method, any special command-line arguments, and the `sys.path`.

You can see an example of what is generated by running `multiprocessing.spawn.get_preparation_data(name)`:

```
>>> import multiprocessing.spawn
>>> import pprint
>>> pprint.pprint(multiprocessing.spawn.get_preparation_data("example"))
{'authkey': b'\x90\xaa_\x22[\x18\ri\xbcag]\x93\xfe\xf5\xe5@[wJ\x99p#\x00'
            b'\xce\xd4)1j.\xc3c',
 'dir': '/Users/anthonyshaw',
 'log_to_stderr': False,
```

239

```
'name': 'example',
'orig_dir': '/Users/anthonyshaw',
'start_method': 'spawn',
'sys_argv': [''],
'sys_path': [
  '/Users/anthonyshaw',
  ]}
```

The second object written is the `BaseProcess` child class instance. Depending on how multiprocessing was called and which operating system is being used, one of the child classes of `BaseProcess` will be the instance serialized.

Both the preparation data and process object are serialized using the `pickle` module and written to the parent process's pipe stream:

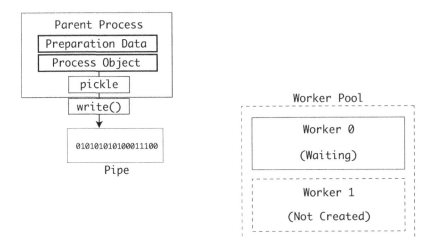

> **Note**
>
> The POSIX implementation of the child process spawning and serialization process is located in `Lib` ▸ `multiprocessing` ▸ `popen_spawn_posix.py`.
>
> The Windows implementation is located in `Lib` ▸ `multiprocessing` ▸ `popen_spawn_win32.py`.

Executing the Child Process

The entry point of the child process, `multiprocessing.spawn.spawn_main()`, takes the argument `pipe_handle` and either `parent_pid` for Windows or `tracked_fd` for POSIX:

```python
def spawn_main(pipe_handle, parent_pid=None, tracker_fd=None):
    '''
    Run code specified by data received over pipe
    '''
    assert is_forking(sys.argv), "Not forking"
```

For Windows, the function will call the parent PID's `OpenProcess` API. This is used to create a file handle, `fd`, of the parent process pipe:

```python
if sys.platform == 'win32':
    import msvcrt
    import _winapi

    if parent_pid is not None:
        source_process = _winapi.OpenProcess(
            _winapi.SYNCHRONIZE | _winapi.PROCESS_DUP_HANDLE,
            False, parent_pid)
    else:
        source_process = None
    new_handle = reduction.duplicate(pipe_handle,
                                source_process=source_process)
    fd = msvcrt.open_osfhandle(new_handle, os.O_RDONLY)
    parent_sentinel = source_process
```

For POSIX, the pipe_handle becomes the file descriptor, fd, and is duplicated to become the parent_sentinel value:

```
else:
    from . import resource_tracker
    resource_tracker._resource_tracker._fd = tracker_fd
    fd = pipe_handle
    parent_sentinel = os.dup(pipe_handle)
```

Next, _main() is called with the parent pipe file handle, fd, and the parent process sentinel, parent_sentinel. The return value of _main() becomes the exit code for the process and the interpreter is terminated:

```
exitcode = _main(fd, parent_sentinel)
sys.exit(exitcode)
```

_main() is called with fd and parent_sentinel to check if the parent process has exited while executing the child process.

_main() deserializes the binary data on the fd byte stream. Remember, this is the pipe file handle. The deserialization uses the same pickle library that the parent process used:

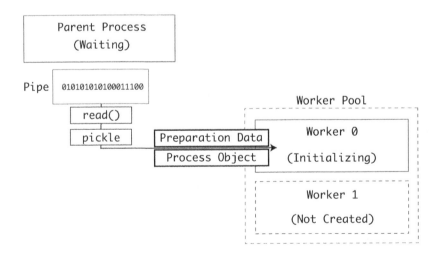

The first value is a `dict` containing the preparation data. The second value is an instance of `SpawnProcess`, which is then used as the instance to call `_bootstrap()` upon:

```
def _main(fd, parent_sentinel):
    with os.fdopen(fd, 'rb', closefd=True) as from_parent:
        process.current_process()._inheriting = True
        try:
            preparation_data = reduction.pickle.load(from_parent)
            prepare(preparation_data)
            self = reduction.pickle.load(from_parent)
        finally:
            del process.current_process()._inheriting
    return self._bootstrap(parent_sentinel)
```

`_bootstrap()` handles the instantiation of a `BaseProcess` instance from the deserialized data, and then the target function is called with the arguments and keyword arguments. This final task is completed by `BaseProcess.run()`:

```
def run(self):
    '''
    Method to be run in subprocess; can be overridden in subclass
    '''
    if self._target:
        self._target(*self._args, **self._kwargs)
```

The exit code of `self._bootstrap()` is set as the exit code, and the child process is terminated.

This process allows the parent process to serialize the module and the executable function. It also allows the child process to deserialize that instance, execute the function with arguments, and return.

It does not allow data to be exchanged once the child process has started. This task is done using the extension of the `Queue` and `Pipe` objects.

If processes are being created in a pool, then the first process will be ready and in a waiting state. The parent process repeats the process and sends the data to the next worker:

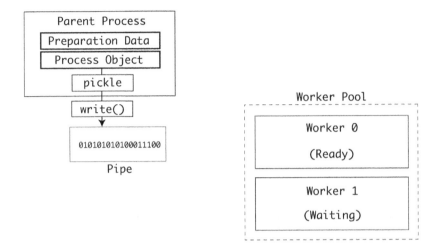

The next worker receives the data and initializes its state and runs the target function:

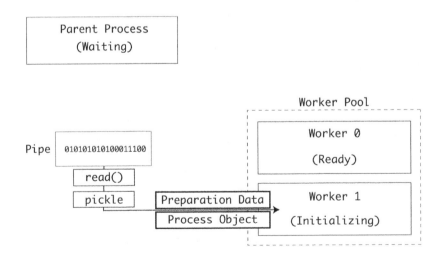

To share any data beyond initialization, queues and pipes must be used.

Exchanging Data With Queues and Pipes

In the previous section you saw how child processes are spawned and then the pipe is used as a serialization stream to tell the child process what function to call with arguments.

There are two types of communication between processes, depending on the nature of the task: **queues** and **pipes**. Before learning about each, you'll take a quick look at how operating systems protect access to resources using variables called **semaphores**.

Semaphores

Many of the mechanisms in multiprocessing use semaphores as a way of signaling that resources are locked, are being waited on, or are not used. Operating systems use binary semaphores as a simple variable type for locking resources like files, sockets, and others.

If one process is writing to a file or to a network socket, then you don't want another process to suddenly start writing to the same file. The data would instantly become corrupt.

Instead, operating systems put a lock on resources by using a semaphore. Processes can also signal that they're waiting for that lock to be released so that when it is, they get a message to say it's ready and that they can start using it.

In the real world, semaphores are a signaling method that uses flags to transmit messages. So, you can imagine that the semaphore signals for a resource's waiting, locked, and not-used states look like this:

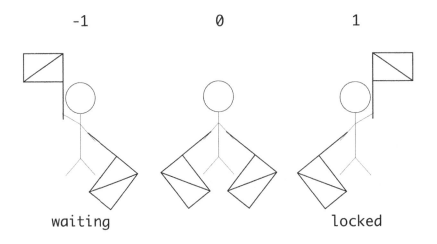

The semaphore API differs between operating systems, so there's an abstraction class, `multiprocessing.synchronize.Semaphore`.

Semaphores are used by CPython for multiprocessing because they're both thread-safe and process-safe. The operating system handles any potential deadlocks of reading or writing to the same semaphore.

The implementation of these semaphore API functions is located in a C extension module `Modules ‣ _multiprocessing ‣ semaphore.c`. This extension module offers a single method for creating, locking, and releasing semaphores along with other operations.

The call to the operating system is made through a series of macros, which are compiled into different implementations depending on the operating system platform.

For Windows, the macros use the `<winbase.h>` API functions for semaphores:

```
#define SEM_CREATE(name, val, max) CreateSemaphore(NULL, val, max, NULL)
#define SEM_CLOSE(sem) (CloseHandle(sem) ? 0 : -1)
#define SEM_GETVALUE(sem, pval) _GetSemaphoreValue(sem, pval)
#define SEM_UNLINK(name) 0
```

For POSIX, the macros use the `<semaphore.h>` API:

```
#define SEM_CREATE(name, val, max) sem_open(name, O_CREAT | O_EXCL, 0600,...
#define SEM_CLOSE(sem) sem_close(sem)
#define SEM_GETVALUE(sem, pval) sem_getvalue(sem, pval)
#define SEM_UNLINK(name) sem_unlink(name)
```

Queues

Queues are a great way of sending small data to and from multiple processes.

You can adapt the multiprocessing example from earlier to use a multiprocessing `Manager()` instance and create two queues:

1. **inputs** to hold the Fahrenheit input values

2. **outputs** to hold the resulting Celsius values

Change the pool size to 2 so that there are two workers:

cpython-book-samples ▸ 33 ▸ pool_queue_celsius.py

```python
import multiprocessing as mp


def to_celsius(input: mp.Queue, output: mp.Queue):
    f = input.get()
    # Time-consuming task ...
    c = (f - 32) * (5/9)
    output.put(c)


if __name__ == '__main__':
    mp.set_start_method('spawn')
    pool_manager = mp.Manager()
    with mp.Pool(2) as pool:
        inputs = pool_manager.Queue()
        outputs = pool_manager.Queue()
        input_values = list(range(110, 150, 10))
        for i in input_values:
            inputs.put(i)
```

```
pool.apply(to_celsius, (inputs, outputs))

for f in input_values:
    print(outputs.get(block=False))
```

This prints the returned list of tuples to the outputs queue:

```
$ python pool_queue_celsius.py
43.333333333333336
48.88888888888889
54.44444444444445
60.0
```

The parent process first puts the input values onto the inputs queue. The first worker then takes an item from the queue. Each time an item is taken from the queue using .get(), a semaphore lock is used on the queue object:

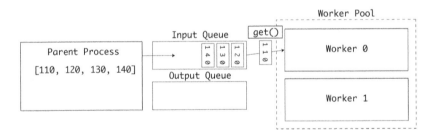

While this worker is busy, the second worker then takes another value from the queue:

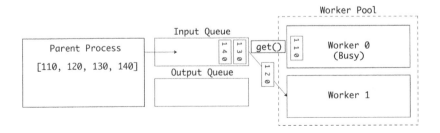

The first worker has completed its calculation and puts the resulting value onto the outputs queue:

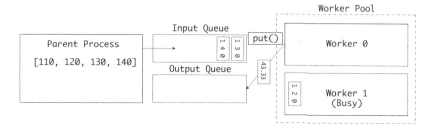

Two queues are in use to separate the input and output values. Eventually, all input values have been processed, and the outputs queue is full. The values are then printed by the parent process:

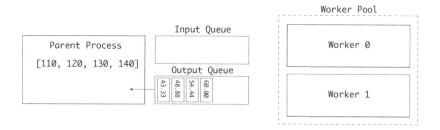

This example shows how a pool of workers could receive a queue of small, discrete values and process them in parallel to send the resulting data back to the host process.

In practice, converting Celsius to Fahrenheit is a small, trivial calculation unsuited for parallel execution. If the worker process were doing a different, CPU-intensive calculation, then this would provide significant performance improvement on a multi-CPU or multicore computer.

For streaming data instead of discrete queues, you can use pipes instead.

Pipes

Within the `multiprocessing` package, there is a type `Pipe`. Instantiating a pipe returns two connections, a parent and a child. Both can send and receive data:

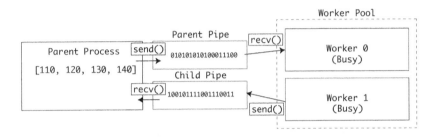

In the queue example, a lock is implicitly placed on the queue when data is sent and received. Pipes don't have that behavior, so you have to be careful that two processes don't try to write to the same pipe at the same time.

To adapt the last example to work with a pipe, it will require changing `pool.apply()` to `pool.apply_async()`. This changes the execution of the next process to a non-blocking operation:

cpython-book-samples ▸ 33 ▸ pool_pipe_celsius.py

```python
import multiprocessing as mp

def to_celsius(child_pipe: mp.Pipe):
    f = child_pipe.recv()
    # time-consuming task ...
    c = (f - 32) * (5/9)
    child_pipe.send(c)


if __name__ == '__main__':
    mp.set_start_method('spawn')
    pool_manager = mp.Manager()
```

```
with mp.Pool(2) as pool:
    parent_pipe, child_pipe = mp.Pipe()
    results = []
    for input in range(110, 150, 10):
        parent_pipe.send(input)
        results.append(pool.apply_async(to_celsius, args=(child_pipe,)))
        print("Got {0:}".format(parent_pipe.recv()))
    parent_pipe.close()
    child_pipe.close()
```

There's a risk of two or more processes trying to read from the parent pipe at the same time in this line:

```
f = child_pipe.recv()
```

There's also a risk of two or more processes trying to write to the child pipe at the same time:

```
child_pipe.send(c)
```

If this situation occurred, then data would be corrupted in either the receive or send operations:

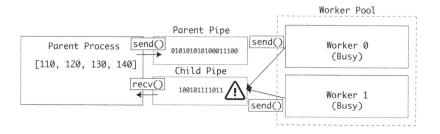

To avoid this, you can implement a semaphore lock on the operating system. Then all child processes will check with the lock before reading or writing to the same pipe.

There are two locks required, one on the receiving end of the parent pipe and another on the sending end of the child pipe:

cpython-book-samples ▶ 33 ▶ pool_pipe_locks_celsius.py

```python
import multiprocessing as mp

def to_celsius(child_pipe: mp.Pipe, child_lock: mp.Lock):
    child_lock.acquire(blocking=False)
    try:
        f = child_pipe.recv()
    finally:
        child_lock.release()
    # time-consuming task ... release lock before processing
    c = (f - 32) * (5/9)
    # reacquire lock when done
    child_lock.acquire(blocking=False)
    try:
        child_pipe.send(c)
    finally:
        child_lock.release()

if __name__ == '__main__':
    mp.set_start_method('spawn')
    pool_manager = mp.Manager()
    with mp.Pool(2) as pool:
        parent_pipe, child_pipe = mp.Pipe()
        child_lock = pool_manager.Lock()
        results = []
        for i in range(110, 150, 10):
            parent_pipe.send(i)
            results.append(pool.apply_async(
                to_celsius, args=(child_pipe, child_lock)))
            print(parent_pipe.recv())
        parent_pipe.close()
        child_pipe.close()
```

Now the worker processes will wait to acquire a lock before receiving data and wait again to acquire another lock to send data:

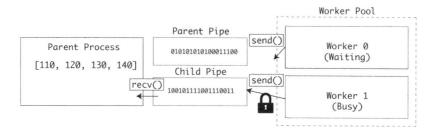

This example would suit situations where the data going over the pipe is large because the chance of a collision is higher.

Shared State Between Processes

So far, you've seen how data can be shared between child and parent processes.

There may be scenarios in which you want to share data between child processes. In this situation, the multiprocessing package provides two solutions:

1. A performant shared memory API using shared memory maps and shared C types

2. A flexible server process API supporting complex types via the Manager class

Example Application

As a demonstration application, throughout the rest of this chapter, you'll be refactoring a TCP port scanner for different concurrency and parallelism techniques.

Over a network, a host can be contacted on ports, which are numbered from 1 through 65535. Common services have standard ports. For example, HTTP operates on port 80 and HTTPS operates on 443. TCP port scanners are a common network testing tool for checking that packets can be sent over a network.

This code example uses the `Queue` interface, a thread-safe queue implementation similar to the one you used in the multiprocessing examples. The code also uses the `socket` package to try connecting to a remote port with a short one-second timeout.

`check_port()` will see if the `host` responds on the given `port`. If it does, then `check_port()` will add the port number to the `results` queue.

When the script is executed, `check_port()` is called in sequence for port numbers 80 to 100. After this has completed, the `results` queue is emptied out, and the results are printed on the command line. So you can compare the difference, it will print the execution time at the end:

cpython-book-samples ▸ 33 ▸ portscanner.py

```python
from queue import Queue
import socket
import time
timeout = 1.0


def check_port(host: str, port: int, results: Queue):
    sock = socket.socket(socket.AF_INET, socket.SOCK_STREAM)
    sock.settimeout(timeout)
    result = sock.connect_ex((host, port))
    if result == 0:
        results.put(port)
    sock.close()


if __name__ == '__main__':
    start = time.time()
    host = "localhost"  # Replace with a host you own
    results = Queue()
    for port in range(80, 100):
        check_port(host, port, results)
    while not results.empty():
        print("Port {0} is open".format(results.get()))
    print("Completed scan in {0} seconds".format(time.time() - start))
```

The execution will print out the open ports and the time taken:

```
$ python portscanner.py
Port 80 is open
Completed scan in 19.623435020446777 seconds
```

You can refactor this example to use multiprocessing. Swap the `Queue` interface for `multiprocessing.Queue` and scan the ports together using a pool executor:

cpython-book-samples ▸ 33 ▸ portscanner_mp_queue.py

```python
import multiprocessing as mp
import time
import socket

timeout = 1


def check_port(host: str, port: int, results: mp.Queue):
    sock = socket.socket(socket.AF_INET, socket.SOCK_STREAM)
    sock.settimeout(timeout)
    result = sock.connect_ex((host, port))
    if result == 0:
        results.put(port)
    sock.close()


if __name__ == '__main__':
    start = time.time()
    processes = []
    scan_range = range(80, 100)
    host = "localhost"  # Replace with a host you own
    mp.set_start_method('spawn')
    pool_manager = mp.Manager()
    with mp.Pool(len(scan_range)) as pool:
        outputs = pool_manager.Queue()
        for port in scan_range:
            processes.append(pool.apply_async(check_port,
                                              (host, port, outputs)))
        for process in processes:
```

```
        process.get()
    while not outputs.empty():
        print("Port {0} is open".format(outputs.get()))
    print("Completed scan in {0} seconds".format(time.time() - start))
```

As you might expect, this application is much faster because it tests each port in parallel:

```
$ python portscanner_mp_queue.py
Port 80 is open
Completed scan in 1.556523084640503 seconds
```

Multiprocessing Summary

Multiprocessing offers a scalable parallel execution API for Python. Data can be shared between processes, and CPU-intensive work can be broken into parallel tasks to take advantage of multicore or multi-CPU computers.

Multiprocessing isn't a suitable solution when the task to be completed is I/O bound rather than CPU intensive. For example, if you spawned four worker processes to read and write to the same files, then one would do all the work, and the other three would wait for the lock to be released.

Multiprocessing also isn't suitable for short-lived tasks because of the time and processing overhead required to start a new Python interpreter.

In both of those scenarios, you main find one of the next approaches more suitable.

Multithreading

CPython provides both a high-level API and a low-level API for creating, spawning, and controlling threads from Python.

To understand Python threads, you should first understand how operating system threads work. There are two implementations of threading in CPython:

1. `pthreads:` POSIX threads for Linux and macOS

2. `nt threads:` NT threads for Windows

In the section "The Structure of a Process," you saw that a process has the following features:

- A **stack** of subroutines

- A **heap** of memory

- Access to **files**, **locks**, and **sockets** on the operating system

The biggest limitation to scaling a single process is that the operating system will have a single **program counter** for that executable.

To get around this, modern operating systems allow processes to signal the operating system to branch their execution into multiple threads.

Each thread will have its own program counter but use the same resources as the host process. Each thread also has its own call stack, so it can be executing a different function.

Because multiple threads can read and write to the same memory space, collisions can occur. The solution to this is **thread safety**, which involves making sure that memory space is locked by a single thread before it's accessed.

A single process with three threads would have this structure:

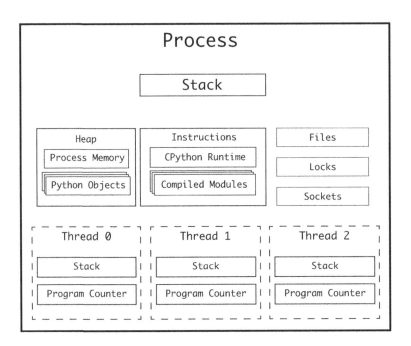

See Also

For an introductory tutorial on the Python threading API, check out *Real Python*'s "Intro to Python Threading."[a]

[a]https://realpython.com/intro-to-python-threading/

The GIL

If you're familiar with NT threads or POSIX threads from C, or if you've used another high-level language, then you may expect multithreading to be parallel.

In CPython, the threads are based on the C APIs but are Python threads. This means that every Python thread needs to execute Python bytecode through the evaluation loop.

The Python evaluation loop is not thread-safe. There are many parts of the interpreter state, such as the garbage collector, that are shared and global. To get around this, the CPython developers implemented a mega-lock called the **global interpreter lock (GIL)**. Before any opcode is executed in the frame-evaluation loop, the GIL is acquired by the thread. Once the opcode has been executed, the GIL is released.

Although it provides global thread safety to every operation in Python, this approach has a major drawback. Any operations that take a long time to execute will leave other threads waiting for the GIL to be released before they can execute. This means that only one thread can execute a Python bytecode operation at any given time.

To acquire the GIL, a call is made to take_gil(). To release it, a call is made to drop_gil(). The GIL acquisition is made within the core frame evaluation loop, _PyEval_EvalFrameDefault().

To stop a single frame execution from permanently holding the GIL, the evaluation loop state stores a flag, gil_drop_request. After every bytecode operation has completed in a frame, this flag is checked, and the GIL is temporarily released before being reacquired:

```
if (_Py_atomic_load_relaxed(&ceval->gil_drop_request)) {
    /* Give another thread a chance */
    if (_PyThreadState_Swap(&runtime->gilstate, NULL) != tstate) {
        Py_FatalError("ceval: tstate mix-up");
    }
    drop_gil(ceval, tstate);

    /* Other threads may run now */

    take_gil(ceval, tstate);

    /* Check if we should make a quick exit. */
    exit_thread_if_finalizing(tstate);

    if (_PyThreadState_Swap(&runtime->gilstate, tstate) != NULL) {
        Py_FatalError("ceval: orphan tstate");
```

```
        }
    }
    ...
```

Despite the limitations that the GIL enforces on parallel execution, it makes multithreading in Python very safe and ideal for running I/O-bound tasks concurrently.

Related Source Files

Here are the source files related to threading:

File	Purpose
Include ▸ pythread.h	PyThread API and definition
Lib ▸ threading.py	High-level threading API and standard library module
Modules ▸ _threadmodule.c	Low-level threading API and standard library module
Python ▸ thread.c	C extension for the thread module
Python ▸ thread_nt.h	Windows threading API
Python ▸ thread_pthread.h	POSIX threading API
Python ▸ ceval_gil.h	GIL lock implementation

Starting Threads in Python

To demonstrate the performance gains of having multithreaded code (in spite of the GIL), you can implement a simple network port scanner in Python.

You'll start by cloning the previous script but changing the logic to spawn a thread for each port using threading.Thread(). This is similar to the multiprocessing API, where it takes a callable, target, and a tuple, args.

Start the threads inside the loop, but don't wait for them to complete. Instead, append the thread instance to a list, threads:

```
for port in range(80, 100):
    t = Thread(target=check_port, args=(host, port, results))
    t.start()
    threads.append(t)
```

Once all threads have been created, iterate through the threads list and call .join() to wait for them to complete:

```
for t in threads:
    t.join()
```

Next, exhaust all the items in the results queue and print them to the screen:

```
while not results.empty():
    print("Port {0} is open".format(results.get()))
```

Here's the entire script:

cpython-book-samples ▸ 33 ▸ portscanner_threads.py

```
from threading import Thread
from queue import Queue
import socket
import time


timeout = 1.0


def check_port(host: str, port: int, results: Queue):
    sock = socket.socket(socket.AF_INET, socket.SOCK_STREAM)
    sock.settimeout(timeout)
    result = sock.connect_ex((host, port))
    if result == 0:
        results.put(port)
    sock.close()


def main():
    start = time.time()
    host = "localhost"  # Replace with a host you own
```

```python
    threads = []
    results = Queue()
    for port in range(80, 100):
        t = Thread(target=check_port, args=(host, port, results))
        t.start()
        threads.append(t)
    for t in threads:
        t.join()
    while not results.empty():
        print("Port {0} is open".format(results.get()))
    print("Completed scan in {0} seconds".format(time.time() - start))

if __name__ == '__main__':
    main()
```

When you call this threaded script at the command line, it will execute more than ten times as fast as the single-threaded example:

```
$ python portscanner_threads.py
Port 80 is open
Completed scan in 1.0101029872894287 seconds
```

This also runs 50 to 60 percent faster than the multiprocessing example. Remember that multiprocessing has an overhead for starting the new processes. Threading does have an overhead, but it's much smaller.

You may be wondering, If the GIL means that only a single operation can execute at once, then why is this faster?

Here's the statement that takes 1–1000 ms:

```python
    result = sock.connect_ex((host, port))
```

In the C extension module Modules ▸ socketmodule.c, this function implements the connection:

Modules ▸ socketmodule.c line 3245

```
static int
internal_connect(PySocketSockObject *s, struct sockaddr *addr, int addrlen,
                 int raise)
{
    int res, err, wait_connect;

    Py_BEGIN_ALLOW_THREADS
    res = connect(s->sock_fd, addr, addrlen);
    Py_END_ALLOW_THREADS
```

Surrounding the system connect() call are the Py_BEGIN_ALLOW_THREADS and Py_END_ALLOW_THREADS macros. These macros are defined as follows in Include ▸ ceval.h:

```
#define Py_BEGIN_ALLOW_THREADS { \
                        PyThreadState *_save; \
                        _save = PyEval_SaveThread();
#define Py_BLOCK_THREADS        PyEval_RestoreThread(_save);
#define Py_UNBLOCK_THREADS      _save = PyEval_SaveThread();
#define Py_END_ALLOW_THREADS    PyEval_RestoreThread(_save); \
                    }
```

So, when Py_BEGIN_ALLOW_THREADS is called, it calls PyEval_SaveThread(). This function changes the thread state to NULL and **drops** the GIL:

Python ▸ ceval.c line 444

```
PyThreadState *
PyEval_SaveThread(void)
{
    PyThreadState *tstate = PyThreadState_Swap(NULL);
    if (tstate == NULL)
        Py_FatalError("PyEval_SaveThread: NULL tstate");
    assert(gil_created());
    drop_gil(tstate);
    return tstate;
}
```

Because the GIL is dropped, any other executing thread can continue. This thread will sit and wait for the system call without blocking the evaluation loop.

Once `connect()` has succeeded or timed out, the `Py_END_ALLOW_THREADS` macro runs `PyEval_RestoreThread()` with the original thread state. The thread state is recovered and the GIL is retaken. The call to `take_gil()` is a blocking call, waiting on a semaphore:

Python ▸ `ceval.c` line 458

```
void
PyEval_RestoreThread(PyThreadState *tstate)
{
    if (tstate == NULL)
        Py_FatalError("PyEval_RestoreThread: NULL tstate");
    assert(gil_created());

    int err = errno;
    take_gil(tstate);
    /* _Py_Finalizing is protected by the GIL */
    if (_Py_IsFinalizing() && !_Py_CURRENTLY_FINALIZING(tstate)) {
        drop_gil(tstate);
        PyThread_exit_thread();
        Py_UNREACHABLE();
    }
    errno = err;

    PyThreadState_Swap(tstate);
}
```

This isn't the only system call wrapped by the non-GIL-blocking pair `Py_BEGIN_ALLOW_THREADS` and `Py_END_ALLOW_THREADS`. There are over three hundred uses of it in the standard library, including:

- Making HTTP requests
- Interacting with local hardware

- Encrypting data

- Reading and writing files

Thread State

CPython provides its own implementation of thread management. Because threads need to execute Python bytecode in the evaluation loop, running a thread in CPython isn't as simple as spawning an operating system thread.

Python threads are called PyThread. You covered them briefly in the "CPython Evaluation Loop" chapter.

Python threads execute code objects and are spawned by the interpreter.

To recap:

- CPython has a single runtime, which has its own **runtime state**.

- CPython can have one or many interpreters.

- An interpreter has a state called the **interpreter state**.

- An interpreter will take a **code object** and convert it into a series of **frame objects**.

- An interpreter has at least one **thread**, and each thread has a **thread state**.

- Frame objects are executed in a stack called the **frame stack**.

- CPython references variables in a **value stack**.

- The **interpreter state** includes a linked list of its threads.

A single-threaded, single-interpreter runtime would have the following states:

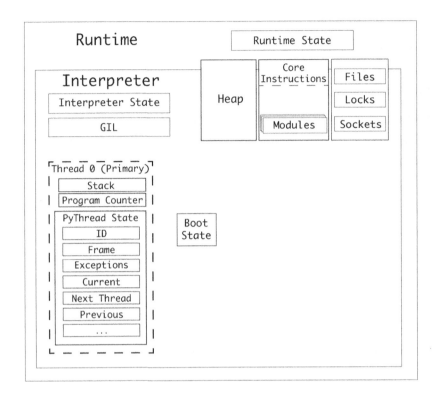

The thread state type, PyThreadState, has over thirty properties, including:

- A unique identifier
- A linked list to the other thread states
- The interpreter state it was spawned by
- The currently executing frame
- The current recursion depth
- Optional tracing functions
- The exception currently being handled
- Any async exception currently being handled
- A stack of exceptions raised

- A GIL counter

- Async generator counters

Like the multiprocessing **preparation data**, threads have a boot state. However, threads share the same memory space, so there's no need to serialize data and send it over a file stream.

Threads are instantiated with the `threading.Thread` type. This is a high-level module that abstracts the `PyThread` type. `PyThread` instances are managed by the C extension module `_thread`.

The `_thread` module has the entry point for executing a new thread, `thread_PyThread_start_new_thread()`. `start_new_thread()` is a method on an instance of the type `Thread`.

New threads are instantiated in this sequence:

1. The `bootstate` is created, linking to the `target`, with arguments `args` and `kwargs`.

2. The `bootstate` is linked to the interpreter state.

3. A new `PyThreadState` is created, linking to the current interpreter.

4. The GIL is enabled, if not already, with a call to `PyEval_InitThreads()`.

5. The new thread is started on the operating system—specific implementation of `PyThread_start_new_thread`.

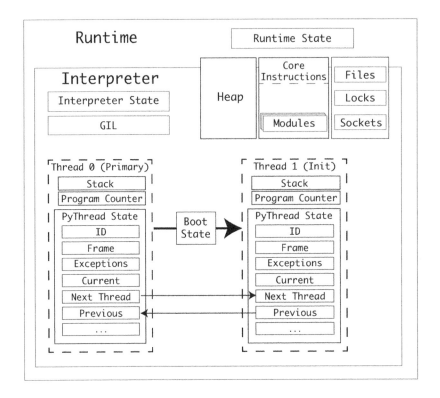

The thread `bootstate` has the following properties:

Field	Type	Purpose
interp	PyInterpreterState*	Link to the interpreter managing this thread
func	PyObject * (callable)	Link to the callable to execute upon running the thread
args	PyObject * (tuple)	Arguments to call func with
keyw	PyObject * (dict)	Keyword arguments to call func with
tstate	PyThreadState *	Thread state for the new thread

With the thread `bootstate`, there are two implementations of `PyThread`:

1. **POSIX threads** for Linux and macOS
2. **NT threads** for Windows

Both of these implementations create the operating system thread, set its attribute, and then execute the callback `t_bootstrap()` from within the new thread.

This function is called with the single argument `boot_raw`, assigned to the `bootstate` constructed in `thread_PyThread_start_new_thread()`.

The `t_bootstrap()` function is the interface between a low-level thread and the Python runtime. The bootstrap will initialize the thread, then execute the `target` callable using `PyObject_Call()`.

Once the callable target has been executed, the thread will exit:

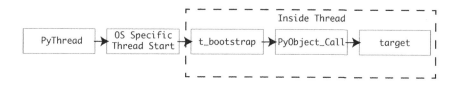

POSIX Threads

POSIX threads, named `pthreads`, have an implementation in Python ▸ `thread_pthread.h`. This implementation abstracts the `<pthread.h>` C API with some additional safeguards and optimizations.

Threads can have a configured stack size. Python has its own stack frame construct, as you explored in the chapter on the evaluation loop. If there's an issue causing a recursive loop, and the frame execution hits the depth limit, then Python will raise a `RecursionError`, which you can handle with a `try...except` block in Python code.

Because `pthreads` have their own stack size, the max depth of Python and the stack size of the `pthread` might conflict. If the thread stack size is smaller than the max frame depth in Python, then the entire Python process will crash before a `RecursionError` is raised.

The max depth in Python can be configured at runtime using `sys.setrecursionlimit()`. To avoid crashes, the CPython `pthread` implementation sets the stack size to the `pythread_stacksize` value of the interpreter state.

Most modern POSIX-compliant operating systems support system scheduling of `pthreads`. If `PTHREAD_SYSTEM_SCHED_SUPPORTED` is defined in `pyconfig.h`, then the `pthread` is set to `PTHREAD_SCOPE_SYSTEM`, meaning that the priority of the thread on the operating system scheduler is decided against the other threads on the system, not just the ones within the Python process.

Once the thread properties have been configured, the thread is created using the `pthread_create()` API. This runs the bootstrap function from inside the new thread.

Lastly, the thread handle, `pthread_t`, is cast into an `unsigned long` and returned to become the thread ID.

Windows Threads

Windows threads implemented in `Python ▸ thread_nt.h` follow a similar but simpler pattern.

The stack size of the new thread is configured to the interpreter `pythread_stacksize` value (if set). The thread is then created using the `_beginthreadex()` Windows API using the bootstrap function as the callback. Finally, the thread ID is returned.

Multithreading Summary

This was not an exhaustive tutorial on Python threads. Python's thread implementation is extensive and offers many mechanisms for sharing data between threads, locking objects, and resources.

Threads are a great, efficient way of improving the runtime of your Python applications when they're I/O bound. In this section, you've seen what the GIL is, why it exists, and which parts of the standard library may be exempt from its constraints.

Asynchronous Programming

Python offers many ways of accomplishing concurrent programming without using threads or multiprocessing. These features have been added, expanded, and often replaced with better alternatives.

For the target version of this book, 3.9, the `@coroutine` decorator is deprecated.

The following systems are still available:

- Creating futures from `async` keywords
- Running coroutines using the `yield from` keywords

Generators

Python generators are functions that return a `yield` statement and can be called continually to generate further values.

Generators are often used as a more memory-efficient way of looping through values in a large block of data, like a file, a database, or over a network. Generator objects are returned in place of a **value** when `yield` is used instead of `return`. The generator object is created from the `yield` statement and returned to the caller.

This simple generator function will yield the letters a through z:

cpython-book-samples ▸ 33 ▸ letter_generator.py

```python
def letters():
    i = 97  # Letter 'a' in ASCII
    end = 97 + 26  # Letter 'z' in ASCII
    while i < end:
        yield chr(i)
        i += 1
```

If you call `letters()`, then it won't return a value. Instead, it will return a generator object:

```
>>> from letter_generator import letters
>>> letters()
<generator object letters at 0x1004d39b0>
```

Built into the syntax of the `for` statement is the ability to iterate through a generator object until it stops yielding values:

```
>>> for letter in letters():
...     print(letter)
a
b
c
d
...
```

This implementation uses the iterator protocol. Objects that have a `__next__()` method can be looped over by `for` and `while` loops or using the built-in `next()`.

All container types (like lists, sets, and tuples) in Python implement the iterator protocol. Generators are unique because the implementation of the `__next__()` method recalls the generator function from its last state.

Generators aren't executed in the background—they're paused. When you request another value, they resume execution. Within the generator object structure is the frame object as it was at the last `yield` statement.

Generator Structure

Generator objects are created by a template macro, `_PyGenObject_HEAD(prefix)`.

This macro is used by the following types and prefixes:

- **Generator objects:** `PyGenObject` (`gi_`)
- **Coroutine objects:** `PyCoroObject` (`cr_`)

- **Async generator objects:** PyAsyncGenObject (ag_)

You'll cover coroutine and async generator objects later in this chapter.

The PyGenObject type has these base properties:

Field	Type	Purpose
[x]_code	PyObject * (PyCodeObject*)	Compiled function that yields the generator
[x]_exc_state	_PyErr_StackItem	Exception data if the generator call raises an exception
[x]_frame	PyFrameObject*	Current frame object for the generator
[x]_name	PyObject * (str)	Name of the generator
[x]_qualname	PyObject * (str)	Qualified name of the generator
[x]_running	char	Set to 0 or 1 if the generator is currently running
[x]_weakreflist	PyObject * (list)	List of weak references to objects inside the generator function

On top of the base properties, the PyCoroObject type has this property:

Field	Type	Purpose
cr_origin	PyObject * (tuple)	Tuple containing the originating frame and caller

On top of the base properties, the PyAsyncGenObject type has these properties:

Field	Type	Purpose
ag_closed	int	Flag to mark that the generator is closed
ag_finalizer	PyObject *	Link to the finalizer method
ag_hooks_inited	int	Flag to mark that the hooks have been initialized
ag_running_async	int	Flag to mark that the generator is running

Related Source Files

Here are the source files related to generators:

File	Purpose
Include ▸ genobject.h	Generator API and PyGenObject definition
Objects ▸ genobject.c	Generator object implementation

Creating Generators

When a function containing a `yield` statement is compiled, the resulting code object has an additional flag, `CO_GENERATOR`.

In the "Constructing Frame Objects" section of the chapter on the evaluation loop, you explored how a compiled code object is converted into a frame object when it's executed. In this process, there's a special case for generators, coroutines, and async generators.

`_PyEval_EvalCode()` checks the code object for the `CO_GENERATOR`, `CO_COROUTINE`, and `CO_ASYNC_GENERATOR` flags. If it finds any of these flags, then instead of evaluating the code object inline, the function creates a frame and turns it into a generator, coroutine, or async generator object using `PyGen_NewWithQualName()`, `PyCoro_New()`, or `PyAsyncGen_New()`, respectively:

```
PyObject *
_PyEval_EvalCode(PyObject *_co, PyObject *globals, PyObject *locals, ...

    ...
    /* Handle generator/coroutine/asynchronous generator */
    if (co->co_flags & (CO_GENERATOR | CO_COROUTINE | CO_ASYNC_GENERATOR)) {
        PyObject *gen;
        PyObject *coro_wrapper = tstate->coroutine_wrapper;
        int is_coro = co->co_flags & CO_COROUTINE;

        ...
        /* Create a new generator that owns the ready-to-run frame
         * and return that as the value. */
        if (is_coro) {
```

```
>>>             gen = PyCoro_New(f, name, qualname);
        } else if (co->co_flags & CO_ASYNC_GENERATOR) {
>>>             gen = PyAsyncGen_New(f, name, qualname);
        } else {
>>>             gen = PyGen_NewWithQualName(f, name, qualname);
        }
        ...
        return gen;
    }
...
```

The generator factory, PyGen_NewWithQualName(), takes the frame and completes some steps to populate the generator object fields:

1. Sets the gi_code property to the compiled code object

2. Sets the generator to not running (gi_running = 0)

3. Sets the exception and weakref lists to NULL

You can also see that gi_code is the compiled code object for the generator function by importing the dis module and disassembling the bytecode inside:

```
>>> from letter_generator import letters
>>> gen = letters()
>>> import dis
>>> dis.disco(gen.gi_code)
  2            0 LOAD_CONST            1 (97)
               2 STORE_FAST            0 (i)
...
```

In the chapter on the evaluation loop, you explored the frame object type. Frame objects contain locals and globals, the last executed instructions, and the code to be executed.

The built-in behavior and state of frame objects allow generators to pause and resume on demand.

Executing Generators

Whenever __next__() is called on a generator object, gen_iternext() is called with the generator instance, which immediately calls gen_send_ex() inside Objects ▸ genobject.c.

gen_send_ex() is the function that converts a generator object into the next yielded result. You'll see many similarities to the way frames are constructed from a code object as these functions have similar tasks.

gen_send_ex() is shared with generators, coroutines, and async generators and has the following steps:

1. The current thread state is fetched.

2. The frame object from the generator object is fetched.

3. If the generator is running when __next__() is called, then raise a ValueError.

4. If the frame inside the generator is at the top of the stack:
   - If this is a coroutine, and the coroutine is not already marked as closing, then a RuntimeError is raised.
   - If this is an async generator, then a StopAsyncIteration is raised.
   - If this is a standard generator, then a StopIteration is raised.

5. If the last instruction in the frame (f->f_lasti) is still -1 because it's just been started, and if this is a coroutine or an async generator, then any value other than None can't be passed as an argument, and an exception is raised.

6. Else, this is the first time it's being called, and arguments are allowed. The value of the argument is pushed to the frame's value stack.

7. The f_back field of the frame is the caller to which return values are sent, so this is set to the current frame in the thread. This means that the return value is sent to the caller, not to the creator of the generator.

8. The generator is marked as running.

9. The last exception in the generator's exception info is copied from the last exception in the thread state.

10. The thread state exception info is set to the address of the generator's exception info. This means that if the caller enters a breakpoint around the execution of a generator, then the stack trace goes through the generator and the offending code is clear.

11. The frame inside the generator is executed within the Python ▸ ceval.c main execution loop, and the value is returned.

12. The thread state last exception info is reset to the value before the frame was called.

13. The generator is marked as not running.

14. The following cases then match the return value and any exceptions thrown by the call to the generator. Remember that generators should raise a StopIteration when they're exhausted, either manually or by not yielding a value:

    • If no result was returned from the frame, then a StopIteration is raised for generators and a StopAsyncIteration is raised for async generators.

    • If a StopIteration was explicitly raised, but this is a coroutine or an async generator, then a RuntimeError is raised as this is not allowed.

    • If a StopAsyncIteration was explicitly raised and this is an async generator, then a RuntimeError is raised as this is not allowed.

15. Lastly, the result is returned back to the caller of __next__().

Bringing this all together, you can see how the generator expression is a powerful syntax in which a single keyword, yield, triggers a whole flow to create a unique object, copy a compiled code object as a property, set a frame, and store a list of variables in the local scope.

Coroutines

Generators have a major limitation: they can yield values only to their immediate caller.

An additional syntax, the `yield from` statement, was added to Python to overcome this limitation. Using this syntax, you can refactor generators into utility functions and then `yield from` them.

For example, the letter generator can be refactored into a utility function in which the starting letter is an argument. Using `yield from`, you can choose which generator object to return:

cpython-book-samples ▶ 33 ▶ letter_coroutines.py

```python
def gen_letters(start, x):
    i = start
    end = start + x
    while i < end:
        yield chr(i)
        i += 1


def letters(upper):
    if upper:
        yield from gen_letters(65, 26)   # A--Z
    else:
        yield from gen_letters(97, 26)   # a--z


for letter in letters(False):
    # Lowercase a--z
    print(letter)


for letter in letters(True):
    # Uppercase A--Z
    print(letter)
```

Generators are also great for lazy sequences, in which they can be called multiple times.

Building on the behaviors of generators, such as being able to pause and resume execution, the concept of a **coroutine** was iterated in Python over multiple APIs.

Generators are a limited form of coroutine because you can send data to them using the .send() method. It's possible to send messages bidirectionally between the caller and the target. Coroutines also store the caller in the cr_origin attribute.

Coroutines were initially available via a decorator, but this has since been deprecated in favor of "native" coroutines using the keywords async and await.

To mark that a function returns a coroutine, you must precede the function with the async keyword. The async keyword makes it explicit that, unlike generators, this function returns a coroutine and not a value.

To create a coroutine, you define a function with the keyword async def. In this example, you add a timer using the asyncio.sleep() function and return a wake-up string:

```
>>> import asyncio
>>> async def sleepy_alarm(time):
...     await asyncio.sleep(time)
...     return "wake up!"
>>> alarm = sleepy_alarm(10)
>>> alarm
<coroutine object sleepy_alarm at 0x1041de340>
```

When you call the function, it returns a coroutine object.

There are many ways to execute a coroutine. The easiest is using asyncio.run(coro). Run asyncio.run() with your coroutine object, then after 10 seconds it will sound the alarm:

```
>>> asyncio.run(alarm)
'wake up'
```

The benefit of coroutines is that you can run them concurrently. Because the coroutine object is a variable that you can pass to a function, these objects can be linked together and chained, or created in a sequence.

For example, if you wanted to have ten alarms with different intervals and start them all at the same time, then you could convert these coroutine objects into tasks.

The task API is used to schedule and execute multiple coroutines concurrently. Before tasks are scheduled, an event loop must be running. The job of the event loop is to schedule concurrent tasks and connect events such as completion, cancellation, and exceptions with callbacks.

When you called `asyncio.run()` (in Lib ▸ asyncio ▸ runners.py), the function performed these tasks for you:

1. Start a new event loop.

2. Wrap the coroutine object in a task.

3. Set a callback on the completion of the task.

4. Loop over the task until it completes.

5. Return the result.

Related Source Files

Here's the source file related to coroutines:

File	Purpose
Lib ▸ asyncio	Python standard library implementation for asyncio

Event Loops

Event loops are the glue that holds async code together. Written in pure Python, event loops are objects containing tasks.

Any of the tasks in the loop can have callbacks. The loop will run the callbacks if a task completes or fails:

```
loop = asyncio.new_event_loop()
```

Inside a loop is a sequence of tasks, represented by the type `asyncio.Task`. Tasks are scheduled onto a loop, and then once the loop is running, it loops over all the tasks until they're complete.

You can convert the single timer into a task loop:

cpython-book-samples ▸ 33 ▸ sleepy_alarm.py

```python
import asyncio

async def sleepy_alarm(person, time):
    await asyncio.sleep(time)
    print(f"{person} -- wake up!")

async def wake_up_gang():
    tasks = [
        asyncio.create_task(sleepy_alarm("Bob", 3), name="wake up Bob"),
        asyncio.create_task(sleepy_alarm("Yudi", 4), name="wake up Yudi"),
        asyncio.create_task(sleepy_alarm("Doris", 2), name="wake up Doris"),
        asyncio.create_task(sleepy_alarm("Kim", 5), name="wake up Kim")
    ]
    await asyncio.gather(*tasks)

asyncio.run(wake_up_gang())
```

This will print the following output:

```
Doris -- wake up!
Bob -- wake up!
Yudi -- wake up!
Kim -- wake up!
```

The event loop will run over each of the coroutines to see if they're completed. Similarly to how the `yield` keyword can return multiple values from the same frame, the `await` keyword can return multiple states.

The event loop will execute the `sleepy_alarm()` coroutine objects again and again until the `await asyncio.sleep()` yields a completed result and `print()` is able to execute.

For this to work, you need to use `asyncio.sleep()` instead of the blocking (and not async-aware) `time.sleep()`.

Example

You can convert the multithreaded port scanner example to `asyncio` with these steps:

- Change `check_port()` to use a socket connection from `asyncio.open_connection()`, which creates a future instead of an immediate connection.

- Use the socket connection future in a timer event with `asyncio.wait_for()`.

- Append the port to the results list if successful.

- Add a new function, `scan()`, to create the `check_port()` coroutines for each port and add them to a `tasks` list.

- Merge all the `tasks` into a new coroutine using `asyncio.gather()`.

- Run the scan using `asyncio.run()`.

Here's the code:

cpython-book-samples ▸ 33 ▸ portscanner_async.py

```
import time
import asyncio

timeout = 1.0
```

```python
async def check_port(host: str, port: int, results: list):
    try:
        future = asyncio.open_connection(host=host, port=port)
        r, w = await asyncio.wait_for(future, timeout=timeout)
        results.append(port)
        w.close()
    except OSError:  # pass on port closure
        pass
    except asyncio.TimeoutError:
        pass  # Port is closed, skip and continue


async def scan(start, end, host):
    tasks = []
    results = []
    for port in range(start, end):
        tasks.append(check_port(host, port, results))
    await asyncio.gather(*tasks)
    return results


if __name__ == '__main__':
    start = time.time()
    host = "localhost"  # Pick a host you own
    results = asyncio.run(scan(80, 100, host))
    for result in results:
        print("Port {0} is open".format(result))
    print("Completed scan in {0} seconds".format(time.time() - start))
```

This scan completes in just over one second:

```
$ python portscanner_async.py
Port 80 is open
Completed scan in 1.0058400630950928 seconds
```

Asynchronous Generators

The concepts you've learned so far, generators and coroutines, can be combined into **asynchronous generators**.

If a function is declared with the `async` keyword and contains a `yield` statement, then it's converted into an async generator object when called.

Like generators, async generators must be executed by something that understands the protocol. In place of __next__(), async generators have an __anext__() method.

A regular `for` loop wouldn't understand an async generator, so instead you use the `async for` statement.

You can refactor `check_port()` into an async generator that yields the next open port until it hits the last port or finds a specified number of open ports:

```python
async def check_ports(host: str, start: int, end: int, max=10):
    found = 0
    for port in range(start, end):
        try:
            future = asyncio.open_connection(host=host, port=port)
            r, w = await asyncio.wait_for(future, timeout=timeout)
            yield port
            found += 1
            w.close()
            if found >= max:
                return
        except asyncio.TimeoutError:
            pass # Closed
```

To execute this, use the `async for` statement:

```python
async def scan(start, end, host):
    results = []
    async for port in check_ports(host, start, end, max=1):
        results.append(port)
    return results
```

See `cpython-book-samples` ▸ 33 ▸ `portscanner_async_generators.py` for the full example.

Subinterpreters

So far, you've covered:

- Parallel execution with multiprocessing

- Concurrent execution with threads and async

The downsides of multiprocessing are that interprocess communication using pipes and queues is slower than with shared memory, and the overhead to start a new process is significant.

Threading and async have a small overhead but don't offer truly parallel execution because of the thread-safety guarantees in the GIL.

A fourth option is `subinterpreters`, which have a smaller overhead than `multiprocessing` and allow a GIL for each subinterpreter. After all, it's the global **interpreter** lock.

Within the CPython runtime, there's always one interpreter. The interpreter holds the interpreter state, and within an interpreter you can have one or many Python threads. The interpreter is the container for the evaluation loop. It also manages its own memory, reference counter, and garbage collection.

CPython has low-level C APIs for creating interpreters, like `Py_NewInterpreter()`:

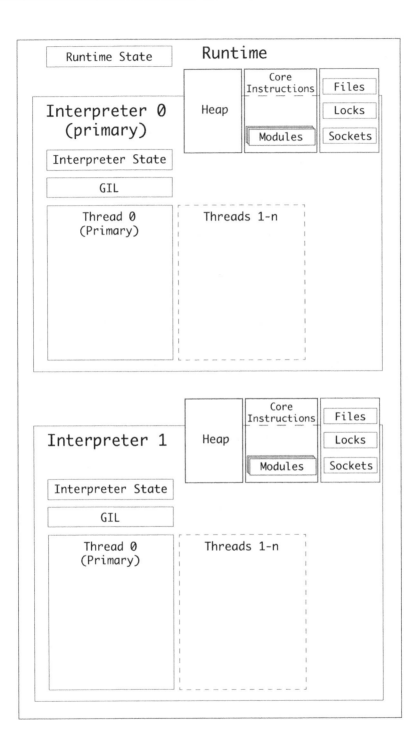

> **Note**
>
> The `subinterpreters` module is still experimental in 3.9, so the API is subject to change and the implementation is still buggy.

Because the interpreter state contains the memory allocation arena—a collection of all pointers to Python objects (local and global)—subinterpreters can't access the global variables of other interpreters.

Similarly to multiprocessing, to share objects between interpreters, you must serialize them or use `ctypes` and use a form of IPC (network, disk, or shared memory).

Related Source Files

Here are the source files related to subinterpreters:

File	Purpose
Lib ▸ _xxsubinterpreters.c	C implementation of the `subinterpreters` module
Python ▸ pylifecycle.c	C implementation of the interpreter management API

Example

In the final example application, the actual connection code has to be captured in a string. In 3.9, subinterpreters can be executed only with a string of code.

To start each of the subinterpreters, a list of threads is started with a callback to a function, `run()`.

This function will:

- Create a communication channel
- Start a new subinterpreter

- Send the subinterpreter the code to execute

- Receive data over the communication channel

- If the port connection succeeds, add it to the thread-safe queue

cpython-book-samples ▸ 33 ▸ portscanner_subinterpreters.py

```python
import time
import _xxsubinterpreters as subinterpreters
from threading import Thread
import textwrap as tw
from queue import Queue


timeout = 1  # In seconds


def run(host: str, port: int, results: Queue):
    # Create a communication channel
    channel_id = subinterpreters.channel_create()
    interpid = subinterpreters.create()
    subinterpreters.run_string(
        interpid,
        tw.dedent(
            """
import socket; import _xxsubinterpreters as subinterpreters
sock = socket.socket(socket.AF_INET, socket.SOCK_STREAM)
sock.settimeout(timeout)
result = sock.connect_ex((host, port))
subinterpreters.channel_send(channel_id, result)
sock.close()
            """),
        shared=dict(
            channel_id=channel_id,
            host=host,
            port=port,
            timeout=timeout
        ))
    output = subinterpreters.channel_recv(channel_id)
    subinterpreters.channel_release(channel_id)
    if output == 0:
```

```
        results.put(port)

if __name__ == '__main__':
    start = time.time()
    host = "127.0.0.1"  # Pick a host you own
    threads = []
    results = Queue()
    for port in range(80, 100):
        t = Thread(target=run, args=(host, port, results))
        t.start()
        threads.append(t)
    for t in threads:
        t.join()
    while not results.empty():
        print("Port {0} is open".format(results.get()))
    print("Completed scan in {0} seconds".format(time.time() - start))
```

Because of the reduced overheads compared with multiprocessing, this example should execute 30 to 40 percent faster and with fewer memory resources:

```
$ python portscanner_subinterpreters.py
Port 80 is open
Completed scan in 1.3474230766296387 seconds
```

Conclusion

Congratulations on getting through the biggest chapter in the book! You've covered a lot of ground. Let's recap some of the concepts and their applications.

For truly **parallel execution**, you need multiple CPUs or cores. You also need to use either the `multiprocessing` or the `subinterpreters` package so that the Python interpreter can be executed in parallel.

Remember that startup time is significant, and each interpreter has a big memory overhead. If the tasks that you want to execute are short-lived, then use a pool of workers and a queue of tasks.

If you have multiple I/O-bound tasks and want them to run **concurrently**, then you should use multithreading or coroutines with the `asyncio` package.

All four of these approaches require an understanding of how to safely and efficiently transfer data between processes or threads. The best way to reinforce what you've learned is to look at an application you've written and see how it can be refactored to leverage these techniques.

Objects and Types

CPython comes with a collection of basic types like strings, lists, tuples, dictionaries, and objects. All these types are built in. You don't need to import any libraries, not even from the standard library.

For example, to create a new list, you can call `list()`:

```
lst = list()
```

Or you can use square brackets:

```
lst = []
```

Strings can be instantiated from a string literal by using either double or single quotes. In the chapter "The Python Language and Grammar," you explored the grammar definitions that cause the compiler to interpret double quotes as a string literal.

All types in Python inherit from `object`, a built-in base type. Even strings, tuples, and lists inherit from `object`.

In `Objects ▸ object.c`, the base implementation of the `object` type is written in pure C code. There are some concrete implementations of basic logic, like shallow comparisons.

You can think of a Python object as consisting of two things:

1. The core data model, with pointers to compiled functions

2. A dictionary with any custom attributes and methods

Much of the base object API is declared in `Objects ▸ object.c`, like the implementation of the built-in `repr()` function, `PyObject_Repr`. You'll also find `PyObject_Hash()` and other APIs.

All these functions can be overridden in a custom object by implementing **dunder methods** on a Python object:

```python
class MyObject(object):
    def __init__(self, id, name):
        self.id = id
        self.name = name

    def __repr__(self):
        return "<{0} id={1}>".format(self.name, self.id)
```

Together, these built-in functions are called the Python data model.[29] Not all methods in a Python object are part of the data model, which allows Python objects to contain class or instance attributes as well as methods.

> **See Also**
>
> One of the great resources for the Python data model is *Fluent Python, 2nd Edition,* by Luciano Ramalho.

Examples in This Chapter

Throughout this chapter, each type explanation will include an example. In the example, you'll implement the almost-equal operator that you built in earlier chapters.

If you haven't yet implemented the changes detailed in the chapters on the CPython grammar and compiler, then be sure to go back and do that before proceeding. They're required for implementing the examples below.

---

[29]https://docs.python.org/3/reference/datamodel.html

Built-in Types

The core data model is defined in the `PyTypeObject`, and the functions are defined in Objects ▸ `typeobject.c`.

Each of the source files has a corresponding header in `Include`. For example, `Objects/rangeobject.c` has a header file Include ▸ `rangeobject.h`.

Here's a list of the source files and their corresponding types:

Source file	Type
Objects ▸ object.c	Built-in methods and base object
Objects ▸ boolobject.c	bool type
Objects ▸ bytearrayobject.c	byte[] type
Objects ▸ bytesobject.c	bytes type
Objects ▸ cellobject.c	cell type
Objects ▸ classobject.c	Abstract class type used in meta-programming
Objects ▸ codeobject.c	Built-in code object type
Objects ▸ complexobject.c	Complex numeric type
Objects ▸ iterobject.c	Iterator type
Objects ▸ listobject.c	list type
Objects ▸ longobject.c	long numeric type
Objects ▸ memoryobject.c	Base memory type
Objects ▸ methodobject.c	Class method type
Objects ▸ moduleobject.c	Module type
Objects ▸ namespaceobject.c	Namespace type
Objects ▸ odictobject.c	Ordered dictionary type
Objects ▸ rangeobject.c	Range generator type
Objects ▸ setobject.c	set type
Objects ▸ sliceobject.c	Slice reference type
Objects ▸ structseq.c	struct.Struct type
Objects ▸ tupleobject.c	tuple type
Objects ▸ typeobject.c	type type
Objects ▸ unicodeobject.c	str type
Objects ▸ weakrefobject.c	weakref type

You'll explore some of these types in this chapter.

Object and Variable Object Types

Because C isn't an object-oriented language like Python,[30] objects in C don't inherit from one another. `PyObject` is the initial data segment for every Python object and `PyObject *` represents a pointer to it.

When defining Python types, the `typedef` uses one of two macros:

1. `PyObject_HEAD` (`PyObject`) for a simple type

2. `PyObject_VAR_HEAD` (`PyVarObject`) for a container type

The simple type `PyObject` has the following fields:

Field	Type	Purpose
ob_refcnt	Py_ssize_t	Instance reference counter
ob_type	_typeobject*	Object type

For example, the `cellobject` declares one additional field, `ob_ref`, and the base fields:

```
typedef struct {
    PyObject_HEAD
    PyObject *ob_ref;       /* Content of the cell or NULL when empty */
} PyCellObject;
```

The variable type, `PyVarObject`, extends the `PyObject` type and also has the following fields:

Field	Type	Purpose
ob_base	PyObject	Base type
ob_size	Py_ssize_t	Number of items it contains

For example, the `int` type, `PyLongObject`, has the following declaration:

---

[30]https://realpython.com/python3-object-oriented-programming/

```
struct _longobject {
    PyObject_VAR_HEAD
    digit ob_digit[1];
}; /* PyLongObject */
```

The type Type

In Python, objects have an ob_type property. You can get the value of this property using the built-in function type():

```
>>> t = type("hello")
>>> t
<class 'str'>
```

The result from type() is an instance of a PyTypeObject:

```
>>> type(t)
<class 'type'>
```

Type objects are used to define the implementation of abstract base classes.

For example, objects always implement the __repr__() method:

```
>>> class example:
...     x = 1
>>> i = example()
>>> repr(i)
'<__main__.example object at 0x10b418100>'
```

The implementation of __repr__() is always at the same address in the type definition of any object. This position is known as a **type slot**.

295

Type Slots

All the type slots are defined in Include ▸ cpython ▸ object.h.

Each type slot has a property name and a function signature. The
__repr__() function for example is called tp_repr and has a signature
reprfunc:

```
struct PyTypeObject
---
typedef struct _typeobject {

    ...

    reprfunc tp_repr;

    ...

} PyTypeObject;
```

The signature reprfunc is defined in Include ▸ cpython ▸ object.h as having
a single argument of PyObject* (self):

```
typedef PyObject *(*reprfunc)(PyObject *);
```

As an example, the cellobject implements the tp_repr slot with the
function cell_repr:

```
PyTypeObject PyCell_Type = {
    PyVarObject_HEAD_INIT(&PyType_Type, 0)
    "cell",
    sizeof(PyCellObject),
    0,
    (destructor)cell_dealloc,          /* tp_dealloc */
    0,                                 /* tp_vectorcall_offset */
    0,                                 /* tp_getattr */
    0,                                 /* tp_setattr */
    0,                                 /* tp_as_async */
    (reprfunc)cell_repr,               /* tp_repr */
    ...
};
```

Beyond the basic PyTypeObject type slots, denoted with the tp_ prefix,
there are other type slot definitions:

Type slot	Prefix
PyNumberMethods	nb_
PySequenceMethods	sq_
PyMappingMethods	mp_
PyAsyncMethods	am_
PyBufferProcs	bf_

All type slots are given a unique number, defined in Include ▸ types-lots.h. When referring to, or fetching, a type slot on an object, you should use these constants.

For example, tp_repr has a constant position of 66, and the constant Py_tp_repr always matches the type slot position. These constants are useful when checking if an object implements a particular type slot function.

Working With Types in C

Within C extension modules and the core CPython code, you'll frequently be working with the PyObject* type.

For example, if you run x[n] on a subscriptable object like a list or a string, then it will call PyObject_GetItem(), which looks at the object x to determine how to subscript it:

Objects ▸ abstract.c line 146

```
PyObject *
PyObject_GetItem(PyObject *o, PyObject *key)
{
    PyMappingMethods *m;
    PySequenceMethods *ms;
...
```

PyObject_GetItem() serves both mapping types, like dictionaries, and sequence types, like lists and tuples.

If the instance, o, has sequence methods, then o->ob_type->tp_as_sequence will evaluate to true. Also, if the instance has a sq_item slot function defined, then it's assumed that it has correctly implemented the sequence protocol.

The value of key is evaluated to check that it's an integer, and the item is requested from the sequence object using PySequence_GetItem():

```
ms = o->ob_type->tp_as_sequence;
if (ms && ms->sq_item) {
 if (PyIndex_Check(key)) {
        Py_ssize_t key_value;
        key_value = PyNumber_AsSsize_t(key, PyExc_IndexError);
        if (key_value == -1 && PyErr_Occurred())
            return NULL;
        return PySequence_GetItem(o, key_value);
    }
    else {
        return type_error("sequence index must "
                          "be integer, not '%.200s'", key);
    }
}
```

Type Property Dictionaries

Python supports defining new types with the class keyword. User-defined types are created by type_new() in the type object module.

User-defined types will have a property dictionary, accessed by __dict__(). Whenever a property is accessed on a custom class, the default __getattr__() implementation looks in this property dictionary. Class methods, instance methods, class properties, and instance properties are all located in this dictionary.

PyObject_GenericGetDict() implements the logic to fetch the dictionary instance for a given object. PyObject_GetAttr() implements the default __getattr__() implementation, and PyObject_SetAttr() implements __setattr__().

> ### See Also
>
> There are many layers to custom types, and they've been extensively documented. One could write an entire book on metaclasses, but in this book you'll stick to the implementation.
>
> If you want to learn more about metaprogramming, check out *Real Python*'s "Python Metaclasses."[a]
>
> ---
> [a]https://realpython.com/python-metaclasses/

The `bool` and `long` Types

The `bool` type is the most straightforward implementation of the built-in types. It inherits from `long` and has the predefined constants `Py_True` and `Py_False`. These constants are **immutable** instances, created on the instantiation of the Python interpreter.

Inside `Objects ▸ boolobject.c`, you can see the helper function to create a `bool` instance from a number:

`Objects ▸ boolobject.c` line 28

```c
PyObject *PyBool_FromLong(long ok)
{
    PyObject *result;

    if (ok)
        result = Py_True;
    else
        result = Py_False;
    Py_INCREF(result);
    return result;
}
```

This function uses the C evaluation of a numeric type to assign `Py_True` or `Py_False` to a result and increment the reference counters.

299

The numeric functions for and, xor, and or are implemented, but addition, subtraction, and division are dereferenced from the base long type since it would make no sense to divide two Boolean values.

The implementation of and for a bool value first checks if a and b are Booleans. If they aren't, then they're cast as numbers, and the and operation is run on the two numbers:

Objects ▸ boolobject.c line 61

```
static PyObject *
bool_and(PyObject *a, PyObject *b)
{
    if (!PyBool_Check(a) || !PyBool_Check(b))
        return PyLong_Type.tp_as_number->nb_and(a, b);
    return PyBool_FromLong((a == Py_True) & (b == Py_True));
}
```

The long Type

The long type is a bit more complex than bool. In the transition from Python 2 to Python 3, CPython dropped support for the int type and instead used the long type as the primary integer type.

Python's long type is quite special in that it can store a variable-length number. The maximum length is set in the compiled binary.

The data structure of a Python long consists of the PyObject variable header and a list of digits. The list of digits, ob_digit, is initially set to have one digit, but it later expands to a longer length when initialized:

Include ▸ longintrepr.h line 85

```
struct _longobject {
    PyObject_VAR_HEAD
    digit ob_digit[1];
};
```

For example, the number 1 would have ob_digit [1], and the number 24601 would have ob_digit [2, 4, 6, 0, 1].

Memory is allocated to a new long through _PyLong_New(). This function takes a fixed length and makes sure it's smaller than MAX_LONG_DIGITS. Then it reallocates the memory for ob_digit to match the length.

To convert a C long type to a Python long type, the C long is converted to a list of digits, the memory for the Python long is assigned, and then each of the digits is set.

For single-digit numbers, the long object is initialized with ob_digit already at a length of 1. Then the value is set without the memory being allocated:

Objects ▶ longobject.c line 297

```
PyObject *
PyLong_FromLong(long ival)
{
    PyLongObject *v;
    unsigned long abs_ival;
    unsigned long t;  /* unsigned so >> doesn't propagate sign bit */
    int ndigits = 0;
    int sign;

    CHECK_SMALL_INT(ival);
...
    /* Fast path for single-digit ints */
    if (!(abs_ival >> PyLong_SHIFT)) {
        v = _PyLong_New(1);
        if (v) {
            Py_SIZE(v) = sign;
            v->ob_digit[0] = Py_SAFE_DOWNCAST(
                abs_ival, unsigned long, digit);
        }
        return (PyObject*)v;
    }
```

...

```
/* Larger numbers: loop to determine number of digits */
t = abs_ival;
while (t) {
    ++ndigits;
    t >>= PyLong_SHIFT;
}
v = _PyLong_New(ndigits);
if (v != NULL) {
    digit *p = v->ob_digit;
    Py_SIZE(v) = ndigits*sign;
    t = abs_ival;
    while (t) {
        *p++ = Py_SAFE_DOWNCAST(
            t & PyLong_MASK, unsigned long, digit);
        t >>= PyLong_SHIFT;
    }
}
return (PyObject *)v;
}
```

To convert a double-point floating-point to a Python `long`, `PyLong_FromDouble()` does the math for you.

The remainder of the implementation functions in `Objects ▸ longobject.c` have utilities, such as converting a Unicode string into a number with `PyLong_FromUnicodeObject()`.

Example

The rich-comparison type slot for `long` is set to `long_richcompare()`. This function wraps `long_compare()`:

Objects ▸ longobject.c line 3031

```
static PyObject *
long_richcompare(PyObject *self, PyObject *other, int op)
{
    Py_ssize_t result;
    CHECK_BINOP(self, other);
    if (self == other)
        result = 0;
    else
        result = long_compare((PyLongObject*)self, (PyLongObject*)other);
    Py_RETURN_RICHCOMPARE(result, 0, op);
}
```

long_compare() will first check the length (number of digits) of the two variables a and b. If the lengths are the same, then it will loop through each digit to see if they're equal to each other.

long_compare() returns one of three types of values:

1. If a < b, then it returns a negative number.

2. If a == b, then it returns 0.

3. If a > b, the it returns a positive number.

For example, when you execute 1 == 5, the result is -4. For 5 == 1, the result is 4.

You can implement the following code block before the Py_RETURN_RICHCOMPARE macro to return True when the absolute value of result is <=1. It uses the macro Py_ABS(), which returns the absolute value of a signed integer:

```
if (op == Py_AlE) {
    if (Py_ABS(result) <= 1)
        Py_RETURN_TRUE;
    else
        Py_RETURN_FALSE;
}
```

```
    Py_RETURN_RICHCOMPARE(result, 0, op);
}
```

After recompiling Python, you should see the effect of the change:

```
>>> 2 == 1
False
>>> 2 ~= 1
True
>>> 2 ~= 10
False
```

The Unicode String Type

Python Unicode strings are complicated. Cross-platform Unicode types in any platform are complicated.

The cause of this complexity is the number of encodings that are on offer and the different default configurations on the platforms that Python supports.

The Python 2 string type was stored in C using the char type. The single-byte char type sufficiently stores any of the ASCII (American Standard Code for Information Interchange) characters and has been used in computer programming since the 1970s.

ASCII doesn't support the thousands of languages and character sets that are in use across the world. Also, there are extended glyph character sets like emojis that it can't support.

To address these issues, a standard system of coding and a database of characters known as the Unicode Standard was introduced by the Unicode Consortium in 1991. The modern Unicode Standard includes characters for all written languages as well as extended glyphs and characters.

The **Unicode Character Database** (UCD) contains 143,859 named characters as of version 13.0, compared with just 128 in ASCII. The

Unicode Standard defines these characters in a character table called the **Universal Character Set (UCS)**. Each character has a unique identifier known as a **code point**.

There are many different **encodings** that use the Unicode Standard and convert the code point into a binary value.

Python Unicode strings support three lengths of encodings:

1. 1-byte (8-bit)
2. 2-byte (16-bit)
3. 4-byte (32-bit)

These variable-length encodings are referred to within the implementation as the following:

1. 1-byte Py_UCS1, stored as 8-bit unsigned `int` type `uint8_t`
2. 2-byte Py_UCS2, stored as 16-bit unsigned `int` type `uint16_t`
3. 4-byte Py_UCS4, stored as 32-bit unsigned `int` type `uint32_t`

Related Source Files

Here are the source files related to strings:

File	Purpose
Include ▸ unicodeobject.h	Unicode string object definition
Include ▸ cpython ▸ unicodeobject.h	Unicode string object definition
Objects ▸ unicodeobject.c	Unicode string object implementation
Lib ▸ encodings	encodings package containing all the possible encodings
Lib ▸ codecs.py	Codecs module
Modules ▸ _codecsmodule.c	Codecs module C extensions, implements OS-specific encodings
Modules ▸ _codecs	Codec implementations for a range of alternative encodings

Processing Unicode Code Points

CPython doesn't contain a copy of the UCD, nor does it have to update whenever scripts and characters are added to the Unicode standard.

Unicode strings in CPython only have to care about the encodings. The operating system handles the task of representing the code points in the correct scripts.

The Unicode Standard includes the UCD and is updated regularly with new scripts, emojis, and characters. Operating systems take these updates to Unicode and update their software via a patch. These patches include the new UCD code points and support the various Unicode encodings. The UCD is split into sections called **code blocks**.

The Unicode code charts are published on the Unicode website.[31]

Another point of support for Unicode is the web browser. Web browsers decode HTML binary data in the encoding-marked HTTP encoding headers. If you're working with CPython as a web server, then your Unicode encodings must match the HTTP headers being sent to your users.

UTF-8 vs UTF-16

There are two common encodings:

1. **UTF-8** is an 8-bit character encoding that supports all possible characters in the UCD with a 1- to 4-byte code point

2. **UTF-16** is a 16-bit character encoding, similar to UTF-8, but is not compatible with 7- or 8-bit encodings like ASCII.

UTF-8 is the most commonly used Unicode encoding.

In all Unicode encodings, the code points can be represented using a hexadecimal shorthand. Here are a few examples:

[31]https://unicode.org/charts/

- **U+00F7** for the division character ('÷')

- **U+0107** for the Latin small letter c with acute ('ć')

In Python, Unicode code points can be encoded directly into the code using the \u escape symbol and the hexadecimal value of the code point:

```
>>> print("\u0107")
ć
```

CPython doesn't attempt to pad this data, so if you tried \u107, then it would give the following exception:

```
print("\u107")
  File "<stdin>", line 1
SyntaxError: (unicode error) 'unicodeescape' codec can't decode
    bytes in position 0-4: truncated \uXXXX escape
```

Both XML and HTML support Unicode code points with a special escape character &#val;, where val is the decimal value of the code point. If you need to encode Unicode code points into XML or HTML, then you can use the xmlcharrefreplace error handler in the .encode() method:

```
>>> "\u0107".encode('ascii', 'xmlcharrefreplace')
b'&#263;'
```

The output will contain HTML- or XML-escaped code points. All modern browsers will decode this escape sequence into the correct character.

ASCII Compatibility

If you're working with ASCII-encoded text, then it's important to understand the difference between UTF-8 and UTF-16. UTF-8 has the major benefit of being compatible with ASCII-encoded text. ASCII encoding is a 7-bit encoding.

The first 128 code points on the Unicode Standard represent the existing 128 characters of the ASCII standard. For example, the Latin letter "a" is the 97th character in ASCII and the 97th character in Unicode. Decimal 97 is equivalent to 61 in hexadecimal, so the Unicode code point for "a" is U+0061.

In the REPL, you can create the binary code for the letter "a":

```
>>> letter_a = b'a'
>>> letter_a.decode('utf8')
'a'
```

This can correctly be decoded into UTF-8.

UTF-16 works with 2- to 4-byte code points. The 1-byte representation of the letter "a" will not decode:

```
>>> letter_a.decode('utf16')
Traceback (most recent call last):
  File "<stdin>", line 1, in <module>
UnicodeDecodeError: 'utf-16-le' codec can't decode
    byte 0x61 in position 0: truncated data
```

This is important to note when selecting an encoding mechanism. UTF-8 is a safer option if you need to import ASCII-encoded data.

Wide Character Type

If you're handling Unicode string input in an unknown encoding within the CPython source code, then the wchar_t C type will be used.

wchar_t is the C standard for a wide-character string and is sufficient to store Unicode strings in memory. After PEP 393, the wchar_t type was selected as the Unicode storage format. The Unicode string object provides PyUnicode_FromWideChar(), a utility function that will convert a wchar_t constant to a string object.

For example, the pymain_run_command() used by python -c converts the -c argument into a Unicode string:

Modules ▸ main.c line 226

```
static int
pymain_run_command(wchar_t *command, PyCompilerFlags *cf)
{
    PyObject *unicode, *bytes;
    int ret;

    unicode = PyUnicode_FromWideChar(command, -1);
```

Byte Order Markers

When decoding an input, such as a file, CPython can detect the byte order from a byte order mark (BOM). BOMs are special characters that appear at the beginning of a Unicode byte stream. They tell the receiver which byte order the data is stored in.

Different computer systems can encode with different byte orders. If you use the wrong byte order, even with the right encoding, then the data will be garbled. A **big-endian** ordering places the most significant byte first. A **little-endian** ordering places the least significant byte first.

The UTF-8 specification does support a BOM, but it has no effect. The UTF-8 BOM can appear at the beginning of a encoded data sequence, represented as b'\xef\xbb\xbf', and will indicate to CPython that the data stream is most likely UTF-8. UTF-16 and UTF-32 support little- and big-endian BOMs.

The default byte order in CPython is set by the sys.byteorder global value:

```
>>> import sys; print(sys.byteorder)
little
```

The encodings Package

The encodings package in Lib ▸ encodings comes with more than one hundred built-in supported encodings for CPython. Whenever the .encode() or .decode() method is called on a string or byte string, the encoding is looked up from this package.

Each encoding is defined as a separate module. For example, ISO2022_JP is a widely used encoding for Japanese email systems and is declared in Lib ▸ encodings ▸ iso2022_jp.py.

Every encoding module will define a function getregentry() and register the following characteristics:

- Its unique name
- Its encode and decode functions from a codec module
- Its incremental encoder and decoder classes
- Its stream reader and stream writer classes

Many of the encoding modules share the same codecs from either the codecs module or the _mulitbytecodec module. Some encoding modules use a separate codec module in C, from Modules ▸ cjkcodecs.

For example, the ISO2022_JP encoding module imports a C extension module, _codecs_iso2022, from Modules ▸ cjkcodecs ▸ _codecs_iso2022.c:

```python
import _codecs_iso2022, codecs
import _multibytecodec as mbc

codec = _codecs_iso2022.getcodec('iso2022_jp')

class Codec(codecs.Codec):
    encode = codec.encode
    decode = codec.decode

class IncrementalEncoder(mbc.MultibyteIncrementalEncoder,
                         codecs.IncrementalEncoder):
    codec = codec

class IncrementalDecoder(mbc.MultibyteIncrementalDecoder,
                         codecs.IncrementalDecoder):
    codec = codec
```

The `encodings` package also has a module, Lib ▸ encodings ▸ aliases.py, that contains an `aliases` dictionary. This dictionary is used to map encodings in the registry by alternative names. For example, utf8, utf-8 and u8 are all aliases of the utf_8 encoding.

The Codecs Module

The `codecs` module handles the translation of data with a specific encoding. The encode or decode function of a particular encoding can be fetched using `getencoder()` and `getdecoder()`, respectively:

```
>>> iso2022_jp_encoder = codecs.getencoder('iso2022_jp')
>>> iso2022_jp_encoder('\u3072\u3068')  # hi-to
(b'\x1b$B$R$H\x1b(B', 2)
```

The encode function will return the binary result and the number of bytes in the output as a tuple. `codecs` also implements the built-in function `open()` for opening file handles from the operating system.

Codec Implementations

The Unicode object (Objects ▸ unicodeobject.c) implementation contains the following encoding methods:

Codec	Encoder
ascii	PyUnicode_EncodeASCII()
latin1	PyUnicode_EncodeLatin1()
UTF7	PyUnicode_EncodeUTF7()
UTF8	PyUnicode_EncodeUTF8()
UTF16	PyUnicode_EncodeUTF16()
UTF32	PyUnicode_EncodeUTF32()
unicode_escape	PyUnicode_EncodeUnicodeEscape()
raw_unicode_escape	PyUnicode_EncodeRawUnicodeEscape()

All decode methods would have similar names, but with Decode in place of Encode.

All decode methods would have similar names, but with Decode in place of `Encode`.

The implementation of the other encodings is within `Modules`▸`_codecs` to avoid cluttering the main Unicode string object implementation. The `unicode_escape` and `raw_unicode_escape` codecs are internal to CPython.

Internal Codecs

CPython comes with a number of internal encodings. These are unique to CPython and are useful for some of the standard library functions as well as when working with producing source code.

These text encodings can be used with any text input or output:

Codec	Purpose
idna	Implements RFC 3490
mbcs	Encode according to the ANSI codepage (Windows only)
raw_unicode_escape	Convert to a string for raw literal in Python source code
string_escape	Convert to a string literal for Python source code
undefined	Try default system encoding
unicode_escape	Convert to Unicode literal for Python source code
unicode_internal	Return the internal CPython representation

There are also several binary-only encodings that need to be used with `codecs.encode()` or `codecs.decode()` with byte string inputs, such as the following:

```
>>> codecs.encode(b'hello world', 'base64')
b'aGVsbG8gd29ybGQ=\n'
```

Here's a list of the binary-only encodings:

Codec	Aliases	Purpose
base64_codec	base64, base-64	Convert to MIME base64
bz2_codec	bz2	Compress the string using bz2
hex_codec	hex	Convert to hexadecimal representation, with two digits per byte
quopri_codec	quoted-printable	Convert operand to MIME quoted-printable
rot_13	rot13	Return the Caesar-cypher encryption (position 13)
uu_codec	uu	Convert using uuencode
zlib_codec	zip, zlib	Compress using gzip

Example

The `tp_richcompare` type slot is allocated to `PyUnicode_RichCompare()` in the `PyUnicode_Type`. This function does the comparison of strings and can be adapted to use the ~= operator. The behavior you'll implement is a case-insensitive comparison of the two strings.

First, add an additional case statement to check when the left and right strings have binary equivalence:

Objects ▸ unicodeobject.c line 11361

```
PyObject *
PyUnicode_RichCompare(PyObject *left, PyObject *right, int op)
{
    ...
    if (left == right) {
        switch (op) {
        case Py_EQ:
        case Py_LE:
>>>     case Py_AlE:
        case Py_GE:
            /* a string is equal to itself */
            Py_RETURN_TRUE;
```

Then add a new `else` `if` block to handle the Py_AIE operator. This will perform the following actions:

1. Convert the left string to a new uppercase string.

2. Convert the right string to a new uppercase string.

3. Compare the two.

4. Dereference both of the temporary strings so they get deallocated.

5. Return the result.

Your code should look like this:

```
else if (op == Py_EQ || op == Py_NE) {
    ...
}
/* Add these lines */
else if (op == Py_AIE){
    PyObject* upper_left = case_operation(left, do_upper);
    PyObject* upper_right = case_operation(right, do_upper);
    result = unicode_compare_eq(upper_left, upper_right);
    Py_DECREF(upper_left);
    Py_DECREF(upper_right);
    return PyBool_FromLong(result);
}
```

After you recompile, your case-insensitive string matching should give the following results on the REPL:

```
>>> "hello" ~= "HEllo"
True
>>> "hello?" ~= "hello"
False
```

The Dictionary Type

Dictionaries are a fast and flexible mapping type. They're used by developers to store and map data as well as by Python objects to store properties and methods.

Python dictionaries are also used for local and global variables, for keyword arguments, and for many other use cases. Python dictionaries are **compact**, meaning the hash table stores only mapped values.

The hashing algorithm that is part of all immutable built-in types is fast. It's what gives Python dictionaries their speed.

Hashing

All immutable built-in types provide a hashing function. This is defined in the tp_hash type slot or, for custom types, using the __hash__() magic method. Hash values are the same size as a pointer (64-bit for 64-bit systems, 32-bit for 32-bit systems), but they don't represent the memory address of their values.

The resulting hash for any Python Object shouldn't change during it's lifecycle. Hashes for two immutable instances with identical values should be equal:

```
>>> "hello".__hash__() == ("hel" + "lo").__hash__()
True
```

There should be no hash collisions. Two objects with different values should not produce the same hash.

Some hashes are simple, like Python longs:

```
>>> (401).__hash__()
401
```

Long hashes get more complex for longer values:

```
>>> (401123124389798989898).__hash__()
2212283795829936375
```

Many of the built-in types use the Python▸pyhash.c module, which provides the following hashing helper functions:

- **Bytes:** _Py_HashBytes(const void*, Py_ssize_t)

- **Doubles:** _Py_HashDouble(double)

- **Pointers:** _Py_HashPointer(void*)

Unicode strings, for example, use _Py_HashBytes() to hash the byte data of the string:

```
>>> ("hello").__hash__()
4894421526362833592
```

Custom classes can define a hashing function by implementing __hash__(). Instead of implementing a custom hash, custom classes should use a **unique** property. Make sure it's immutable by making it a read-only property, then hash it using the built-in hash():

```
class User:
    def __init__(self, id: int, name: str, address: str):
        self._id = id

    def __hash__(self):
        return hash(self._id)

    @property
    def id(self):
        return self._id
```

Instances of this class can now be hashed:

```
>>> bob = User(123884, "Bob Smith", "Townsville, QLD")
>>> hash(bob)
123884
```

This instance can now be used as a dictionary key:

```
>>> sally = User(123823, "Sally Smith", "Cairns, QLD")
>>> near_reef = {bob: False, sally: True}
>>> near_reef[bob]
False
```

Sets will reduce duplicate hashes of this instance:

```
>>> {bob, bob}
{<__main__.User object at 0x10df244b0>}
```

Related Source Files

Here are the source files related to dictionaries:

File	Purpose
Include ▸ dictobject.h	Dictionary object API definition
Include ▸ cpython ▸ dictobject.h	Dictionary object types definition
Objects ▸ dictobject.c	Dictionary object implementation
Objects ▸ dict-common.h	Definition of key entry and key objects
Python ▸ pyhash.c	Internal hashing algorithm

Dictionary Structure

A dictionary object, PyDictObject, comprises the following elements:

1. The dictionary object properties, containing the size, a version tag, and the keys and values

2. A dictionary key table object, PyDictKeysObject, containing the keys and hash values of all entries

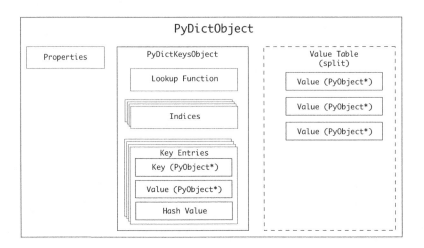

The `PyDictObject` has the following properties:

Field	Type	Purpose
ma_keys	PyDictKeysObject*	Dictionary key table object
ma_used	Py_ssize_t	Number of items in the dictionary
ma_values	PyObject**	Optional value array (see note)
ma_version_tag	uint64_t	Version number of the dictionary

Note

Dictionaries can have one of two states: split or combined. When dictionaries are combined, the pointers to the dictionary values are stored in the keys object.

When the dictionary is split, the values are stored in an extra property, `ma_values`, as a value table of `PyObject*`.

The dictionary key table, `PyDictKeysObject`, has the following properties:

Field	Type	Purpose
dk_entries	PyDictKeyEntry[]	Allocated array of dictionary key entries
dk_indices	char[]	Hash table and mapping to dk_entries
dk_lookup	dict_lookup_func	The lookup function (see next section)
dk_nentries	Py_ssize_t	The number of used entries in the entry table
dk_refcnt	Py_ssize_t	Reference counter
dk_size	Py_ssize_t	The size of the hash table
dk_usable	Py_ssize_t	The number of usable entries in the entry table—when 0, dictionary is resized

A dictionary key entry, `PyDictKeyEntry`, contains the following properties:

Field	Type	Purpose
me_hash	Py_ssize_t	Cached hash code of me_key
me_key	PyObject*	Pointer to the key object
me_value	PyObject*	Pointer to the value object (if combined)

Lookups

For a given key object, there is a generic lookup function: `lookdict()`.

Dictionary lookups need to cater to three scenarios:

1. The memory address of the key exists in the key table.
2. The hash value of the object exists in the key table.
3. The key does not exist in the dictionary.

> **See Also**
>
> The lookup function is based on Donald Knuth's famous book *The Art of Computer Programming*. See chapter 6, section 4, on hashing.

319

Here's the sequence of the lookup function:

1. Get the hash value of `ob`.

2. Look up the hash value of `ob` in the dictionary keys and get the index, `ix`.

3. If `ix` is empty, then return `DKIX_EMPTY` (not found).

4. Get the key entry, `ep`, for the given index.

5. If the key values match because the object, then `ob` is the same pointer at the key value. Return the result.

6. If the key hashes match because the object, `ob`, resolves to the same hash value as `ep->me_mash`, then return the result.

> **Note**
>
> `lookupdict()` is one of few **hot** functions in the CPython source code:
>
> > The `hot` attribute is used to inform the compiler that a function is a hot spot of the compiled program. The function is optimized more aggressively and on many targets it is placed into special subsection of the text section so all hot functions appear close together, improving locality.
> >
> > — GCC documentation, "Common Function Attributes"
>
> This is specific to GNU C compilers, but when compiled with PGO, this function is likely to be optimized by the compiler automatically.

Conclusion

Now that you've seen the implementation of some built-in types, you're ready to explore others.

When exploring Python classes, it's important to remember that there are built-in types written in C and classes inheriting from those types written in Python or C.

Some libraries have types written in C instead of inheriting from the built-in types. One example is NumPy, a library for numeric arrays. The `nparray` type is written in C and is highly efficient and performant.

In the next chapter, you'll explore the classes and functions defined in the standard library.

The Standard Library

Python has always come *batteries included*. This means that a standard CPython distribution includes libraries for working with files, threads, networks, websites, music, keyboards, screens, text, and a whole range of utilities.

Some of the batteries that come with CPython are like AA batteries, useful for almost any occasion. Examples include the `collections` module and the `sys` module. But some of them are a bit more obscure, making them more like small watch batteries: you never know when you might need them.

There are two types of modules in the CPython standard library:

1. Those written in pure Python that provide a utility
2. Those written in C with Python wrappers

You'll explore both types in this chapter.

Python Modules

The modules written in pure Python are all located in the `Lib` directory in the source code. Some of the larger modules have submodules in subfolders, like the `email` module.

A straightforward module that you may not have come across before is the `colorsys` module. It's only a hundred lines of Python code and contains some utility functions for converting color scales.

When you install a Python distribution from source, standard library modules are copied from the Lib folder into the distribution folder. This folder is always part of your path when you start Python, so you can import the modules without having to worry about where they're located.

For example, here's how you import and use colorsys:

```
>>> import colorsys
>>> colorsys
<module 'colorsys' from '/usr/shared/lib/python3.7/colorsys.py'>

>>> colorsys.rgb_to_hls(255,0,0)
(0.0, 127.5, -1.007905138339921)
```

You can see the source code of rgb_to_hls() inside Lib ▸ colorsys.py:

```
# HLS: Hue, Luminance, Saturation
# H: position in the spectrum
# L: color lightness
# S: color saturation


def rgb_to_hls(r, g, b):
    maxc = max(r, g, b)
    minc = min(r, g, b)
    # XXX Can optimize (maxc+minc) and (maxc-minc)
    l = (minc+maxc)/2.0
    if minc == maxc:
        return 0.0, l, 0.0
    if l <= 0.5:
        s = (maxc-minc) / (maxc+minc)
    else:
        s = (maxc-minc) / (2.0-maxc-minc)
    rc = (maxc-r) / (maxc-minc)
    gc = (maxc-g) / (maxc-minc)
    bc = (maxc-b) / (maxc-minc)
    if r == maxc:
        h = bc-gc
```

```
elif g == maxc:
    h = 2.0+rc-bc
else:
    h = 4.0+gc-rc
h = (h/6.0) % 1.0
return h, l, s
```

There's nothing special about this function—it's just standard Python. You'll find a similar situation for all the pure Python standard library modules. They're just written in plain Python, well laid out and uncomplicated to understand.

You may even spot improvements or bugs in standard library modules. If so, you can make changes and contribute them to the Python distribution. You'll cover that toward the end of this book.

Python and C Modules

The remainder of modules are written in C or a combination of Python and C. The source code is in Lib for the Python component and in Modules for the C component. There are two exceptions:

1. The **sys** module, found in Python ▶ sysmodule.c

2. The **__builtins__** module, found in Python ▶ bltinmodule.c

Because the sys module is so specific to the interpreter and the internals of CPython, it's found inside the Python directory. It's also marked as an "implementation detail" of CPython and not found in other distributions.

Python will import * from __builtins__ when an interpreter is instantiated, so all the built-in functions like print(), chr(), format(), and so forth are found within Python ▶ bltinmodule.c.

The built-in function print() was probably the first feature you learned to use in Python. So what exactly happens when you type print("Hello, World")?

Here's a breakdown:

1. The compiler converts the argument `"Hello, World"` from a string constant to a `PyUnicodeObject`.

2. `builtin_print()` is executed with one argument and `NULL` kwnames

3. The `file` variable is set to `PyId_stdout`, the system's stdout handle.

4. Each argument is sent to `file`.

5. A line break (`\n`) is sent to `file`.

Here's how it works:

Python ▸ `bltinmodule.c` line 1828

```c
static PyObject *
builtin_print(PyObject *self, PyObject *const *args,
    Py_ssize_t nargs, PyObject *kwnames)
{
    ...
    if (file == NULL || file == Py_None) {
        file = _PySys_GetObjectId(&PyId_stdout);
        ...
    }
    ...
    for (i = 0; i < nargs; i++) {
        if (i > 0) {
            if (sep == NULL)
                err = PyFile_WriteString(" ", file);
            else
                err = PyFile_WriteObject(sep, file,
                                    Py_PRINT_RAW);
            if (err)
                return NULL;
        }
        err = PyFile_WriteObject(args[i], file, Py_PRINT_RAW);
        if (err)
            return NULL;
    }
```

```
    if (end == NULL)
        err = PyFile_WriteString("\n", file);
    else
        err = PyFile_WriteObject(end, file, Py_PRINT_RAW);
    ...
    Py_RETURN_NONE;
}
```

The contents of some modules written in C expose operating system functions. Because the CPython source code needs to compile to macOS, Windows, Linux, and other *nix-based operating systems, there are some special cases.

The time module is a good example. The way that Windows keeps and stores time in the operating system is fundamentally different from Linux and macOS. This is one of the reasons the accuracy of the clock functions differs between operating systems.[32]

In Modules ▸ timemodule.c, the operating system time functions for Unix-based systems are imported from <sys/times.h>:

```
#ifdef HAVE_SYS_TIMES_H
#include <sys/times.h>
#endif
...
#ifdef MS_WINDOWS
#define WIN32_LEAN_AND_MEAN
#include <windows.h>
#include "pythread.h"
#endif /* MS_WINDOWS */
...
```

Later in the file, time_process_time_ns() is defined as a wrapper for _Py-Time_GetProcessTimeWithInfo():

[32]https://docs.python.org/3/library/time.html#time.clock_gettime_ns

```
static PyObject *
time_process_time_ns(PyObject *self, PyObject *unused)
{
    _PyTime_t t;
    if (_PyTime_GetProcessTimeWithInfo(&t, NULL) < 0) {
        return NULL;
    }
    return _PyTime_AsNanosecondsObject(t);
}
```

_PyTime_GetProcessTimeWithInfo() is implemented multiple different ways in the source code, but only certain parts are compiled into the binary for the module depending on the operating system. Windows systems will call GetProcessTimes(), and Unix systems will call clock_gettime().

Other modules that have multiple implementations for the same API are the threading module,[33] the file system module, and the networking modules. Because the operating systems behave differently, the CPython source code implements the same behavior as best as it can and exposes it using a consistent, abstracted API.

---

[33]https://realpython.com/intro-to-python-threading/

The Test Suite

CPython has a robust test suite covering the core interpreter, the standard library, the tooling, and the distribution for Windows, Linux, and macOS. It's located in Lib ▸ test and is written mostly in Python. The full test suite is a Python package, so you can run it using the Python interpreter that you've compiled.

Running the Test Suite on Windows

On Windows, use the rt.bat script inside the PCBuild folder. For example, here's how to run the quick mode against the Debug configuration on an x64 architecture:

```
> cd PCbuild
> rt.bat -q -d -x64

== CPython 3.9
== Windows-10-10.0.17134-SP0 little-endian
== cwd: C:\repos\cpython\build\test_python_2784
== CPU count: 2
== encodings: locale=cp1252, FS=utf-8
Run tests sequentially
0:00:00 [  1/420] test_grammar
0:00:00 [  2/420] test_opcodes
0:00:00 [  3/420] test_dict
0:00:00 [  4/420] test_builtin
  ...
```

329

To run the regression test suite against the Release configuration, remove the -d flag from the command line.

Running the Test Suite on Linux or macOS

On Linux and macOS, run the test make target to compile and run the tests:

```
$ make test
== CPython 3.9
== macOS-10.14.3-x86_64-i386-64bit little-endian
== cwd: /Users/anthonyshaw/cpython/build/test_python_23399
== CPU count: 4
== encodings: locale=UTF-8, FS=utf-8
0:00:00 load avg: 2.14 [  1/420] test_opcodes passed
0:00:00 load avg: 2.14 [  2/420] test_grammar passed
 ...
```

Alternatively, use the python or python.exe compiled binary path with the test package:

```
$ ./python -m test
== CPython 3.9
== macOS-10.14.3-x86_64-i386-64bit little-endian
== cwd: /Users/anthonyshaw/cpython/build/test_python_23399
== CPU count: 4
== encodings: locale=UTF-8, FS=utf-8
0:00:00 load avg: 2.14 [  1/420] test_opcodes passed
0:00:00 load avg: 2.14 [  2/420] test_grammar passed
 ...
```

There are additional make targets for testing:

Target	Purpose
test	Run a basic set of regression tests
testall	Run the full test suite twice—once without .pyc files and once with
quicktest	Run a faster set of regression tests, excluding the tests that take a long time
testuniversal	Run the test suite for both architectures in a universal build on OSX
coverage	Compile and run tests with gcov
coverage-lcov	Create coverage HTML reports

Test Flags

Some tests require certain flags or else they're skipped. For example, many of the IDLE tests require a GUI.

To see a list of test suites in the configuration, use the --list-tests flag:

```
$ ./python -m test --list-tests
```

```
test_grammar
test_opcodes
test_dict
test_builtin
test_exceptions
...
```

Running Specific Tests

You can run specific tests by providing the test suite as the first argument.

Here's an example on Linux or macOS:

```
$ ./python -m test test_webbrowser

Run tests sequentially
0:00:00 load avg: 2.74 [1/1] test_webbrowser

== Tests result: SUCCESS ==

1 test OK.

Total duration: 117 ms
Tests result: SUCCESS
```

Here's an example on Windows:

```
> rt.bat -q -d -x64 test_webbrowser
```

You can also see a detailed list of tests that were executed, along with the result, using the -v argument:

```
$ ./python -m test test_webbrowser -v

== CPython 3.9
== macOS-10.14.3-x86_64-i386-64bit little-endian
== cwd: /Users/anthonyshaw/cpython/build/test_python_24562
== CPU count: 4
== encodings: locale=UTF-8, FS=utf-8
Run tests sequentially
0:00:00 load avg: 2.36 [1/1] test_webbrowser
test_open (test.test_webbrowser.BackgroundBrowserCommandTest) ...ok
test_register (test.test_webbrowser.BrowserRegistrationTest) ...ok
test_register_default (test.test_webbrowser.BrowserRegistrationTest) ...ok
test_register_preferred (test.test_webbrowser.BrowserRegistrationTest) ...ok
test_open (test.test_webbrowser.ChromeCommandTest) ...ok
test_open_new (test.test_webbrowser.ChromeCommandTest) ...ok
...
test_open_with_autoraise_false (test.test_webbrowser.OperaCommandTest) ...ok

-----------------------------------------------------------------------
```

```
Ran 34 tests in 0.056s

OK (skipped=2)

== Tests result: SUCCESS ==

1 test OK.

Total duration: 134 ms
Tests result: SUCCESS
```

Understanding how to use the test suite and check the state of the version you've compiled is very important if you wish to make changes to CPython. Before you start making changes, you should run the whole test suite and make sure everything passes.

Testing Modules

For C extension or Python modules, you can import and test them using the unittest module. Tests are assembled by module or package.

For example, the Python Unicode string type has tests in Lib ▸ test ▸ test_unicode.py. The asyncio package has a test package in Lib ▸ test ▸ test_asyncio.

> ### See Also
>
> If you're new to the unittest module or testing in Python, then check out *Real Python*'s "Getting Started With Testing in Python."[a]
>
> ---
> [a]https://realpython.com/python-testing/

Here's an excerpt from the `UnicodeTest` class:

```
class UnicodeTest(string_tests.CommonTest,
        string_tests.MixinStrUnicodeUserStringTest,
        string_tests.MixinStrUnicodeTest,
        unittest.TestCase):
...
    def test_casefold(self):
        self.assertEqual('hello'.casefold(), 'hello')
        self.assertEqual('hELlo'.casefold(), 'hello')
        self.assertEqual('ß'.casefold(), 'ss')
        self.assertEqual('fi'.casefold(), 'fi')
```

You can extend the almost-equal operator that you implemented for Python Unicode strings in earlier chapters by adding a new test method inside the `UnicodeTest` class:

```
    def test_almost_equals(self):
        self.assertTrue('hello' ~= 'hello')
        self.assertTrue('hELlo' ~= 'hello')
        self.assertFalse('hELlo!' ~= 'hello')
```

You can run this particular test module on Windows:

```
> rt.bat -q -d -x64 test_unicode
```

Or you can run it on macOS or Linux:

```
$ ./python -m test test_unicode -v
```

Test Utilities

By importing the `test.support.script_helper` module, you can access some helper functions for testing the Python runtime:

- **assert_python_ok(*args, **env_vars)** executes a Python process with the specified arguments and returns a (return code, `stdout`, `stderr`) tuple.

- **assert_python_failure(*args, **env_vars)** is similar to assert_python_ok() but asserts that it fails to execute.

- **make_script(script_dir, script_basename, source)** makes a script in script_dir with the script_basename and the source, then returns the script path. It's useful to combine with assert_python_ok() or assert_python_failure().

If you want to create a test that will be skipped if the module wasn't built, then you can use the test.support.import_module() utility function. It will raise a SkipTest and signal the test runner to skip this test package. Here's an example:

```
import test.support

_multiprocessing = test.support.import_module('_multiprocessing')

# Your tests...
```

Conclusion

The Python regression test suite is full of two decades' worth of tests for strange edge cases, bug fixes, and new features. Outside of this, there's still a large part of the CPython standard library that has little or no testing. If you want to get involved in the CPython project, then writing or extending unit tests is a great place to start.

If you're going to modify any part of CPython or add additional functionality, then you'll need to have written or extended tests as part of your patch.

Debugging

CPython comes with a built-in debugger, pdb, for debugging Python applications. The pdb debugger is excellent for debugging crashes inside a Python application, as well as for writing tests and inspecting local variables.

When it comes to CPython, though, you need a second debugger—one that understands C.

In this chapter, you'll learn how to:

• Attach a debugger to the CPython interpreter

• Use the debugger to see inside a running CPython process

There are two types of debugger: console and visual. **Console debuggers** (like pdb) give you a command prompt and custom commands to explore variables and the stack. **Visual debuggers** are GUI applications that present the data in grids.

The following debuggers are covered in this chapter:

Debugger	Type	Platform
LLDB	Console	macOS
GDB	Console	Linux
Visual Studio debugger	Visual	Windows
CLion debugger	Visual	Windows, macOS, Linux

Using the Crash Handler

In C, if an application tries to read or write to an area of memory that it shouldn't, then a **segmentation fault** is raised. This fault halts the running process immediately to stop it from doing any damage to other applications. Segmentation faults can also happen when you try to read from memory that contains no data or an invalid pointer.

If CPython causes a segmentation fault, then you get very little information about what happened:

```
[1]    63476 segmentation fault  ./python portscanner.py
```

CPython comes with a built-in fault handler. If you start CPython with -X faulthandler or -X dev, then instead of printing the system segmentation fault message, the fault handler will print the running threads and the Python stack trace to where the fault occurred:

```
Fatal Python error: Segmentation fault
Thread 0x0000000119021dc0 (most recent call first):
  File "/cpython/Lib/threading.py", line 1039 in _wait_for_tstate_lock
  File "/cpython/Lib/threading.py", line 1023 in join
  File "/cpython/portscanner.py", line 26 in main
  File "/cpython/portscanner.py", line 32 in <module>
[1]    63540 segmentation fault  ./python -X dev portscanner.py
```

This feature is also helpful when developing and testing C extensions for CPython.

Compiling Debug Support

To get meaningful information from the debugger, you must compile the debug symbols into CPython. Without these symbols, the stack traces within a debug session won't contain the correct function names, variable names, or filenames.

Windows

Following the same steps as you did in the Windows section of the chapter on Compiling CPython, ensure that you've compiled in the Debug configuration to get the debug symbols:

```
> build.bat -p x64 -c Debug
```

Remember, the Debug configuration produces the executable python_d.exe, so make sure you use this executable for debugging.

macOS or Linux

The steps in the chapter on Compiling CPython specify to run the ./configure script with the --with-pydebug flag. If you didn't include this flag, then go back and run ./configure again with your original options and the --with-pydebug flag. This will produce the correct executable and symbols for debugging.

Using LLDB for macOS

The LLDB debugger comes with the Xcode developer tools, so you should already have it installed.

Start LLDB and load the CPython compiled binary as the target:

```
$ lldb ./python.exe
(lldb) target create "./python.exe"
Current executable set to './python.exe' (x86_64).
```

You'll now have a prompt where you can enter some commands for debugging.

Creating Breakpoints

To create a breakpoint, use the break set command with the file (relative to the root) and the line number:

```
(lldb) break set --file Objects/floatobject.c --line 532
Breakpoint 1: where = python.exe`float_richcompare + 2276 at
    floatobject.c:532:26, address = 0x000000010006a974
```

> **Note**
>
> There's also a shorthand for setting breakpoints: `(lldb) b Ob-
> jects/floatobject.c:532`

You can add multiple breakpoints using the `break set` command. To
list the current breakpoints, use the `break list` command:

```
(lldb) break list
Current breakpoints:
1: file = 'Objects/floatobject.c', line = 532, exact_match = 0, locations = 1
   1.1: where = python.exe`float_richcompare + 2276 at floatobject.c:532:26,
             address = python.exe[...], unresolved, hit count = 0
```

Starting CPython

To start CPython, use the `process launch --` command with the
command-line options you would normally use for Python.

To start Python with a string, such as `python -c "print(1)"`, use the
following command:

```
(lldb) process launch -- -c "print(1)"
```

To start python with a script, use the following command:

```
(lldb) process launch -- my_script.py
```

Attaching to a Running CPython Interpreter

If you already have a CPython interpreter running, then you can attach to it.

From inside the LLDB session, run `process attach --pid` with the process ID:

```
(lldb) process attach --pid 123
```

You can get the process ID from the Activity Monitor or by using `os.getpid()` in Python.

Any breakpoints set up before or after this point will halt the process.

Handling a Breakpoint

To see how breakpoints are handled, set a breakpoint on the `Objects`▸ `floatobject.c float_richcompare()` function.

Next, run the process and compare two float values using the almost-equal operator that you developed in previous chapters:

```
(lldb) process launch -- -c "1.0~=1.1"
Process 64421 launched: '/cpython/python.exe' (x86_64)
Process 64421 stopped
* thread #1, queue = '...', stop reason = breakpoint 1.1
    frame #0: 0x000000010006a974 python.exe`float_richcompare(v=1.0,
        w=1.1, op=6) at floatobject.c:532:26
   529              break;
   530      case Py_AlE: {
   531              double diff = fabs(i - j);
-> 532              const double rel_tol = 1e-9;
   533              const double abs_tol = 0.1;
   534              r = (((diff <= fabs(rel_tol * j)) ||
Target 0: (python.exe) stopped.
```

LLDB will give you a prompt again. You can see the local variables by using the `v` command:

```
(lldb) v
(PyObject *) v = 0x000000010111b370 1.0
(PyObject *) w = 0x000000010111b340 1.1
(int) op = 6
(double) i = 1
(double) j = 1.1000000000000001
```

```
(int) r = 0
(double) diff = 0.10000000000000009
(const double) rel_tol = 2.1256294105914498E-314
(const double) abs_tol = 0
```

You can evaluate a C expression using the expr command with any valid C command. The variables in scope can be used. For example, to call fabs(rel_tol) and cast to a double, run the following command:

```
(lldb) expr (double)fabs(rel_tol)
(double) $1 = 2.1256294105914498E-314
```

This prints the resulting variable and assigns it an identifier ($1). You can reuse this identifier as a temporary variable.

You may also want to explore PyObject instances:

```
(lldb) expr v->ob_type->tp_name
(const char *) $6 = 0x000000010034fc26 "float"
```

To get a traceback from the breakpoint, use the bt command:

```
(lldb) bt
* thread #1, queue = '...', stop reason = breakpoint 1.1
  * frame #0: ...
        python.exe`float_richcompare(...) at floatobject.c:532:26
    frame #1: ...
        python.exe`do_richcompare(...) at object.c:796:15
    frame #2: ...
        python.exe`PyObject_RichCompare(...) at object.c:846:21
    frame #3: ...
        python.exe`cmp_outcome(...) at ceval.c:4998:16
```

To step in, use the step command or s.

To step over or continue to the next statement, use the next command or n.

To continue execution, use the continue command or c.

To exit the session, use the `quit` command or `q`.

> **See Also**
>
> The LLDB Documentation Tutorial[a] contains a more exhaustive list of commands.
>
> ---
> [a]https://lldb.llvm.org/use/tutorial.html

Using the `cpython_lldb` Extension

LLDB supports extensions written in Python. There's an open source extension, `cpython_lldb`, that prints additional information in the LLDB session for native CPython objects.

To install it, run these commands:

```
$ mkdir -p ~/.lldb
$ cd ~/.lldb && git clone https://github.com/malor/cpython-lldb
$ echo "command script import ~/.lldb/cpython-lldb/cpython_lldb.py" \
  >> ~/.lldbinit
$ chmod +x ~/.lldbinit
```

Now, whenever you see variables in LLDB, you'll also see some additional information to the right, such as the numeric value for integers and floating-point numbers or the text for Unicode strings. Within a LLDB console, you also have an additional command, `py-bt`, that prints the stack trace for Python frames.

Using GDB

GDB is a commonly used debugger for C/C++ applications written on Linux platforms. It's also very popular with the CPython core development team.

When CPython is compiled, it generates a script, `python-gdb.py`. Don't execute this script directly. Instead, GDB will discover it and run it automatically once configured.

To configure this stage, edit the .gdbinit file inside your home path (~/.gdbinit) and add the following line, where /path/to/checkout is the path to the cpython git checkout:

```
add-auto-load-safe-path /path/to/checkout
```

To start GDB, run it with the argument pointing to your compiled CPython binary:

```
$ gdb ./python
```

GDB will load the symbols for the compiled binary and give you a command prompt. GDB has a set of built-in commands, and the CPython extensions bundle some additional commands.

Creating Breakpoints

To set a breakpoint, use the b <file>:<line> command relative to the path of the executable:

```
(gdb) b Objects/floatobject.c:532
Breakpoint 1 at 0x10006a974: file Objects/floatobject.c, line 532.
```

You can set as many breakpoints as you wish.

Starting CPython

To start the process, use the run command followed by arguments to start the Python interpreter.

For example, use the following command to start with a string:

```
(gdb) run -c "print(1)"
```

To start python with a script, use the following command:

```
(gdb) run my_script.py
```

Attaching to a Running CPython Interpreter

If you already have a CPython interpreter running, then you can attach to it.

From inside the GDB session, run `attach` with the process ID:

```
(gdb) attach 123
```

You can get the process ID from the Activity Monitor or by using `os.getpid()` in Python.

Any breakpoints set up before or after this point will halt the process.

Handling a Breakpoint

When GDB hits a breakpoint, you can use the `print` command or `p` to print a variable:

```
(gdb) p *(PyLongObject*)v
$1 = {ob_base = {ob_base = {ob_refcnt = 8, ob_type = ...}, ob_size = 1},
ob_digit = {42}}
```

To step into the next statement, use the `step` command or `s`.

To step over the next statement, use the `next` command or `n`.

Using the `python-gdb` Extension

The `python-gdb` extension will load an additional command set into the GDB console:

Command	Purpose
py-print	Look up a Python variable and print it
py-bt	Print a Python stack trace
py-locals	Print the result of `locals()`
py-up	Go down one Python frame
py-down	Go up one Python frame
py-list	Print the Python source code for the current frame

345

Using Visual Studio Debugger

Microsoft Visual Studio comes bundled with a visual debugger. This debugger is powerful and supports a frame stack visualizer, a watch list, and the ability to evaluate expressions.

To use it, open Visual Studio and the PCBuild ▸ pcbuild.sln solution file.

Adding Breakpoints

To add a new breakpoint, navigate to the file you want in the solution window, then click in the gutter to the left of the line number.

This adds a red circle to indicate you've set a breakpoint on the line:

```
354     */
355
356     static PyObject*
357   ⊟float_richcompare(PyObject *v, PyObject *w, int op)
358     {
359         double i, j;
360         int r = 0;
361
●  362         assert(PyFloat_Check(v));
363         i = PyFloat_AS_DOUBLE(v);
364
365   ⊟     /* Switch on the type of w.  Set i and j to doubles to be compared,
366          * and op to the richcomp to use.
367          */
368         if (PyFloat_Check(w))
369             j = PyFloat_AS_DOUBLE(w);
370
371   ⊟     else if (!Py_IS_FINITE(i)) {
```

When you hover over the red circle, a cog appears. Click this cog to configure conditional breakpoints. Add one or more conditional expressions that must evaluate before this breakpoint hits:

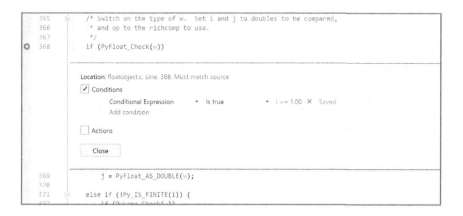

Starting the Debugger

From the top menu, select Debug >> Start Debugger or press F5 .

Visual Studio will start a new Python runtime and REPL.

Handling a Breakpoint

When you hit a breakpoint, you can step forward and into statements using the navigation buttons or the following shortcuts:

- **Step into:** F11
- **Step over:** F10
- **Step out:** Shift + F11

You'll see a call stack at the bottom. You can select frames in the stack to change the navigation and inspect variables in other frames:

347

In the code editor, you can highlight any variable or expression to see its value. You can also right-click and select $\boxed{\text{Add Watch}}$. This adds the variable to the Watch window, where you can quickly see the values of variables you need to help you debug:

Using CLion Debugger

The CLion IDE comes bundled with a powerful visual debugger. It works with LLDB on macOS and GDB on macOS, Windows, and Linux.

To configure the debugger, go to Preferences and select $\boxed{\text{Build, Execution, Deployment} \gg \text{Toolchains}}$:

There is a selection box for the target debugger. Select the appropriate option for your operating system:

- **macOS:** Bundled LLDB
- **Windows or Linux:** Bundled GDB

> **Important**
>
> Both the LLDB and GDB options benefit from the `cpython_lldb` and `python-gdb` extensions, respectively. Read the LLDB and GDB sections in this chapter for information on how to install and enable these extensions.

Debugging a Make Application

From CLion 2020.2, you can compile and debug any makefile-based project, including CPython.

To start debugging, complete the steps in the "Setting Up JetBrains CLion" section in the chapter "Setting Up Your Development Environment."

After completing these steps, you'll have a Make Application target. Select Run ⟩ Debug from the top menu to start the process and start debugging.

Alternatively, you can attach the debugger to a running CPython process.

Attaching the Debugger

To attach the CLion debugger to a running CPython process, select Run ⟩ Attach to Process.

A list of running processes will pop up. Find the Python process you want to attach to and select Attach. The debugging session will begin.

Important

If you have the Python plugin installed, it will show the Python process at the top. Don't select this one!

This uses the Python debugger, not the C debugger:

Instead, scroll further down into the Native list and find the correct Python process.

Creating Breakpoints

To create a breakpoint, navigate to the file and line you want, then click in the gutter between the line number and the code. A red circle will appear to indicate the breakpoint is set:

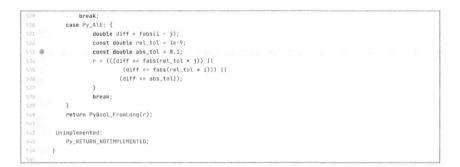

Right-click the breakpoint to attach a condition:

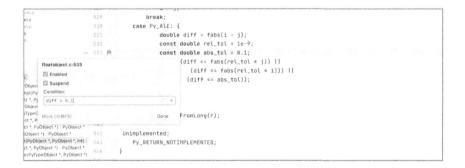

To see and manage all current breakpoints, navigate from the top menu to `Run` ⟩ `View Breakpoints`:

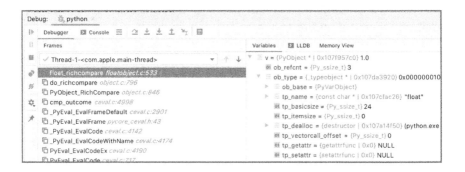

You can enable and disable breakpoints as well as disable them once another breakpoint has been hit.

Handling Breakpoints

Once a breakpoint has been hit, CLion will set up the Debug panel. Inside the Debug panel is a call stack showing where the breakpoint hit. You can select other frames in the call stack to switch between them.

Next to the call stack are the local variables. You can expand the properties of pointers and type structures, and the value of simple types will be shown:

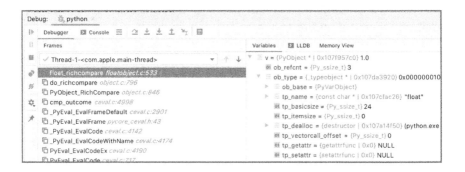

Within a break, you can evaluate expressions to get more information about the local variables. You can find the Evaluate window in `Run` `Debugging Actions` `Evaluate Expression` or in a shortcut icon in the Debug window.

Inside the Evaluate window, you can type expressions, and CLion will type-ahead with the property names and types:

You can also cast expressions, which is useful for casting `PyObject*` into the actual type, such as into a `PyFloatObject*`:

Conclusion

In this chapter, you've seen how to set up a debugger on all the major operating systems. While the initial setup is time-consuming, the reward is great. Being able to set breakpoints and explore variables and memory for a running CPython process will give you superpowers.

You can use this skill to extend CPython, optimize existing parts of the codebase, or track down nasty bugs.

Benchmarking, Profiling, and Tracing

When making changes to CPython, you need to verify that your changes don't have a significant detrimental impact on performance. You may even want to make changes to CPython that improve performance.

There are solutions for profiling that you'll cover in this chapter:

1. Using the `timeit` module to check a simple Python statement thousands of times for the median execution speed

2. Running `pyperformance`, the Python Benchmark Suite, to compare multiple versions of Python

3. Using `cProfile` to analyze execution times of frames

4. Profiling the CPython execution with probes

The choice of solution depends on the type of task:

- A **benchmark** will produce an average or median runtime of a fixed code snippet so that you can compare multiple Python runtimes.

- A **profiler** will produce a call graph with execution times so that you can understand which function is the slowest.

Profilers are available at a C level or a Python level. If you're profiling a function, module, or script written in Python, then you want to use a Python profiler. If you're profiling a C extension module or a modification to the C code in CPython, then you need to use a C profiler or a combination of C and Python profilers.

Here is a summary of some of the tools available:

Tool	Category	Level	OS support
timeit	Benchmarking	Python	All
pyperformance	Benchmarking	Python	All
cProfile	Profiling	Python	All
DTrace	Tracing/profiling	C	Linux, macOS

> **Important**
>
> Before you run any benchmarks, it's best to close down all applications on your computer so the CPU is dedicated to the benchmark.

Using `timeit` for Microbenchmarks

The Python Benchmark Suite is a thorough test of CPython's runtime with multiple iterations. If you want to run a quick, simple comparison of a specific snippet, then use the `timeit` module instead.

To run `timeit` for a short script, run the compiled CPython with the `-m` `timeit` module and a script in quotes:

```
$ ./python -m timeit -c "x=1; x+=1; x**x"
1000000 loops, best of 5: 258 nsec per loop
```

To run a smaller number of loops, use the -n flag:

```
$ ./python -m timeit -n 1000 "x=1; x+=1; x**x"
1000 loops, best of 5: 227 nsec per loop
```

`timeit` **Example**

In this book, you've introduced changes to the `float` type by supporting the almost-equal operator.

Try this test to see the current performance of comparing two float values:

```
$ ./python -m timeit -n 1000 "x=1.0001; y=1.0000; x~=y"
1000 loops, best of 5: 177 nsec per loop
```

The implementation of this comparison is in `float_richcompare()`, inside Objects ▸ floatobject.c:

Objects ▸ floatobject.c line 358

```
static PyObject*
float_richcompare(PyObject *v, PyObject *w, int op)
{
    ...
    case Py_AlE: {
            double diff = fabs(i - j);
            double rel_tol = 1e-9;
            double abs_tol = 0.1;
            r = (((diff <= fabs(rel_tol * j)) ||
                    (diff <= fabs(rel_tol * i))) ||
                    (diff <= abs_tol));
        }
        break;
    }
```

Notice that the `rel_tol` and `abs_tol` values are constant but haven't been marked as such. Change them to the following:

```
const double rel_tol = 1e-9;
const double abs_tol = 0.1;
```

Now compile CPython again and rerun the test:

```
$ ./python -m timeit -n 1000 "x=1.0001; y=1.0000; x~=y"
1000 loops, best of 5: 172 nsec per loop
```

You might notice a minor (1 to 5 percent) improvement in performance. Experiment with different implementations of the comparison to see if you can improve it further.

Using the Python Benchmark Suite for Runtime Benchmarks

The Python Benchmark Suite is the tool to use when you want to compare the complete performance of Python. The Python Benchmark suite is a collection of Python applications designed to test multiple aspects of the Python runtime under load.

The Benchmark Suite tests are pure Python, so they can be used to test multiple runtimes, such as PyPy and Jython. They're also compatible with Python 2.7 up to the latest version.

Any commits to the master branch on github.com/python/cpython will be tested using the benchmark tool, and the results will be uploaded to the Python Speed Center:[34]

---

[34]https://speed.python.org

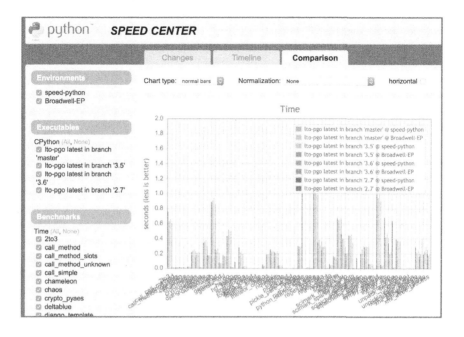

You can compare commits, branches, and tags side by side using the Speed Center. The benchmarks use both the profile-guided optimization and regular builds with a fixed hardware configuration to produce stable comparisons.

You can install the Python Benchmark Suite from PyPI using a Python runtime (other than the one you're testing) in a virtual environment:

```
(venv) $ pip install pyperformance
```

Next, you need to create a configuration file and an output directory for the test profile. It's recommended that you create this directory outside of your Git working directory. This will also allow you to check out multiple versions.

In the configuration file, for example `~/benchmarks/benchmark.cfg`, add the following lines:

cpython-book-samples ▸ 62 ▸ benchmark.cfg

```
[config]
# Path to output json files
json_dir = ~/benchmarks/json

# If True, then compile CPython in Debug mode (LTO and PGO disabled),
# run benchmarks with --debug-single-sample, and disable upload.
#
# Use this option to quickly test a configuration.
debug = False


[scm]
# Directory of CPython source code (Git repository)
repo_dir = ~/cpython

# Update the Git repository (git fetch)?
update = False

# Name of the Git remote, used to create revision of
# the Git branch.
git_remote = remotes/origin


[compile]
# Create files in bench_dir:
bench_dir = ~/benchmarks/tmp

# Link-time optimization (LTO)?
lto = True

# Profile-guided optimization (PGO)?
pgo = True

# The space-separated list of libraries that are package only
pkg_only =

# Install Python? If False, then run Python from the build directory
install = True
```

```
[run_benchmark]
# Run "sudo python3 -m pyperf system tune" before running benchmarks?
system_tune = True

# --benchmarks option for 'pyperformance run'
benchmarks =

# --affinity option for 'pyperf system tune' and 'pyperformance run'
affinity =

# Upload generated JSON file?
upload = False

# Configuration to upload results to a Codespeed website
[upload]
url =
environment =
executable =
project =

[compile_all]
# List of CPython Git branches
branches = default 3.6 3.5 2.7

# List of revisions to benchmark by compile_all
[compile_all_revisions]
# List of 'sha1=' (default branch: 'master') or 'sha1=branch'
# used by the "pyperformance compile_all" command
```

Executing the Benchmark

Once you've set up your configuration file, you can run the benchmark with the following command:

```
$ pyperformance compile -U ~/benchmarks/benchmark.cfg HEAD
```

361

This will compile CPython in the `repo_dir` directory you specified and create the JSON output with the benchmark data in the directory specified in the config file.

Comparing Benchmarks

If you want to compare JSON results, the Python Benchmark Suite doesn't come with a graphing solution. Instead, you can use the following script from within a virtual environment.

First, install the dependencies:

```
$ pip install seaborn pandas pyperformance
```

Then create a `profile.py` script:

cpython-book-samples ▸ 62 ▸ profile.py

```python
import argparse
from pathlib import Path
from perf._bench import BenchmarkSuite

import seaborn as sns
import pandas as pd

sns.set(style="whitegrid")

parser = argparse.ArgumentParser()
parser.add_argument("files", metavar="N", type=str, nargs="+",
                    help="files to compare")
args = parser.parse_args()

benchmark_names = []
records = []
first = True
for f in args.files:
    benchmark_suite = BenchmarkSuite.load(f)
    if first:
```

```python
            # Initialize the dictionary keys to the benchmark names
            benchmark_names = benchmark_suite.get_benchmark_names()
            first = False
        bench_name = Path(benchmark_suite.filename).name
    for name in benchmark_names:
        try:
            benchmark = benchmark_suite.get_benchmark(name)
            if benchmark is not None:
                records.append({
                    "test": name,
                    "runtime": bench_name.replace(".json", ""),
                    "stdev": benchmark.stdev(),
                    "mean": benchmark.mean(),
                    "median": benchmark.median()
                })
        except KeyError:
            # Bonus benchmark! Ignore.
            pass

df = pd.DataFrame(records)

for test in benchmark_names:
    g = sns.factorplot(
        x="runtime",
        y="mean",
        data=df[df["test"] == test],
        palette="YlGnBu_d",
        size=12,
        aspect=1,
        kind="bar")
    g.despine(left=True)
    g.savefig("png/{}-result.png".format(test))
```

Then, to create a graph, run the script from the interpreter with the
JSON files you've created:

```
$ python profile.py ~/benchmarks/json/HEAD.json ...
```

This will produce a series of graphs in the subdirectory png/ for each executed benchmark.

Profiling Python Code With cProfile

The standard library comes with two profilers for Python code:

1. **profile:** A pure Python profiler
2. **cProfile:** A faster profiler written in C

In most cases, cProfile is the best module to use.

You can use cProfile to analyze a running application and collect deterministic profiles on the evaluated frames. You can display a summary of the output from cProfile on the command line or save it to a .pstat file for analysis in an external tool.

In the chapter "Parallelism and Concurrency," you wrote a port scanner application in Python. Try profiling that application in cProfile.

To run the cProfile module, run python at the command line with the -m cProfile argument. The second argument is the script to execute:

```
$ python -m cProfile portscanner_threads.py
Port 80 is open
Completed scan in 19.8901150226593 seconds
        6833 function calls (6787 primitive calls) in 19.971 seconds

   Ordered by: standard name

   ncalls  tottime  percall  cumtime  percall filename:lineno(function)
        2    0.000    0.000    0.000    0.000 ...
```

The output will print a table with the following columns:

Column	Purpose
`ncalls`	Number of calls
`tottime`	Total time spent in the function (minus subfunctions)
`percall`	Quotient of `tottime` divided by `ncalls`
`cumtime`	Total time spent in the function (including subfunctions)
`percall`	Quotient of `cumtime` divided by primitive calls
`filename:lineno(function)`	Data of each function

You can add the `-s` argument and the column name to sort the output:

```
$ python -m cProfile -s tottime portscanner_threads.py
```

This command will sort the output by the total time spent in each function.

Exporting Profiles

You can run the `cProfile` module again with the `-o` argument to specify an output file path:

```
$ python -m cProfile -o out.pstat portscanner_threads.py
```

This will create a file, `out.pstat`, that you can load and analyze with the `Stats` class[35] or with an external tool.

Visualizing With SnakeViz

SnakeViz is a free Python package for visualizing profile data inside a web browser.

To install SnakeViz, use `pip`:

```
$ python -m pip install snakeviz
```

---

[35]https://docs.python.org/3.9/library/profile.html#the-stats-class

Then execute `snakeviz` on the command line with the path to the stats file you created:

```
$ python -m snakeviz out.pstat
```

This will open your browser and allow you to explore and analyze the data:

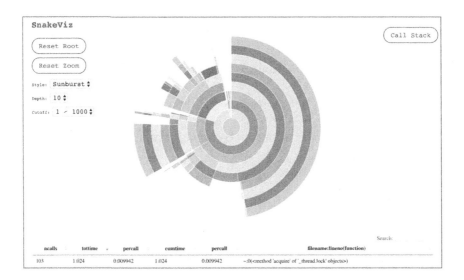

Visualizing With PyCharm

PyCharm has a built-in tool for running `cProfile` and visualizing the results. To execute it, you need to have a Python target configured.

To run the profiler, select your run target, then select `Run` `Profile (target)` from the top menu. This will execute the run target with `cProfile` and open a visualization window with the tabular data and a call graph:

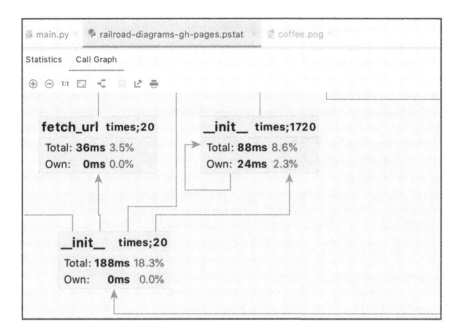

Profiling C Code With DTrace

The CPython source code has several markers for the DTrace tracing tool. DTrace executes a compiled C/C++ binary, then catches and handles events within it using **probes**.

For DTrace to provide meaningful data, the compiled application must have custom **markers** compiled into the application. These are events raised during the runtime. The markers can attach arbitrary data to help with tracing.

For example, the frame evaluation function in Python ▸ ceval.c includes a call to dtrace_function_entry():

```
if (PyDTrace_FUNCTION_ENTRY_ENABLED())
    dtrace_function_entry(f);
```

This raises a marker called function_entry in DTrace every time a function is entered.

CPython has built-in markers for:

- Line execution

- Function entry and return (frame execution)

- Garbage collection start and completion

- Module import start and completion

- Audit hook events from `sys.audit()`

Each of these markers has arguments with more information. For example, the `function_entry` marker has arguments for:

- Filename

- Function name

- Line number

The static marker arguments are defined in the official documentation.[36]

DTrace can execute a script file written in D to execute custom code when probes are triggered. You can also filter out probes based on their attributes.

Related Source Files

Here are the source files related to DTrace:

File	Purpose
Include ▸ `pydtrace.h`	API definition for DTrace markers
Include ▸ `pydtrace.d`	Metadata for the Python provider that DTrace uses
Include ▸ `pydtrace_probes.h`	Auto-generated headers for handling probes

---

[36]https://realpython.com/cpython-static-markers

Installing DTrace

DTrace comes preinstalled on macOS and can be installed on Linux using one of the packaging tools.

Here's the command for YUM-based systems:

```
$ yum install systemtap-sdt-devel
```

Here's the command for APT-based systems:

```
$ apt-get install systemtap-sdt-dev
```

Compiling DTrace Support

DTrace support must be compiled into CPython. You can do this with the ./configuration script.

Run ./configure again with the same arguments you used in the chapter "Compiling CPython," and add the flag --with-dtrace. Once this is complete, run make clean && make to rebuild the binary.

Check that the configuration tool created the probe header:

```
$ ls Include/pydtrace_probes.h
Include/pydtrace_probes.h
```

Important

Newer versions of macOS have kernel-level protection, called System Integrity Protection (SIP), that interferes with DTrace.

The examples in this chapter use the CPython probes. If you want to include libc or syscall probes to get extra information, then you'll need to disable SIP.

369

Using DTrace From CLion

The CLion IDE includes DTrace support. To start tracing, select `Run ⟩` `⟩Attach Profiler to Process` and select the running Python process.

The profiler window will prompt you to start and then stop the tracing session. Once tracing is complete, it will provide you with a flame graph showing execution stacks and call times, a call tree, and a method list:

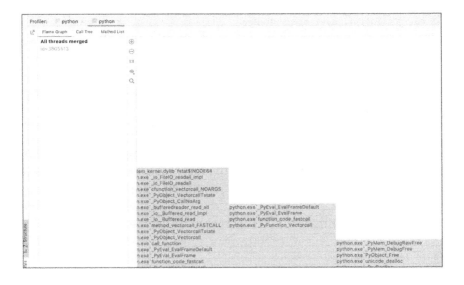

DTrace Example

In this example, you'll test the multithreaded port scanner you created in the chapter "Parallelism and Concurrency."

Create a profile script in D, `profile_compare.d`. To reduce the noise from the interpreter startup, this profiler will start when `portscanner_threads.py:main()` is entered:

cpython-book-samples ▸ 62 ▸ profile_compare.d

```
#pragma D option quiet
self int indent;
```

370

```
python$target:::function-entry
/basename(copyinstr(arg0)) == "portscanner_threads.py"
 && copyinstr(arg1) == "main"/
{
    self->trace = 1;
    self->last = timestamp;
}

python$target:::function-entry
/self->trace/
{
    this->delta = (timestamp - self->last) / 1000;
    printf("%d\t%*s:", this->delta, 15, probename);
    printf("%*s", self->indent, "");
    printf("%s:%s:%d\n", basename(copyinstr(arg0)), copyinstr(arg1), arg2);
    self->indent++;
    self->last = timestamp;
}

python$target:::function-return
/self->trace/
{
    this->delta = (timestamp - self->last) / 1000;
    self->indent--;
    printf("%d\t%*s:", this->delta, 15, probename);
    printf("%*s", self->indent, "");
    printf("%s:%s:%d\n", basename(copyinstr(arg0)), copyinstr(arg1), arg2);
    self->last = timestamp;
}

python$target:::function-return
/basename(copyinstr(arg0)) == "portscanner_threads.py"
 && copyinstr(arg1) == "main"/
{
    self->trace = 0;
}
```

This script will print a line every time a function is executed and time the delta between when the function starts and exits.

You need to execute with the script argument -s profile_compare and the command argument -c './python portscanner_threads.py':

```
$ sudo dtrace -s profile_compare.d -c './python portscanner_threads.py'
0    function-entry:portscanner_threads.py:main:16
28    function-entry: queue.py:__init__:33
18    function-entry:  queue.py:_init:205
29   function-return:  queue.py:_init:206
46    function-entry:   threading.py:__init__:223
33   function-return:   threading.py:__init__:245
27    function-entry:   threading.py:__init__:223
26   function-return:   threading.py:__init__:245
26    function-entry:   threading.py:__init__:223
25   function-return:   threading.py:__init__:245
```

> **Important**
>
> Older versions of DTrace may not have a -c option. In this case, you will have to run DTrace and the Python command in separate shells.

In the output, the first column is the time delta in microseconds since the last event, followed by the event name, filename, and line number. When function calls are nested, the filename will be increasingly indented to the right.

Conclusion

In this chapter, you've explored benchmarking, profiling, and tracing using a number of tools designed for CPython. With the right tooling, you can find bottlenecks, compare performance of multiple builds, and identify improvement opportunities.

Next Steps

In this chapter, you'll look at three possible uses for the information in this book:

1. Writing C or C++ extension modules

2. Improving your Python applications

3. Contributing to the CPython project

The first practical use of this knowledge is to write extension modules in C or C++.

Writing C Extensions for CPython

There are several ways in which you can extend the functionality of Python. One of these is to write your Python module in C or C++. This process can lead to improved performance and better access to C library functions and system calls.

If you want to write a C extension module, then these are some essentials bits of knowledge covered in this book that you can refer back to:

- **How to set up a C compiler and compile C modules** from the chapter "Compiling CPython"

- **How to set up your development environment for C** from the chapter "Setting Up Your Development Environment"

- **How to increment and decrement references to generated objects** from the "Reference Counting" section in the chapter "Memory Management"

- **What PyObject* is and what its interfaces are** from the "Object and Variable Object Types" section in the chapter "Objects and Types" chapter

- **What type slots are and how to access Python type APIs from C** from the "Type Slots" section in the "Objects and Types" chapter

- **How to add breakpoints to C source files for your extension module and debug them** from the "Debugging" chapter

---

See Also

If you haven't written a C extension module before, then check out *Real Python*'s "Building a C Extension Module."[a] The tutorial includes a concrete example of building, compiling, and testing an extension module.

---

[a]https://realpython.com/build-python-c-extension-module

Improving Your Python Applications

There are several important topics covered in this book that can help you improve your applications. Here are some examples:

- **Using parallelism and concurrency techniques to reduce the execution time of your applications** from the "Parallelism and Concurrency" chapter

- **Customizing the garbage collector algorithm to better handle memory in your application by collecting at the end of a task** from the "Garbage Collection" section in the "Memory Management" chapter

- **Using the debuggers to debug C extensions and triage issues** from the "Debugging" chapter

- **Using profilers to profile the execution time of your code** from the "Profiling Python Code with cProfile" section of the "Benchmarking, Profiling, and Tracing" chapter

- **Analyzing frame execution to inspect and debug complex issues** from the "Frame Execution Tracing" section in the "Evaluation Loop" chapter

Contributing to the CPython Project

In twelve months, CPython had twelve new minor releases, hundreds of changes and bug reports, and thousands of commits to the source code.

CPython is one of the biggest, most vibrant, and most open software projects out there. The knowledge you've gained in this book will give you a massive head start to navigating, understanding, and helping improve the CPython project.

The CPython community is eager for more contributors. But before submitting a change, improvement, or fix to CPython, you need to know where to start. Here are a few ideas:

1. Triaging issues raised by developers on bugs.python.org

2. Fixing small, well-described issues

Let's explore each of those in a bit more detail.

Triaging Issues

All bug reports and change requests are first submitted to bugs.python.org, also known as BPO. This website is the bug tracker for the CPython Project. If you want to submit a pull request on GitHub, then you first need a **BPO number**, which is the issue number created by BPO (bugs.python.org).

To get started, register yourself as a user by going to User ⟫ Register on the left menu.

The default view isn't particularly productive and shows both issues raised by users and those raised by core developers, which likely already have a fix.

Instead, after logging in, go to Your Queries ⟩ Edit on the left menu. This page will give you a list of queries for the bug index that you can bookmark:

Query	
Patches	leave out
pending issues	leave out
serverhorror's Reports	leave out
Easy Tasks	leave out
Showstoppers	leave out
Latest issues	include
Release Blockers	leave out
Critical	leave out
py3k-open	leave out
Needs review	leave out
Crashers	leave in
Open Doc Bugs 2.6	leave out
Opened patches	leave out

Change the value to `leave  in` to include these queries in the Your Queries menu.

Here are some of the queries I find useful:

- **Easy Documentation Issues:** Documentation improvements that haven't been made
- **Easy Tasks:** Tasks that have been identified as good for beginners
- **Recently Created:** Recently created issues
- **Reports Without Replies:** Bug reports that never got a reply
- **Unread:** Bug reports that never got read
- **50 Latest Issues:** The fifty most recently updated issues

With these views, you can follow the "Triaging an Issue"[37] guide for the latest process on commenting on issues.

---

[37]https://devguide.python.org/triaging/

Raising a Pull Request to Fix an Issue

When you've settled on an issue, you can get started on creating a fix and submitting it to the CPython project. Here's the process:

1. Make sure you have a BPO number.

2. Create a branch on your fork of CPython. See the "Getting the Source Code" chapter for steps on downloading the source code.

3. Create a test to reproduce the issue. See the "Testing Modules" section of the "Test Suite" chapter for steps.

4. Make your change following the PEP 7 and PEP 8 style guides.

5. Run the regression test suite to confirm all the tests are passing. The regression test suite will automatically run on GitHub when you submit the pull request, but it's better to check it locally first. See the "Test Suite" chapter for steps.

6. Commit and push your changes to GitHub.

7. Go to github.com/python/cpython and create a pull request for your branch.

After you submit your pull request, it will be triaged by one of the triage teams and assigned to a core developer or team for review.

As mentioned earlier, the CPython project needs more contributors. The time between when you submit your change and when it's reviewed could be an hour, a week, or many months. Don't be dismayed if you don't get an immediate response. Most of the core developers are volunteers and tend to review or merge pull requests in batches.

> **Important**
>
> It's important to fix only one issue per pull request. If you see a separate, unrelated issue in some code while writing your patch, make a note and submit it as a second pull request.

To help get your change merged quickly, a good explanation of the problem, the solution, and the fix goes a long way.

Other Contributions

Other than bug fixes, there are some different types of improvements you can make to the CPython project:

- Many of the standard library functions and modules are missing unit tests. You can write some tests and submit them to the project.

- Many of the standard library functions don't have up-to-date documentation. You can update the documentation and submit a change.

Keep Learning

Part of what makes Python so great is the community. Know someone learning Python? Help them out! The only way to know you've really mastered a concept is to explain it to someone else.

Come visit us on the Web and continue your Python journey on the realpython.com website and the @realpython Twitter account.

Weekly Tips for Python Developers

Are you looking for a weekly dose of Python development tips to improve your productivity and streamline your workflows? Good news: we're running a free email newsletter for Python developers just like you.

The newsletter emails we send out are not just your typical list of popular articles. Instead, we aim to share at least one original thought per week in a (short) essay-style format.

If you'd like to see what all the fuss is about, then head on over to realpython.com/newsletter and enter your email address in the signup form. We're looking forward to meeting you!

The Real Python Video Course Library

Become a well-rounded Pythonista with the large (and growing) collection of Python tutorials and in-depth training materials at *Real Python*. With new content published weekly, you'll always find something to boost your skills:

- **Master practical, real-world Python skills:** Our tutorials are created, curated, and vetted by a community of expert Pythonistas. At *Real Python*, you'll get the trusted resources you need on your path to Python mastery.

- **Meet other Pythonistas:** Join the *Real Python* Slack chat and meet the *Real Python* team and other subscribers. Discuss your coding and career questions, vote on upcoming tutorial topics, or just hang out with us at this virtual water cooler.

- **Interactive quizzes & Learning Paths:** See where you stand and practice what you learn with interactive quizzes, hands-on coding challenges, and skill-focused learning paths.

- **Track your learning progress:** Mark lessons as completed or in-progress and learn at your own pace. Bookmark interesting lessons and review them later to boost long-term retention.

- **Completion certificates:** For each course you complete, you receive a shareable (and printable) certificate of completion, hosted privately on the *Real Python* website. Embed your certificates in your portfolio, LinkedIn resume, and other websites to show the world that you're a dedicated Pythonista.

- **Regularly updated:** Keep your skills fresh and keep up with technology. We're constantly releasing new members-only tutorials and update our content regularly.

See what's available at `realpython.com/courses`

Appendix: Introduction to C for Python Programmers

This introduction is intended to get an experienced Python programmer up to speed with the basics of the C language and how it's used in the CPython source code. It assumes you already have an intermediate understanding of Python syntax.

That said, C is a fairly limited language, and most of its usage in CPython falls under a small set of syntax rules. Getting to the point where you understand the code is a much smaller step than being able to write C effectively. This tutorial is aimed at the first goal but not the second.

One of the first things that stands out as a big difference between Python and C is the C preprocessor. Let's look at that first.

The C Preprocessor

The preprocessor, as the name suggests, is run on your source files before the compiler runs. It has very limited abilities, but you can use them to great advantage in building C programs.

The preprocessor produces a new file, which is what the compiler will actually process. All the commands to the preprocessor start at the beginning of a line, with a # symbol as the first non-whitespace character.

The main purpose of the preprocessor is to do text substitution in the source file, but it will also do some basic conditional code with #if or similar statements.

Let's start with the most frequent preprocessor directive: #include.

#include

#include is used to pull the contents of one file into the current source file. There's nothing sophisticated about #include. It reads a file from the file system, runs the preprocessor on that file, and puts the results into the output file. This is done recursively for each #include directive.

For example, if you look at the Modules/_multiprocessing/semaphore.c file, then near the top you'll see the following line:

```
#include "multiprocessing.h"
```

This tells the preprocessor to pull in the entire contents of multiprocessing.h and put them into the output file at this position.

You'll notice two different forms for the #include statement. One of them uses quotes ("") to specify the name of the include file, and the other uses angle brackets (<>). The difference comes from which paths are searched when looking for the file on the file system.

If you use <> for the filename, then the preprocessor will look only at system include files. Using quotes around the filename instead will force the preprocessor to look in the local directory first and then fall back to the system directories.

#define

#define allows you to do simple text substitution and also plays into the #if directives you'll see below.

At its most basic, #define lets you define a new symbol that gets replaced with a text string in the preprocessor output.

Continuing in `semphore.c`, you'll find this line:

```
#define SEM_FAILED NULL
```

This tells the preprocessor to replace every instance of SEM_FAILED below this point with the literal string NULL before the code is sent to the compiler.

#define items can also take parameters as in this Windows-specific version of SEM_CREATE:

```
#define SEM_CREATE(name, val, max) CreateSemaphore(NULL, val, max, NULL)
```

In this case, the preprocessor will expect SEM_CREATE() to look like a function call and have three parameters. This is generally referred to as a **macro**. It will directly replace the text of the three parameters into the output code.

For example, on line 460 of `semphore.c`, the SEM_CREATE macro is used like this:

```
handle = SEM_CREATE(name, value, max);
```

When you're compiling for Windows, this macro will be expanded so that line looks like this:

```
handle = CreateSemaphore(NULL, value, max, NULL);
```

In a later section, you'll see how this macro is defined differently on Windows and other operating systems.

#undef

This directive erases any previous preprocessor definition from #define. This makes it possible to have a #define in effect for only part of a file.

#if

The preprocessor also allows conditional statements, allowing you to either include or exclude sections of text based on certain conditions. Conditional statements are closed with the #endif directive and can also make use of #elif and #else for fine-tuned adjustments.

There are three basic forms of #if that you'll see in the CPython source:

1. #ifdef <macro> includes the subsequent block of text if the specified macro is defined. You may also see it written as #if defined(<macro>).

2. #ifndef <macro> includes the subsequent block of text if the specified macro is **not** defined.

3. #if <macro> includes the subsequent block of text if the macro is defined **and** it evaluates to True.

Note the use of "text" instead of "code" to describe what's included or excluded from the file. The preprocessor knows nothing of C syntax and doesn't care what the specified text is.

#pragma

Pragmas are instructions or hints to the compiler. In general, you can ignore these while reading the code as they usually deal with how the code is compiled, not how the code runs.

#error

Finally, #error displays a message and causes the preprocessor to stop executing. Again, you can safely ignore these for reading the CPython source code.

Basic C Syntax

This section won't cover *all* aspects of C, nor is it intended to teach you how to write C. It will focus on aspects of C that are different or confusing for Python developers the first time they see them.

General

Unlike in Python, whitespace isn't important to the C compiler. The compiler doesn't care if you split statements across lines or jam your entire program into a single, very long line. This is because it uses delimiters for all statements and blocks.

There are, of course, very specific rules for the parser, but in general you'll be able to understand the CPython source just knowing that each statement ends with a semicolon (;), and all blocks of code are surrounded by curly braces ({}).

The exception to this rule is that if a block has only a single statement, then the curly braces can be omitted.

All variables in C must be **declared**, meaning there needs to be a single statement indicating the **type** of that variable. Note that, unlike Python, the data type that a single variable can hold can't change.

Let's look at some examples:

```
/* Comments are included between slash-asterisk and asterisk-slash */
/* This style of comment can span several lines -
   so this part is still a comment. */

// Comments can also come after two slashes
// This type of comment only goes until the end of the line, so new
// lines must start with double slashes (//).

int x = 0; // declares x to be of type 'int' and initializes it to 0

if (x == 0) {
```

```
    // This is a block of code
    int y = 1;  // y is only a valid variable name until the closing }
    // More statements here
    printf("x is %d y is %d\n", x, y);
}


// Single-line blocks do not require curly brackets
if (x == 13)
    printf("x is 13!\n");
printf("past the if block\n");
```

In general, you'll see that the CPython code is very cleanly formatted and typically sticks to a single style within a given module.

if Statements

In C, if works generally like it does in Python. If the condition is true, then the following block is executed. The else and elseif syntax should be familiar enough to Python programmers. Note that C if statements don't need an endif because blocks are delimited by {}.

There's a shorthand in C for short if ... else statements called the **ternary operator**:

```
condition ? true_result : false_result
```

You can find it in semaphore.c where, for Windows, it defines a macro for SEM_CLOSE():

```
#define SEM_CLOSE(sem) (CloseHandle(sem) ? 0 : -1)
```

The return value of this macro will be 0 if the function CloseHandle() returns true and -1 otherwise.

> **Note**
>
> Boolean variable types are supported and used in parts of the CPython source, but they aren't part of the original language. C interprets binary conditions using a simple rule: 0 or NULL is false, and everything else is true.

switch **Statements**

Unlike Python, C also supports switch. Using switch can be viewed as a shortcut for extended if ... elseif chains. This example is from semaphore.c:

```
switch (WaitForSingleObjectEx(handle, 0, FALSE)) {
case WAIT_OBJECT_0:
    if (!ReleaseSemaphore(handle, 1, &previous))
        return MP_STANDARD_ERROR;
    *value = previous + 1;
    return 0;
case WAIT_TIMEOUT:
    *value = 0;
    return 0;
default:
    return MP_STANDARD_ERROR;
}
```

This performs a switch on the return value from WaitForSingleObjectEx(). If the value is WAIT_OBJECT_0, then the first block is executed. The WAIT_TIMEOUT value results in the second block, and anything else matches the default block.

Note that the value being tested, in this case the return value from WaitForSingleObjectEx(), must be an integral value or an enumerated type, and each case must be a constant value.

Loops

There are three looping structures in C:

1. `for` loops

2. `while` loops

3. `do ... while` loops

Let's look at each of these in turn.

`for` loops have syntax that's quite different from Python:

```
for ( <initialization>; <condition>; <increment>) {
    <code to be looped over>
}
```

In addition to the code to be executed in the loop, there are three blocks of code that control the `for` loop:

1. The `<initialization>` section runs exactly once when the loop is started. It's typically used to set a loop counter to an initial value (and possibly to declare the loop counter).

2. The `<increment>` code runs immediately after each pass through the main block of the loop. Traditionally, this will increment the loop counter.

3. Finally, the `<condition>` runs after the `<increment>`. The return value of this code will be evaluated and the loop breaks when this condition returns false.

Here's an example from `Modules/sha512module.c`:

```
for (i = 0; i < 8; ++i) {
    S[i] = sha_info->digest[i];
}
```

This loop will run 8 times, with `i` incrementing from 0 to 7, and will terminate when the condition is checked and `i` is 8.

`while` loops are virtually identical to their Python counterparts. The `do` ... `while` syntax is a little different, however. The condition on a `do` ... `while` loop isn't checked until *after* the body of the loop is executed for the first time.

There are many instances of `for` loops and `while` loops in the CPython code base, but `do` ... `while` is unused.

Functions

The syntax for functions in C is similar to that in Python, with the addition that the return type and parameter types must be specified. The C syntax looks like this:

```
<return_type> function_name(<parameters>) {
    <function_body>
}
```

The return type can be any valid type in C, including built-in types like `int` and `double` as well as custom types like `PyObject`, as in this example from `semaphore.c`:

```
static PyObject *
semlock_release(SemLockObject *self, PyObject *args)
{
  <statements of function body here>
}
```

Here you see a couple of C-specific features in play. First, remember that whitespace doesn't matter. Much of the CPython source code puts the return type of a function on the line above the rest of the function declaration. That's the `PyObject *` part. You'll take a closer look at the use of `*` a little later, but for now it's important to know that there are several modifiers that you can place on functions and variables.

`static` is one of these modifiers. There are some complex rules governing how modifiers operate. For instance, the `static` modifier here means something very different than if you placed it in front of a variable declaration.

Fortunately, you can generally ignore these modifiers while trying to read and understand the CPython source code.

The parameter list for functions is a comma-separated list of variables, similar to what you use in Python. Again, C requires specific types for each parameter, so `SemLockObject *self` says that the first parameter is a pointer to a `SemLockObject` and is called `self`. Note that all parameters in C are positional.

Let's look at what the "pointer" part of that statement means.

To give some context, the parameters that are passed to C functions are all passed by value, meaning the function operates on a copy of the value and not on the original value in the calling function. To work around this, functions will frequently pass in the address of some data that the function can modify.

These addresses are called **pointers** and have types, so `int *` is a pointer to an integer value and is of a different type than `double *`, which is a pointer to a double-precision floating-point number.

Pointers

As mentioned above, pointers are variables that hold the address of a value. These are used frequently in C, as seen in this example:

```
static PyObject *
semlock_release(SemLockObject *self, PyObject *args)
{
  <statements of function body here>
}
```

Here, the `self` parameter will hold the address of, or *a pointer to*, a `SemLockObject` value. Also note that the function will return a pointer to a `PyObject` value.

There's a special value in C called NULL that indicates a pointer doesn't point to anything. You'll see pointers assigned to NULL and checked against NULL throughout the CPython source. This is important since there are very few limitations as to what values a pointer can have, and accessing a memory location that isn't part of your program can cause very strange behavior.

On the other hand, if you try to access the memory at NULL, then your program will exit immediately. This may not seem better, but it's generally easier to figure out a memory bug if NULL is accessed than if a random memory address is modified.

Strings

C doesn't have a string type. There's a convention around which many standard library functions are written, but there's no actual type. Rather, strings in C are stored as arrays of char (for ASCII) or wchar (for Unicode) values, each of which holds a single character. Strings are marked with a **null terminator**, which has a value 0 and is usually shown in code as \0.

Basic string operations like strlen() rely on this null terminator to mark the end of the string.

Because strings are just arrays of values, they cannot be directly copied or compared. The standard library has the strcpy() and strcmp() functions (and their wchar cousins) for doing these operations and more.

Structs

Your final stop on this mini-tour of C is how you can create new types in C: **structs**. The struct keyword allows you to group a set of different data types together into a new, custom data type:

```
struct <struct_name> {
    <type> <member_name>;
    <type> <member_name>;
    ...
};
```

This partial example from `Modules/arraymodule.c` shows a `struct` declaration:

```
struct arraydescr {
    char typecode;
    int itemsize;

    ...
};
```

This creates a new data type called `arraydescr` which has many members, the first two of which are a `char typecode` and an `int itemsize`.

Frequently structs will be used as part of a `typedef`, which provides a simple alias for the name. In the example above, all variables of the new type must be declared with the full name `struct arraydescr x;`.

You'll frequently see syntax like this:

```
typedef struct {
    PyObject_HEAD
    SEM_HANDLE handle;
    unsigned long last_tid;
    int count;
    int maxvalue;
    int kind;
    char *name;
} SemLockObject;
```

This creates a new, custom struct type and gives it the name `SemLockObject`. To declare a variable of this type, you can simply use the alias `SemLockObject x;`.

Conclusion

This wraps up your quick walk through C syntax. Although this description barely scratches the surface of the C language, you now have sufficient knowledge to read and understand the CPython source code.

Python Mastery: We're With You All the Way

When you subscribe to *Real Python*, you'll master **real-world Python skills** with a **community of experts**. Become a well-rounded Pythonista with hands-on resources at your fingertips:

- **Thousands of tutorials, video lessons, and more:** With new content published weekly, you'll always find something to boost your skills.

- **A community of expert Pythonistas:** Discuss your coding and career questions, vote on upcoming tutorial topics, or just hang out with us at the virtual water cooler.

- **Interactive quizzes & learning paths:** See where you stand and practice what you learn with interactive quizzes, hands-on coding challenges, and skill-focused learning paths.

We look forward to meeting you in our private Slack community and hearing all about your Python journey! **Subscribe today at realpython.com/join**

Acknowledgements

Thank you to my wife, Verity, for her support and patience. Without her this wouldn't be possible.

Thank you to everyone who has supported me on this journey.

– Anthony Shaw

We'd like to thank our early access readers for their excellent feedback:

Jürgen Gmach, ES Alexander, Patton Bradford, Michal Porteš, Sam Roberts, Vishnu Sreekumar, Mathias Hjärtström, Sören Weber, Art, Mary Chester-Kadwell, Jonathan Reichelt Gjertsen, Andrey Ferriyan, Guillaume, Micah Lyle, Robert Willhoft, Juan Manuel Gimeno, Błażej Michalik, RWA, Dave, Lionel, Pasi, Thad, Steve Hill, Mauricio, R. Wayne, Carlos, Mary, Anton Zayniev, aleks, Lindsay John Arendse, Vincent Poulailleau, Christian Hettlage, Felipe "Bidu" Rodrigues, Francois, Eugene Latham, Jordan Rowland, Jenn D, Angel, Mauro Fiacco, Rolandas, Radek, Peter, milos, Hans Davidsson, Bernat Gabor, Florian Dahlitz, Anders Bogsnes, Shmuel Kamensky, Matt Clarke, Josh Deiner, Oren Wolfe, R. Wayne Arenz, emily spahn, Eric Ranger, Dave Grunwald, bob desinger, Robert, Peter McDonald, Park Seyoung, Allen Huang, Seyoung Park, Eugene, Kartik, Vegard Stikbakke, Matt Young, Martin Berg Petersen, Jack Camier, Keiichi Kobayashi, Julius Schwartz, Luk, Christian, Axel Voitier, Aleksandr, Javier Novoa Cataño, travis, Najam Syed, Sebastian Nehls, Yi Wei, Branden, paolo, Jim Woodward, Huub van Thienen, Edward Duarte, Ray, Ivan, Chris Gerrish, Spencer, Volodymyr, Rob Pinkerton, Ben Campbell, Francesc, Chris Smith, John Wiederhirn, Jon Peck, Beau Senyard, Rémi MEVAERE, Carlos S Ande, Abhinav Upadhyay, Charles Wegrzyn, Yaroslav Nezval, Ben Hockley, Marin Muso, Karthik, John Bussoletti, Jonathon, Kerby Geffrard, Andrew Montalenti, Mateusz Stawiarski, Evance Soumaoro, Fletcher Graham, André Roberge, Daniel Hao, Kimia. If we've forgotten to mention your name here, then please know we're extremely grateful for your help. Thank you all!